Embroidering Our Heritage

Written and illustrated by

Judy Chicago

Needlework background provided by

Susan Hill

Designed by

Sheila Levrant de Bretteville

with additional technical drawings by
Shannon Hogan
and special photography by Michael Alexander

Embroidering Our Heritage

The Dinner Party Needlework

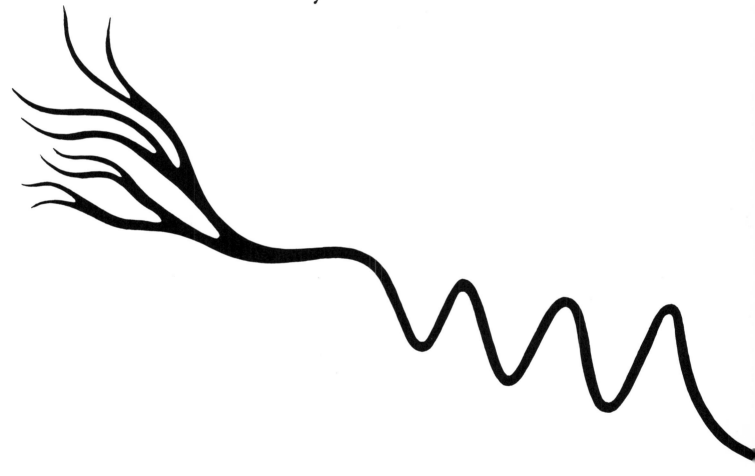

Anchor Books
Anchor Press/Doubleday
Garden City, New York
1980

Dedicated with affection and gratitude
to Kate Amend and Juliet Myers.

Embroidering Our Heritage is
published simultaneously in
hardcover and paperback
editions.
Anchor Books Edition 1980

Library of Congress Cataloging in
Publication Data.

Chicago, Judy, 1939 –
Embroidering Our Heritage.

Includes index.
1. Needlework – Exhibitions.
2. Women in art – Exhibitions.
3. China painting – Exhibitions.
I. Title
NK4605.C45   738   79-6645
Hardcover edition ISBN: 0-385-14568-3
Paperback edition ISBN: 0-385-14569-1
Library of Congress
Catalog Card Number 79-6645
Copyright © 1980 by Judy Chicago
Designed by Sheila Levrant de Bretteville
Set in Baskerville type.

Contents

Part One — Struggle, Process, and Vision

6 — The Development of Our Needlework

Part Two — Embroidering Our Heritage

22 — The Runners as Symbols of Women's History

32 — Wing One: From Pre-History to Rome

Primordial Goddess, 34
Fertile Goddess, 38
Ishtar, 44
Kali, 46
Snake Goddess, 48

Sophia, 50
Amazon, 52
Hatshepsut, 56
Judith, 64

Sappho, 68
Aspasia, 72
Boadaceia, 78
Hypatia, 84

90 — Wing Two: From the Beginning of Christianity to the Reformation

Marcella, 106
Saint Bridget, 112
Theodora, 118
Hrosvitha, 124
Trotula, 132

Eleanor of Aquitaine, 138
Hildegarde of Bingen, 144
Petronilla de Meath, 152
Christine de Pisan, 158

Isabella d'Este, 162
Elizabeth R, 166
Artemisia Gentileschi, 172
Anna van Schurman, 176

182 — Wing Three: From the American Revolution to the Women's Revolution

Anne Hutchinson, 194
Sacajawea, 202
Caroline Herschel, 208
Mary Wollstonecraft, 212
Sojourner Truth, 220

Susan B. Anthony, 226
Elizabeth Blackwell, 232
Emily Dickinson, 234
Ethel Smyth, 242

Margaret Sanger, 246
Natalie Barney, 250
Virginia Woolf, 256
Georgia O'Keeffe, 258

Part Three — The Dinner Party as Sacrament

260 — Our Table Linens and Altar Cloths

Part Four — The Needleworkers' Dictionary

276 — Recognizing Our Community

284 — Glossary/Index of Terms

286 — Attributions and Endnotes

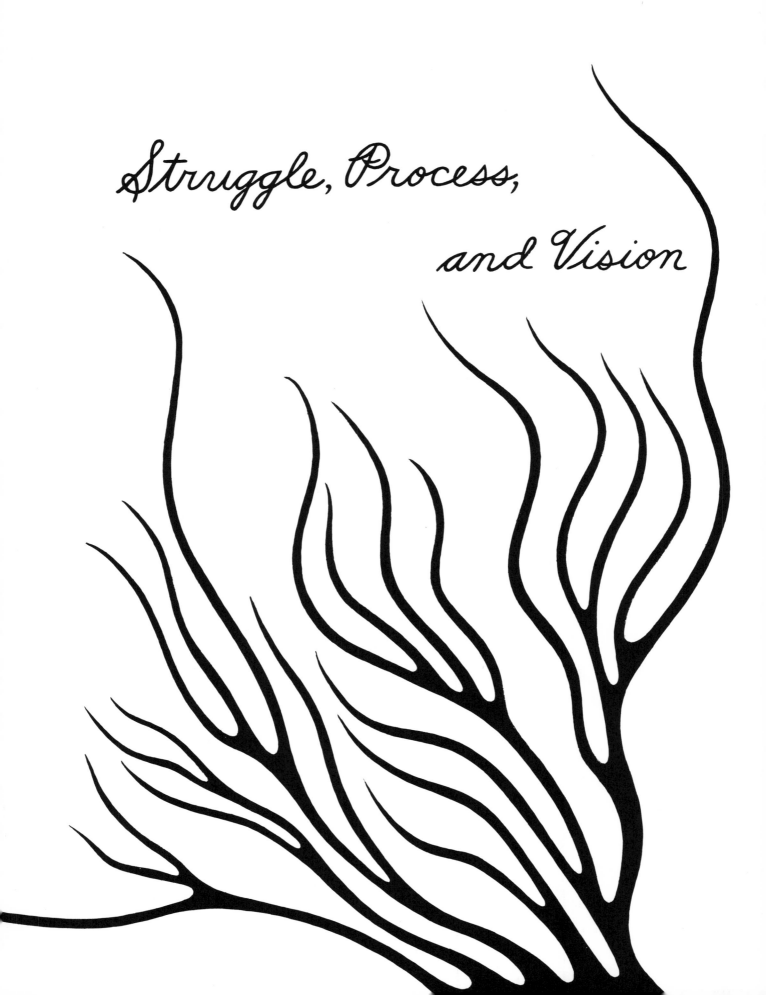

Struggle, Process,

and Vision

The Development of Our Needlework

A dinner party –

In the spring of 1979, after five years of work and the efforts of over four hundred people, *The Dinner Party* opened at the San Francisco Museum of Modern Art. I had begun the first preparatory drawings for this exhibition in June 1974 in a small apartment near a college campus in the Northwest where my then-husband was building a sculpture. What was to be a calm and quiet work period turned into emotional scenes and arguments as my marriage began to disintegrate. Distraught, I forced myself to work as I had so many times in the past, funneling my feelings into the forms that were developing with the strokes of my colored pencils on the paper. As the images began to emerge, I felt an energy coming from within me that seemed totally out of my control. I kept imagining that some dread disease was growing inside my body, and I was terrified. A series of frantic long-distance phone conversations with my friends helped me gain perspective on what was happening in both my personal and artistic life. After calming down, I realized that I was struggling with giving over to the power of my creative drive, which – because it seemed in conflict with my identity as a woman – I was experiencing negatively.

Although my conditioning as a woman had never prevented me from being an artist, it had affected me in other ways. I had always held back from committing myself entirely to my own life and vision, feeling that some part of myself had to be reserved for a relationship with a man. Doing this, however, had not prevented problems in my marriage. This fact, combined with the pressure of the ideas that were developing in my work, pushed me through the emotional blocks of my response, propelling me on a journey that was to change my way of life as well as my sense of self.

From my studies of women's art and literature and my research into women's lives – undertaken as part of my search for my own tradition as a woman and an artist – I had concluded that the general lack of knowledge of our heritage as women was pivotal in our continued oppression. It caused us all to have an unconsciously diminished feeling of self-worth and a lack of pride in women. Because we were educated to think that women had never achieved anything of significance, it was easy to believe that we were incapable of ever accomplishing important work. The absence of female role models in my own development had sometimes made me feel as if my intentions to be a major artist were insane. But a closer examination of history taught me that my ambitions were entirely consistent with those of many women of the past. Women had always made significant contributions to the development of human civilization, but these were consistently ignored, denied, or trivialized.

I decided to create a work of art that could symbolize these achievements and also represent the circumstances women had to overcome to realize their aspirations. The drawings I worked on in Washington state were studies for a series of thirty-nine china-painted plates, each of which was to represent a particular goddess or woman in Western civilization. Over the next year and a half, my conception of this symbolic "history of women" was enlarged. By March of 1975, I had completed the conceptual framework of *The Dinner Party* as well as the first group of china-painted plates. But I could never have realized my conception had I not overcome my conditioned fear – that feeling powerful and living a completely self-motivated life was tantamount to being terminally ill.

The Dinner Party consists of an open, triangular table, 46½ feet on each side. The table, which is covered with fine, white cloths edged in gold, contains thirty-nine place settings – thirteen on each of the three wings. The number thirteen refers to the number of guests present at the Last Supper and to the number of members in a witches' coven. The fact that the number thirteen had both a positive and a negative meaning – i.e., the "holy" table of men versus the "demonic" coven of witches – seemed consistent with the dual meaning of *The Dinner Party*.

Each place setting includes a fourteen-inch china-painted plate, which represents a period in Western civilization as well as the mythological figure or woman who, in my opinion, best exemplifies that period; a set of lustered ceramic flatware; a lustered and gold ceramic chalice; and a napkin with an embroidered gold edge. These rest upon an embroidered runner, which drops over the front and back of the table and incorporates the needlework style and techniques of the time each woman lived. The name of the woman represented, embellished with an illuminated capital letter, is embroidered on the front of the runner.

Installation of *The Dinner Party* at the San Francisco Museum of Modern Art.

Section of Heritage Floor showing groupings of names.

The *Dinner Party* table rests on a large triangular floor comprised of 2300 handcast porcelain tiles. These are inscribed in gold luster with the names of 999 women of achievement grouped around the women represented at the table. These groupings emanate like streams from beneath the place settings and attest to the long tradition of female accomplishment symbolized by each plate.

I decided to learn china-painting in 1972 after seeing an antique porcelain plate and realizing that the quality of its color and surface was perfect for the images I had in mind. I never consciously thought about using a woman's craft in relation to a project on women's history; in fact, I often used techniques that were outside mainstream art sensibility. Over the years I had worked with automotive paint, plastics, or fireworks, as these always seemed to offer unexplored visual possibilities.

Studying china-painting exposed me, for the first time, to the world of women's traditional arts. I learned a great deal from the women with whom I trained – not only about china-painting, but also about a very different way of being an artist. Most china-painters see teaching as part of their work. Their teaching takes a number of forms; they give classes and seminars, but most importantly, at least for me, they teach by example. During exhibitions, they sit in their booths and paint while crowds of people watch them. This act and the public response to it intrigued me; the china-painters' activity was in stark contrast with the isolated and private act of creation associated with twentieth-century "high art." Watching these women work out in the open helped me do the same thing when the *Dinner Party* Project required a studio full of workers. Moreover, the enormous interest of the viewers at these demonstrations suggested that many people craved the opportunity to participate in art.

My learning experience with the china-painters was not totally positive, however. Many of them viewed me suspiciously, were outright hostile, or thought of me as someone who wanted to exploit them – despite all my efforts, both public and private, to honor them. This kind of reaction forced me to confront the conservatism and fear which, along with generosity and warmth, typify the "subculture" of women's crafts.

During my apprenticeship with the china-painters, I often listened to their discussions about why china-painting wasn't considered art. Interestingly, these conversations focused on the technique of china-painting – which is exceedingly difficult – rather than its content. But it is the absence of personal content that distinguishes craft from art. It was as if the conflict I had experienced between my drive to be an artist and my conditioning as a woman mirrored a much deeper conflict in most of these women. Although many of them possessed the visual skills to express personal subject matter, they did not take themselves seriously nor did they believe that their experiences were important enough to express. This lack of self-esteem resulted not only in a continual dependence upon preformed patterns and designs, but also in a resistance to new ideas and unfamiliar thoughts. All this only reinforced my belief in the importance of addressing women's lack of self-worth as a crucial step in creating change and my determination to achieve this through art.

made by a beloved grandmother.

Rosemarie Radmaker teaching Chicago at china-painting show.

Rosemarie Radmaker, a well-known china-painter, was one of my major influences. She personally instructed me, helped build a bridge between me and the traditional china-painters, and also was one of the two people who assisted me in painting the reliefed and dimensional plates.

Chicago's china-painting studio.

Most china-painters work in their homes, sometimes in a bedroom or basement studio, sometimes on the kitchen table. My china-painting studio may lack the warmth of these household workshops, but I still prefer the stark, white-walled space of the "isolated" artist, even after having abandoned the role.

This plate, painted by Radmaker in a traditional style, exemplifies the kind of work being done by many contemporary china-painters. Though I never learned the specific "dot, dash, and comma" system of brushwork necessary for painting flowers like these, I adapted the quality of color and luminosity inherent in this painting style to my own work.

By the summer of 1974, I had set up a clean, well-ventilated white room in my studio specifically for china-painting, and I had begun working on the plates.* As the concept of *The Dinner Party* developed, I realized that it was essential to identify each of the women represented at the table. By this time, I had determined that the plates would be presented on a fully set table covered with fine cloths. Deciding to embroider a circular phrase around each plate, I bought a sophisticated Bernina embroidery machine. Although I struggled valiantly with this piece of equipment – which included cams for twenty different stitches and was guaranteed for twenty-five years – it was quite clear that I was as clumsy with a sewing machine as with a potter's wheel.

*For a description of the development of the plates, see *The Dinner Party: A Symbol of Our Heritage,* by Judy Chicago (New York: Anchor/Doubleday, 1979).

I had worked on *The Dinner Party* alone for about one-and-a-half years before I realized that I could not complete it by myself, but I never imagined the numbers of people the Project would eventually require. At first I looked for a few assistants. Leonard Skuro, a graduate student at UCLA and now a sculptor, began to work with me on the problem of supplementing the flat, painted plates with a number of dimensional images. A few months later Susan Hill, a Los Angeles photographer who had attended one of my lectures, volunteered her time.* I soon discovered that although Susan was not a skilled embroiderer, she came from a family of needlewomen. I happily turned the sewing machine over to her and asked her to solve the problem of embroidering circular phrases on the cloths.

*The third member of the early *Dinner Party* team was Diane Gelon, an art history student. She started out doing historical research, but ultimately became the primary fundraiser and public-relations person for the Project.

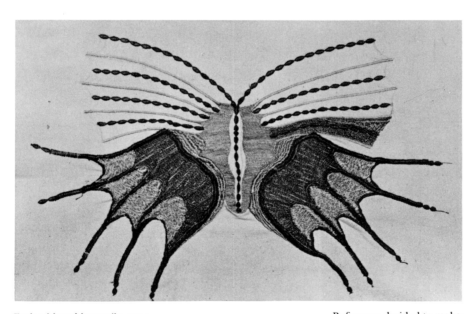

Embroidered butterfly, 1974.

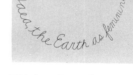

This is a phrase I gave Susan to embroider. It refers to the Primordial Goddess, whose name was changed from a specific figure to a more generalized concept during the course of the Project.

Before we decided to make individual runners for each plate, I had begun experimenting with extending the butterfly imagery of the plates onto fabric. This embroidered butterfly was my most successful effort on the Bernina.

provide an environment of comfort,

Susan – who apprenticed herself to a group of traditional needleworkers, much as I had done with the china-painters – introduced me to the "world of embroidery," which, in many ways, resembled that of the china-painters. She was also responsible for the one change in my original concept of *The Dinner Party,* a change that proved to be extremely significant. After a period of research and some trial-and-error stitching by hand and on the machine, Susan informed me that we could neither manipulate the long tablecloths through the sewing machine thirteen times in a circle nor embroider them over and over again in hoops. Instead, she suggested the idea of embroidering separate cloths to be placed at intervals *over* the tablecloths and under each plate – and thus our "runners" were born.

Hill at ecclesiastical embroidery class.

The Altar Guild embroidery class was held every Thursday from 9:30 to 2:30. I loved learning the techniques and enjoyed being in the group of women, but I felt frustrated by and restless with the lack of focus. Also, I didn't like working on small designs.
—S.H.

an elegant setting, and a nourishing

At first, I thought of the runners only as extensions of or backgrounds for the plates. My initial idea was to embroider descriptive phrases about each woman on colored fabrics that would contrast with or reinforce the colors of each plate. But I was afraid that using too many different hues would create a choppy effect, and therefore I decided to use the same white linen for the runners as we had chosen for the tablecloths. Then Pearl Krause – a needlework designer who was working with us when we began developing the runners – suggested extending the imagery of the plates onto the runners. This corresponded to my earlier interest in embroidering forms similar to those on the plates.

Chicago designing Ishtar runner, using plate as guide.

Place settings for Margaret Sanger (left) and Natalie Barney (right).

Place settings for Margaret Sanger and Natalie Barney, showing change in runner edge – a metaphor for women breaking free of historical constraints.

We set to work painting the designs for the first runners directly on cotton fabric, using the plates as guides. I simply repeated the forms of the plates on the front, back, and side borders of the runners, having no idea how my painted images would translate into embroidery. I approached needlework as I had approached every other media I'd used – in terms of what I wanted to express. But inexperience in textiles actually proved beneficial in the evolution of our needlework, as I had no preconceptions of what could or could not be done.

The other Project members (by then there were about six or eight, most of whom were artists and art students) were also generally unfamiliar with needlework. Susan, who knew somewhat more than the rest of us, always assured me that almost anything I designed could be executed in embroidery. Because she had become the "Head of Needlework" – by virtue of having accepted the responsibility for supervising the making of the tablecloths and runners – I accepted her "authority." Neither of us ever stopped to think how long one of my painted fades would take to interpret in thread.

After completing a number of runner designs, we recruited a group of students who were textile majors. They were challenged by our unusual approach to needlework and concentrated on translating my designs. Susan and I, not knowing what the techniques and stitches they suggested looked like,

14

and esthetically pleasing meal.

asked them to make samples. This resulted in the beginning of our Embroidery Sample Book, which I would study endlessly, trying to determine how the marvelous visual qualities of these different types of embroidery could best be utilized.

As my designs were slowly transformed into embroidered images, I began to feel more confident. Gradually I learned to think in terms of what embroidery could do, particularly after Susan and I made "study trips" to museums in the East. We wanted to expand our knowledge of needlework techniques and historical styles, as, by early 1976, we had both decided that needlework should be more fully incorporated into *The Dinner Party*. When we began to understand the rich tradition of embroidery and perceive its enormous visual potential, we became determined to include as many different techniques and styles as possible as another way of calling attention to women's unrecognized heritage. Moreover, I decided that – in addition to using embroidery to identify the women on the table and extend the imagery on the plates – I would express something about each woman's experience, environment, or context through a combination of symbolic and literal images which create a narrative on the backs of the runners. This led to an expansion of the iconography of the runners generally.

After the first group of runners had been completed, I began to alter the format of the design. Instead of the imagery being restricted to the periphery of the runner, it gradually moved closer to the plate, steadily encroaching on its space. I intended this as a metaphor for the increasing restrictions on women's power that occurred in the development of Western civilization. The relationship between the plates and their runners reflects the varying positions of women in different periods of history. In some cases, the plates dominate the runners; in others, the imagery of the runners engulfs or threatens the plate; sometimes, there is the same congruence between the plate and the runner that the woman experienced between her own aspirations and the prevailing attitudes toward female achievement; and occasionally, there is enormous visual tension between the plate and its runner as a symbol of that woman's rebellion against the constraints of female role.

On the last wing of the table, I made a strong visual change. I wanted to imply an alteration in the historical circumstances of the women represented – particularly after the beginning of the women's revolution, which is marked by the place setting for Mary Wollstonecraft. At this point I began to break the rigid rectilinear form of the runners in the same way that the edges of the plates had been modified to reflect women's growing struggle toward freedom. Additionally, the butterfly image, a consistent motif in the plates, appears for the first time in the needlework of the third wing. A symbol of liberation, the butterfly gradually becomes more prominent in the last place settings, which chronicle women's efforts to gain equal rights and to regain their creative powers.

The making of the runners

1. Embroidery Frames

Usually, embroidery is done on a frame that allows the needleworker to roll up the fabric and work on only one section at a time. But I wanted the runners to be seen as paintings and the needleworkers to deal with the overall picture plane as they worked. Moreover, more than one person at a time had to be able to work on each runner, and the frame needed to tilt in order to be both worked and viewed.

Susan Hill working on traditional embroidery frame.

The construction of the frames – designed and built primarily by Millie Stein – was based on that of traditional quilting or embroidery frames. Made of hardwood in order to withstand pressure without bowing, these adjustable frames rested in specially built stands – designed by Ken Gilliam – to hold the stretched runners in a variety of positions.

Millie Stein making embroidery frames.

2. Stretching the Linen

Stretching the *Dinner Party* linen was an extraordinarily tedious and exacting task, We used a traditional method: pulling threads on all four sides of the linen panel to determine the grain of the fabric, and sewing the linen to tapes that were fixed or laced to the frame. We blocked any piece of linen that was crooked, and, using rulers and right angles to position the fabric, we allowed ourselves only a quarter-inch error in the length or width or a few degrees' variance in what should be a perfect 90-degree corner. These were exceptional standards for work of this scale, but the precision, care, and compulsiveness were typical of studio procedure.

Hill and Connie von Briesen stretching linen.

Needlework loft. Our embroidery frames could be used in various positions and by either individual workers or groups.

3. Designing the Runner

Because I wanted to introduce higher visual standards into embroidery, rigorous technical drawings were made after the design sessions. Those mockups which contained sections of my hand-drawn imagery were carefully redrawn by me on the blue-line graph paper we used. If there were geometric or symmetrical motifs, the graphics team – headed by Helene Simich and later Martie Rotchford – plotted the curves and made sure the patterns were accurately drawn. Each runner name, like the names on the floor, though in a larger scale, was pieced together from individual letters and then taped to the technical drawing. The design was transferred to the linen on our specially built light table with blue pencils.

Chicago painting mockup for Caroline Herschel runner.

4. Embroidering from Mockup

After the mockup had been designed, the needleworkers began tests to work out the translation technique. By the time the technical drawing was finished, we had usually resolved the question of how to embroider the design. Sometimes I would create with a particular technique in mind – as in the case of Caroline Herschel, whose runner I designed specifically for crewel work.

Marjorie Biggs translating Chicago's design for the Herschel runner into crewel embroidery.

5. Capital

Illuminating each woman's first initial was, for me, a way of paying a special tribute to her. I tried to symbolize some aspect of her achievements in these drawings.

The embroidered names are a consistent visual element in the runners; each is identical in size, color, placement, and technique. The small letters are ⅛-inch wide, and the capital letters are ³/₁₆ of an inch. They were embroidered in the split stitch, with two strands of Zwicky gold silk thread, and outlined with #8 Japanese gold. The illuminated letter is distinguished by two rows of gold couching, which makes it slightly wider than the other letters. Silk and metallic threads were combined to give the names the same lustrous, slightly shiny appearance as the china-painted names on the floor. The needleworkers who embroidered the letters developed uniform methods of forming the loops and bars, and, working with clear plexiglas rulers, they constantly checked the width of the work, often stitching with only one thread to fill a curve or smooth a line. When a wing of runners was finished, the names were lined up and surveyed to see that they were visually identical despite the differences in stitching styles. Misshapen or oddly proportioned letters were taken out, redrawn, and stitched again.

L.A. Olson embroidering letter for Christine de Pisan from Chicago's study based on a medieval manuscript illumination.

6. Washing

It became apparent very early that we had to clean the runners. After extensive research in textile conservation, we decided we could wash the linen runners and the others would be dry-cleaned. We built a simple tank that held the runners stretched on their frames for the studio washing process, and then we worked with a dry-cleaning specialist to ensure careful treatment of the others.

Hill washing Hrosvitha runner.

7. Conservation Samples

To ensure proper care of our runners, Susan developed a system for testing all the fabrics and threads we used. Each skein of thread was washed to remove excess dye; every fabric was tested for content; and all thread and fabric were both washed and dry-cleaned to determine the best way of eliminating dirt. Types and colors of thread used on a runner were stitched onto a piece of the runner's fabric, and these – along with records of the materials used and special instructions for certain runners – serve as guides for maintaining and restoring the *Dinner Party* needlework.

8. Fastening

In order to protect *The Dinner Party* from damage or theft, all the various pieces had to be attached in some way. The runners needed to be strapped to the tablecloths, the napkins sewn in place, and all the ceramic pieces bolted to the specially fabricated tabletops. After the runners were finished, holes were cut and bound to accommodate the bolts in the plates, chalices, and flatware.

The implementation of this plan proved to be traumatic to the needleworkers, who – despite their prior knowledge of the fastening system – were horrified at having to "violate" their work. Finally the needleworkers decided that whenever possible, the "runner mother" (the woman who had either executed the runner or supervised its construction) would cut the holes. Eventually, in typical *Dinner Party* fashion, everyone became involved in trying to make the slits as attractive as possible, even though they knew they'd never be seen.

Cutting holes in the runners for the fastening system.

9. Backing

In December 1979 we began the last major needlework task – backing the runners. The procedure was based on a method I learned at the Altar Guild embroidery class: Each runner was lined with hymo, then backed with white linen. Certain runners, however, had to have specially constructed linings to make their surfaces smooth, to protect their delicate embroidery, or to keep them flat and straight.

—*S.H.*

Catherine Stifter backing a runner.

10. Embroidering Names on Back

Because we didn't want to perpetuate the traditional anonymity of needleworkers, we embroidered the signatures of everyone who had contributed significantly to the production of a runner on the back. This embroidery was usually done by the one-day workers or weekend groups from colleges or organizations who volunteered to "do anything" in order to bring *The Dinner Party* to completion.

The making of the tablecloths

Although we didn't use embroidered phrases on the tablecloths, we did end up using an embroidered gold edge. This was stitched and couched along the entire length of each 55-foot tablecloth on both sides. The fabrication of these tablecloths was a major undertaking, and we began planning them early in the Project. Determining the proportions of the table, the length of the tablecloths, and the position of each place setting was crucial in the development of the piece, and in the summer of 1975 we built a mockup of a section of the table in order to work out these problems.

The tablecloth and napkins, like most of the runners, are made of fine linen imported from Switzerland. It took me several months of research to find a wide linen that was both beautiful and affordable. The linen sold at embroidery shops or supplied by importers was rarely wide enough and was about $40 a yard – too expensive. I found no suitable American linen, so I telephoned the Los Angeles embassies for Switzerland, Ireland, and Belgium. I acquired a list of textile manufacturers in each country, wrote to every one, and asked for samples. From what I collected, we chose an "Art Linen" provided by Scheitlin-Worb, a Swiss company established in the seventeenth century. It was 108 inches wide, and it cost $10.00 a yard; we used a hundred yards.

The fabric arrived in four brown paper parcels, each containing a folded piece of linen 9 feet wide by 75 feet long. Three bolts were cut to yield a 6-foot width for the tablecloth and a 3-foot width – later subdivided into 60-inch lengths – for the runners. One bolt was kept in reserve and was eventually cut for runners and backing. No space in the studio was big enough to lay these bolts out flat

for cutting and measuring, so we made arrangements with the management of Century City – a complex of corporate offices and exclusive shops — to use undeveloped office space. They made the top floor of an appropriately triangular office tower available to us. (I wish it had been the thirty-ninth floor, but it was only the thirty-seventh.)

Once the fabric was cut into strips, it had to be shrunk and ironed. I took it to a French laundry recommended by a museum curator. Fortunately we had only one lot of fabric commercially ironed, because the industrial machine aptly called a "mangle" stretched the fabric beyond use. The next morning – when I had recovered from my first lesson in blindly following advice – I decided that we would have to iron all the linen by hand. Just one ironing of all the *Dinner Party* linen required that over 2,000 square feet of fabric be methodically dampened and pressed smooth. It became a favorite joke in the needlework loft that while the hundreds of years of female history were being researched and forged into art, we were *still* washing and ironing!

—*S.H.*

Kathleen Schneider, Judye Keyes, Hill, and Chicago discussing the proportion and scale of the *Dinner Party* tables.

Using real plates and white paper to simulate the tablecloths and runners, we determined the proportions of the table, the scale of the cloths, and the width of the runners.

Cutting the linen.

The tablecloths – which were fabricated under the supervision of Susan Brenner, Marilyn Anderson, and me – were embroidered and then hemmed by Brenner, along with Ellen Dinerman, Charlotte Ranke, and Linda Shelp, using Bernina sewing/ embroidery machines. Each finished tablecloth is 55 feet long and 64 inches wide. The hems were stiffened with a half-inch drapery tape to add weight and prevent the cloths from stretching. The ends of each cloth were carefully cut and fitted to form giant overlapping tabs on the corners of the table. Two layers of white felt serve as padding for the tablecloth. These, which add weight and softness to the appearance of the linen, were patterned on the undercloths or "silence cloths" traditionally used to muffle the noise of plates being set down during the service of the meal.
—S.H.

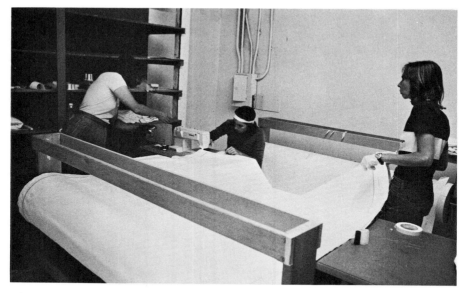

Ranke, Shelp, and Pat Akers sewing tablecloth.

Ironing the linen.

All the edges of the table-cloth were done in a single-needle satin stitch on my trusty Bernina embroidery/sewing machine and then couched with Japanese gold. Because we were reluctant to use any machine embroidery, we initially planned to hand-embroider the entire border – more than three hundred feet – in a week-long "sew-in" involving hundreds of needleworkers. Fortunately, we came to our senses and used the machine instead.

In constructing the table-cloths, we first had to build equipment to handle the fabric and then devise a method to ensure that it would drape smoothly over the tables and fit properly on the angled corners. To handle nearly a thousand square feet of linen during the table-cloths' construction, as well as during shipping and installation, Ken Gilliam – our installation designer – developed an ingenious system. Six special rollers, 6 feet long by 12 inches in diameter, were made from industrial cardboard cylinders and wrapped in acid-free foam. Held in specially built wooden stands at precisely table height, the rollers allowed us to easily unwind and then rewind the fabric as it was moved across the ironing board, through the sewing machine, and later onto the tables.

Embroidering border of tablecloth.

a traditional female act, requiring

From the time other people began to work with me – in the fall of 1975 – to the time *The Dinner Party* was completed – in the spring of 1979 – three-and-a-half years had elapsed. During that period, hundreds of people had been involved in helping transform my vision into a reality. People were drawn to the Project by interest in my philosophy and my work and, most importantly, by the belief that the information embodied in and symbolized by *The Dinner Party* had to reach a wide audience; millions of dollars' worth of labor was volunteered.*

 The Dinner Party cost over $250,000 in materials and fabrication costs. We worked as I had worked for fifteen years: without knowing where the money would come from. I'd sell a drawing, we'd get a small grant, someone would make a donation – and we'd have enough money for another month or two. Diane Gelon gradually assumed the responsibility for fundraising, which meant that there were two of us to share the constant fear that we would never raise sufficient funds to finish the piece.**

 To deal with the numbers of people who eventually participated in the making of *The Dinner Party*, we incorporated certain group-process techniques as well as a set of studio rules. We offered consciousness-raising groups to all Project members. A signup sheet would be posted, and, when eight people had indicated interest, Diane would meet with them and facilitate the formation of a group. These groups, which met weekly, provided people with a sense of connection to other Project members as well as a chance to work out some of their problems as women.

 Additionally, once a week an evening was set aside for discussions, lectures, and potluck dinners. On these Thursday nights I made myself available for questions, confrontations, and casual conversation – something that was not allowed during the week. The studio was organized around work, and we established rules that protected this time. To provide the silence and uninterrupted thought essential to the creative process, we tried to minimize all but work-related talk, discouraged "hanging out" at the studio, and strictly enforced the rule that I was not to be interrupted for trivial or inessential reasons.

 Teaching people to respect others' work and to work themselves was a time-consuming but important aspect of the Project. This was accomplished partly by example – watching me and the other long-term Project members working despite discomfort, boredom, personal problems, or ill health – and partly by means of the Thursday-night discussions, the consciousness-raising groups, and, increasingly, work-related groups.

*The ownership of *The Dinner Party* is in the hands of Through The Flower, a non-profit corporation founded by me and other Project members. The function of the corporation is to handle the traveling, care, and eventual housing of the exhibition.

**Funding came from several sources: all my earnings for five years, $60,000 in assorted grants, and continual donations from people all over the country who wanted to help ensure the completion of *The Dinner Party*.

both generosity and personal sacrifice.

As the Project developed, teams evolved, not only in needlework and ceramics, but in research, graphics, photography, and fabrication as well. Each team had a supervisor who was chosen on the basis of both skill and willingness to make a time commitment, assume leadership, and take responsibility. These supervisors had to deal with the problems of their own groups, often employing consciousness-raising techniques to accomplish this. The studio gradually became a structure of self-sufficient teams, each taking responsibility for itself and building teamwork through shared work and honest dialogue. Diane functioned as a troubleshooter, meeting regularly with team leaders and facilitating communication when problems developed.

One of the things I learned from opening my studio to others was that many of those who worked on the Project had a hunger to understand and be involved in the process of making art. This was similar to what I had witnessed at the china-painting shows. The changes that took place in some of my co-workers, particularly those who worked in the studio for an extended period of time, were astounding. I realized that their development was a result of not only the supportive atmosphere of the studio and the demands we placed on people to grow, but also the inherently life-giving nature of the creative process.

For the last decade, I have struggled to create art that is more accessible and more relevant, and the audience response to *The Dinner Party* confirms all my ideas about the potential power of art. I have always believed that art is profoundly affirming and has the capacity to reveal truth and change consciousness, but I never realized before that offering people the chance to participate in the art-making process was so important. The studio aspect of the *Dinner Party* Project has taught me that if I really want to continue my efforts to expand the role of the artist and redefine the relationship between art and society, both art and the process of producing that art will have to be shared with a wider audience. People, particularly women, need images that affirm their experience. And, if artists are to have a broader social base of support, they need to communicate more clearly how and why they create art.

Chicago worked with architectural renderer Carlos Diniz and structural designer Peter Pearce on this vision of a permanent home for *The Dinner Party*.

I feel that unless *The Dinner Party* is permanently housed I will not have achieved my goal of introducing women's heritage into the culture so that it can never be erased again – I would be content to see it in a simple, triangular room in a museum, cultural institution, or university, or as part of a larger women's institution.

21

Embroidering Our Heritage

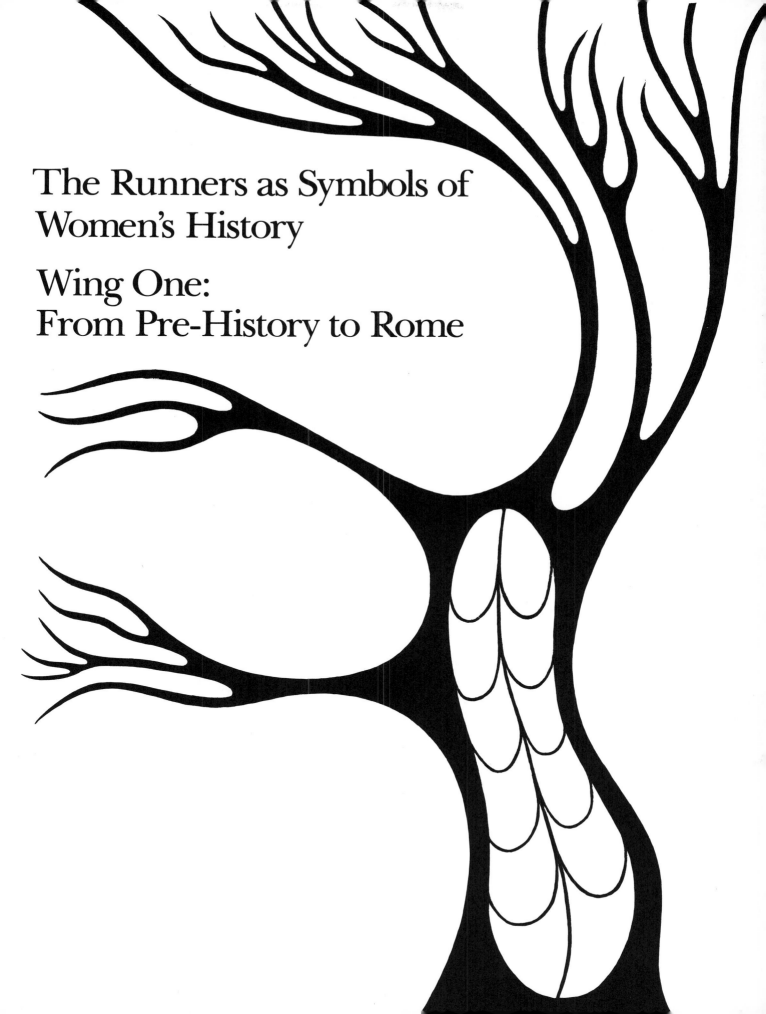

The Runners as Symbols of Women's History

Wing One:
From Pre-History to Rome

We examined the history of needlework – as it is reflected in textiles and costumes, paintings and sculptures, myths and legends, and archaeological evidence – from the point of view of what these revealed about women, the quality of their lives, and their relationship to needlework. We soon learned that women have been associated with the textile arts since the beginning of time. Moreover, we could perceive women's changing position in society through the changes that occurred in needlework. We incorporated this information into our designs so that the runners would comprise a symbolic history of the way women's lives were affected by the development of Western civilization. Each runner – executed in the needlework techniques and/or patterns of the time – is a composite of historical and iconographic information, transformed into a visual image that provides an appropriate context for the plate.

There are very few examples of early textiles. Most of what we learned came from art and archaeology, which indicated that the first textiles were simple body coverings; but these were not necessarily always utilitarian in nature. The embellished figurines that have been unearthed from the remains of ancient civilizations suggest that rudimentary textiles were also used for ritual or decorative purposes.

These sculptures, which in all likelihood are representations of goddesses, were often presented wearing hip belts, knotted bands, or fringe attached to strips around the waist or hips. The belts and bands were probably made of plaited plant fibers or animal hair; the fringe was either made of the same material or made of roving or leather strips. The function of these is unknown, but it is clear that they provided neither warmth nor adequate covering.

One important aspect of many of the ancient goddesses was that of the Eternal Weaver, whose womb was thought to contain the pattern of life. Because the mystery of giving birth was associated with goddesses who "spun life" or "wove destiny," they were regarded as the protectors of women. Among the female deities associated with the textile arts were the Egyptian goddesses Neith, Net, and Isis. Neith was called the Great Weaver, who wove the world on her loom; Net's name may stem from the root *netet,* meaning to knit or to weave; and Isis was credited with the invention of spinning.

Gaea's sacred site at Delphi, thought to be the center or navel of the world, was completely covered with a woven net of threads. In the Cretan myth of Ariadne, there are references to the sacred knot, a symbol that also appears in the knot of Isis – the emblem of her womb – and in the knotted reed bundle of the Sumerian goddess Innana.

The Scandinavian fertility goddess Frigga, in her original form, was described as spinning golden threads and weaving all the clouds. The Norns in Teutonic mythology, like the Greek Fates, spun and wove the web of fate. The Aztec goddess Xochiquetzal was the patron of weavers, and Ixchel, the mother of all the deities, who had power over birth, was believed to have taught the Mayan women to weave.

The bands may have had some connection with the Goddess, as knots were a magic symbol of her protection, and also with fertility, as crossed threads represented sexual union. The fringe – which accentuated the pubic area, especially when tied below the buttocks – seems to have emphasized female sexuality or symbolized the power of the Goddess, who was revered for her capacity to create life.

The Venus of Lespugue, a Paleolithic goddess figure, is depicted as wearing a plaited strip with fringe. Its position on her body emphasizes her bulging buttocks and thighs, an obvious reference to female fecundity. The symbolic importance of this garment is indicated by the fact that it continued to be worn for centuries until woven versions replaced the earlier form.

Fur garments developed during the Paleolithic period and continued to be worn for thousands of years. From the bone and flint tools which have been discovered, it is thought that early women first scraped and cut hides, punched holes with awls, and – using bone needles strung with animal hair or ligaments – sewed the hide or hides into skirts or shawls just as Eskimo women still do today. These were worn alone, as it was customary for women to go bare-breasted. It was not until much later in history that distinctly female or male garments developed, reflecting the increasing sex-role differentiations in society.

In this cave painting, women wearing typical prehistoric fur skirts stand with their naked children near a seemingly docile group of animals. Combined with the absence of either male hunters or weapons, the proximity – as well as the serenity – of the animals suggests their domestication. This image appears to support recent archaeological evidence suggesting that women and their offspring comprised the first human groupings and that it was women who first domesticated animals.

Cave painting.

Enthroned goddess figure.

This bare-breasted goddess is shown wearing a wrapped fabric covered with ornate patterning, including a diamond glyph motif that symbolizes the womb. The design, which is repeated on many prehistoric artifacts, illustrates the close relationship between textiles and the other arts.

Venus of Lespugue.

for warmth and decoration.

The importance of the Goddess in relation to the development of textiles cannot be overemphasized. A variety of ancient myths and legends attribute the invention of spinning and weaving to female deities, who are supposed to have taught these skills to women and sanctified their work. The actual origins of spinning are unknown, although evidence suggests that it was developed by women sometime during the Paleolithic period, and in art, myth, and legend spinning has continuously been portrayed as a female activity. While we saw almost no images of male spinners, there are hundreds of representations of women with spindles or distaffs from early times through the Industrial Revolution reflecting women's domination of this craft.

At first, women probably rolled animal hair or plant fibers between their palms or on their thighs to make strands of thread for fringe or braid. At some point they discovered that if they suspended clay balls from the ends of these strands and set the balls in motion, they could produce stronger and finer thread for joining bands of braiding, making wrapped cords, and even doing simple embroidery. Moreover, this technique allowed the production of larger quantities of thread, which was essential to the development of weaving.

Evidence gathered in archaeological excavations (i.e., the Lake Dwellers in Switzerland) has established that weaving dates back at least to the Stone Age. Flax, wool, string, rope, balls of yarn, and fabrics embellished with images of human figures have been found. Basketry, which probably pre-dated weaving, may have established the basic techniques for plaiting or weaving small sections of fabric by hand.

"They at a task eternal their hands religiously plying,
Held in the left on high, with wool enfolded, a distaff,
Delicate fibers wherefrom, drawn down, were shaped by the right hand –
Poised with perfected whorl, the industrious shaft of the spindle.
Still, as they span, as they span, was the tooth kept nipping and smoothing
And to the withered lip clung morsels of wool as they smoothed it.
Filaments erstwhile rough that stood from the twist of the surface
Close at their feet, meantime, were woven baskets of wicker
Guarding the soft white balls of the wool resplendent within them.
Thus then, parting the strands, these Three with resonant voices
Uttered, in a chant divine, predestined sooth of the future –
Prophecy neither in time, nor yet in eternity, shaken."

—from a Homeric poem

Many ancient goddesses were described as the "spinners of life" or "weavers of destiny," characterizations that continued to be ascribed to various female deities throughout the ages. By the time of Homer, early myths were being recorded – among them the legend of the Fates. Responsible for human destiny, these triple goddesses included Clotho, from whose name the word cloth is derived and who spun the "thread of life"; Tachesis, who determined its length; and Atropos, who terminated it.

When women first invented spinning,

It is thought that the loom was invented eight or ten thousand years ago, but evidence is very sparse and experts disagree. The first loom is likely to have been made by hanging weighted threads from the branches of a tree to create the warp. Other methods may have included tying the thread to a sapling and driving the other end into the ground with pegs or securing both ends with stakes. At first only small pieces could be woven; these were made from either flax or wool and sewn together with spun thread. As more sophisticated styles of looms evolved, larger, wider pieces of fabric were produced and early hide garments were replaced by cloth.

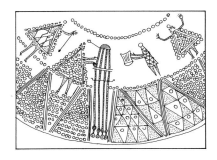

This image, etched on the neck of an old tomb urn, depicts a woman (far left) spinning with weighted threads, another woman (right center) weaving on a one-beam loom with weighted warp threads, and a third woman (right center) playing music. Their activities are watched over by the figure on the far right, whose triangular form and upraised arms suggest one of the traditional poses of the Goddess. The fact that the weaver and spinner also have triangular bodies repeats the familiar association between women, textile activities, and the female deity.

Spindle-whorls, a development from Stone Age clay weights, allowed the thread to be wound around the spindle that was inserted in the center of the disc. This inscribed artifact, however, was probably a votive offering rather than a tool. It was found with similarly decorated vessels and figurines that were dedicated as gifts to the Goddess – another indication of the close relationship between female deities and the textile arts.

Schematic of inscribed spindle-whorl from Diki-litash – near Philipi, north-eastern Greece, East Balkan civilization (c. 4000 B.C.).

Schematic of front and back of inscribed goddess figurine from Vinca mound (c. 4000 B.C.).

Sumerian inlaid work.

These Sumerian women may have been making "Kaunakes cloth" – a transitional type of fabric which was more sophisticated than animal hides but which pre-dated wool. This plush-piled fabric seems to have developed about 2700 B.C. and was like the matted wool worn by the Celts. The Sumerians continued to use it for goddess rituals long after it was outmoded, as the Minoans did with fur skirts. There is a similar type of material made today by an African tribe.

they used their thighs to work the wool.

In some areas, the development of weaving technology provided the basis for the growth of textile industries. As far as records indicate, the earliest of these were in Mesopotamia, Egypt, and Crete. In Crete fabric production remained a household industry within women's domain. But in Mesopotamia and Egypt, small-scale female domestic production gave way to prodigious manufacturing of cloth under the direction of men.

Until this point in history, women were responsible not only for spinning and weaving, but also for most aspects of the creation and decoration of textiles as well as the production of clothes. In early cultures – most of which were relatively egalitarian – women derived social stature from these activities, particularly from spinning and weaving, since they were associated with the Goddess and considered sacred.

By 2000 B.C., however, in Mesopotamia, the act of weaving and the temple of the Goddess were appropriated by men. Priests, who had replaced the priestesses, passed out thread to master weavers and checked the finished work. Moreover, the early textile industries were built upon the labor of both female and male slaves, and although cloth was still special – particularly in Egypt – weavers were not. Women continued to be involved in some aspects of textile production, making and embellishing clothing and continuing to spin thread primarily for commercial use. But in most countries where textile industries developed, women lost control of an occupation that had traditionally been theirs.

When the Jews left Egypt, they were – according to the Bible – directed by God to build a tabernacle in the wilderness and embellish it, using the textile arts they had learned as slaves in Egypt. The Old Testament indicates that the Hebrews bred sheep for wool and that wool-spinning was done by women in accordance with biblical specifications for sacred fabrics. This passage from Exodus describes women embroidering the sacramental linen with pomegranates, which symbolized female fecundity.

"And they made the ephod of gold, blue and purple, and scarlet, and fine twined linen. And they did beat the gold into thin plates and cut it into wires to work it in the blue, and in the purple, and in the scarlet, and in the fine linen, with cunning work.

And they made upon the hems of the robe pomegranates of blue and purple, and scarlet and fine twined linen. And they made bells of pure gold, and put the bells between the pomegranates upon the hem of the robe, round about between the pomegranates."

— *Exodus*

Cretan women or priestesses are pictured here bringing sacrifices to the altar of the Great Goddess, who is represented by a cauldron flanked with pillars in the shape of stylized double axes. These were typical symbols in this goddess-worshiping culture.

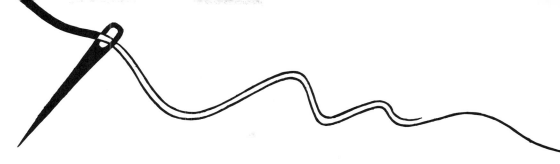

This contemporary image of a group of Navaho weavers demonstrates that whenever there was no developed textile industry in a culture, women's weaving continued to have social and spiritual significance. And, as always, they would pass this sacred tradition on to their daughters along with stories and legends like the following:

"Spider Woman instructed the Navaho women how to weave on a loom which Spider Man told them how to make. The crosspoles were made of sky and earth cords, the warp sticks of sun rays, the healds of rock crystal and sheet lightening. The batten was a sun halo, white shell made the comb. There were four spindles; one a stick of zigzag lightening with a whorl of cannel cloth; one a stick of flash lightening with a whorl of turquoise; a third had a stick of sheet lightening with a whorl of abalone; a rain streamer formed the stick of the fourth, and its whorl was white shell."

Navaho weavers.

Egyptian textile workers.

This bas-relief depicting a Mesopotamian woman spinning is one image which indicates that despite the transformation of weaving from a female craft into a male-dominated industry, women continued to participate in the creation of fabrics. Curiously, the switch from female to male-controlled fabric production coincided with the period in which Hammurabi established codified laws restricting women's rights.

Egyptian textile production was extremely sophisticated by 2500 B.C., and some sources suggest an even earlier date. Although linen, wool, and some cotton were all made for both domestic use and trade, linen was the most important product, and huge quantities were produced – particularly for mummy cloths. These "cerements" were six feet by seventy yards long and were woven using from 160 to 540 warp threads to the inch. (Today, machine-produced linen is capable of a maximum of 300 warp threads to the inch.) All Egyptian textile work was done by male and female slaves, including children. They worked in spinning mills, weaving workshops, and private households, usually under the terrible conditions that have been typical of many textile industries. The slaves were forced to work "in small rooms where the air was thick with the dust of fibers ... the weaver never tastes fresh air. If s/he does not produce the full day's allotment, s/he is beaten."

The origin of embroidery, like that of weaving, is unknown. Myths again recount that needle skills were taught to women by various female deities, and these have certainly been closely associated with women throughout history. Early evidence of embroidery has been found on fragments of cloth and leather. Costume details preserved on prehistoric clay figurines seem to indicate embroidered embellishments. One of the earliest forms of decorative stitches known was the twining stitch, which was probably done with the fingers while the fabric was on the loom.

Pieces of patterned fabrics from Egyptian tombs of the New Kingdom contain embroidery believed to have been introduced into Egypt during the XVIII dynasty. We know that the Egyptians ornamented their fabric with linen thread, silk, gold, and silver, using the chain and outline stitch as well as drawn threadwork.

The Greeks learned embroidery from the Egyptians, from the Jews – who acquired skills when they were enslaved – and as a result of trade with the East. Motifs were borrowed from the Egyptians and the Minoans, whom the Greeks conquered in 1200 B.C. These designs have been found on fragments of embroidered wool that date back to the fourth century B.C. Greek women learned embroidery from the slave women who worked in their household workshops.

Though women ceased to play a major role in textile production in Greece, female deities continued to be identified with needlework. Eileithyia, one of a triad of goddesses also including Artemis and Hera – both of whom had the spindle as their emblem – was a creation goddess associated with weaving. There are many references in Homer to goddesses, women, and the textile arts. In the Odyssey, he relates how Odysseus encountered Calypso and Circe on his wanderings. Both were seated at looms, Calypso holding a golden shuttle and Circe weaving "a great web; imperishable, such as in the handiwork of goddesses, fine of woof and full of grace and splendor."

In his account of the Trojan War, Homer speaks of Helen of Troy "weaving a web full ample, twofold, purple; and into it many a battle she'd woven Battles of Troy's steed tamers and bronze-mailed sons of Achaeans." He recounts Hector's farewell speech to Andromache, in which he warns her that – because Trojan women were valuable to the Greeks for their skills in weaving and embroidering – if he is killed in battle, she will be taken captive. Sorrowfully, he predicts that his wife, "will go to Argos to weave cloth for another and to draw water at the well, with bitterness in [her] heart, under the burden of hard necessity."

It was customary for special garments to be woven at temple workshops, then embroidered by women with images relating to the important events of a deity's life and presented at festivals. This detail from a relief-decorated Greek amphora shows a procession of Trojan women, led by Hecate, bringing an embroidered robe to Athena – the Greek goddess who was particularly associated with the textile arts. In this case, Hecate's efforts to appease Athena were in vain, as Troy was defeated and the women enslaved.

Detail: Greek amphora
c. 660 B.C.

Early Roman garments, which were quite simple, were embroidered with twining. This technique was used to make borders of different widths and colors signifying class and rank. As the Roman Empire developed, the fabrics used for clothing became more luxurious and the embroidery more elaborate. Intricate designs similar to those found in architecture and other arts were worked in gold, silver, and jewels by slaves, freedwomen, and noblewomen, who either stitched themselves or supervised the work in household workshops.

With the expansion of the empire, Romans encouraged indigenous textile production and then took both the products and the workers of these countries back to Rome. When they invaded the British Isles, they set up household workshops based on the *gynacea*. These continued in Britain even after the Roman legions withdrew and may have provided an atmosphere of support for English needlewomen, who later became known for their beautiful embroidery.

Greek and Roman legends abound of bands of independent textile women. According to Herodotus, there was a region in Western Greece – the Isles of Elisha – where all the women were employed as spinners. Other records describe a band of female weavers in Sybaris, which was colonized by the Greeks in 650 B.C. The island retained a female character into Roman times, apparently because the Greeks, who wanted the wool produced by the women, permitted matriarchal rule.

Sixteenth century engraving of Roman workshop.

Although early Greek women had only primitive textile skills, weaving and spinning were a major part of their duties in running a household. In order to build a developed industry, however, Greek troops brought conquered female slaves – particularly those who were sophisticated textile workers – from Troy and Egypt to Athens. They worked in Greek domestic workshops, thus causing a surplus of home production and the beginning of trade.

Details: Greek vase painting showing women weaving and spinning.

In early Roman times, as in Greece, the production of rudimentary wool and linen textiles took place in the household. Later, shops developed in which textiles were manufactured by female slaves and freedwomen under the direction of Roman matrons. These shops, called *gynacea*, derived their name from the *gynaeceum* – the room in Roman houses where women wove, spun, and embroidered, as they are pictured doing in this sixteenth-century engraving.

The decline of the Roman Empire brought an end to the classical world and marked a great change in women's circumstances. The early period of history, when women played a significant role in the development of civilization, gave way to increasing disenfranchisement, restriction, and even sequestering of women. These changes are reflected in the runner designs on the first wing of the table, epitomized by the last image – a symbol of the silencing and punishing of Hypatia, who represents women's efforts to regain some aspects of their earlier position.

This triangular image – which pays homage to an aspect of women's neglected needlework accomplishments – recurs at each of the three corners of the *Dinner Party* table. Embroidered in various whitework techniques, these Millennium triangles combine domestic and religious traditions and infuse the secular dinner party with a sacramental character.

the vision of an equalized world.

And She Gathered All before Her

And She made for them A Sign to See

And lo They saw a Vision

From this day forth Like to like in All things

And then all that divided them merged

And then Everywhere was Eden Once again

These woven banners welcome you to *The Dinner Party*.

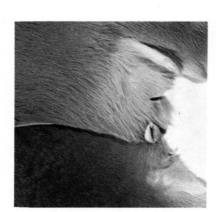

Runner detail.

Illuminated capital.

Primordial Goddess plate.

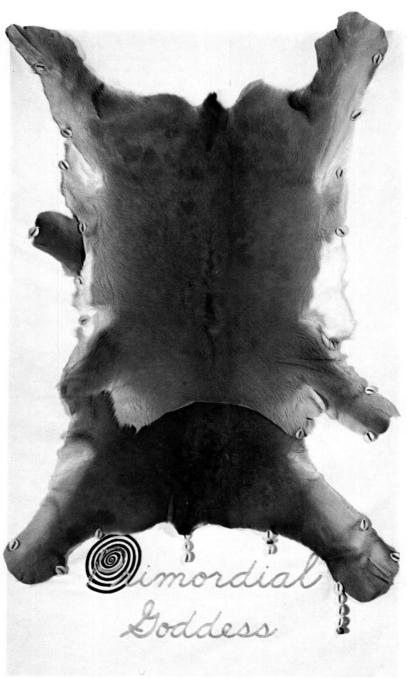

Full runner.

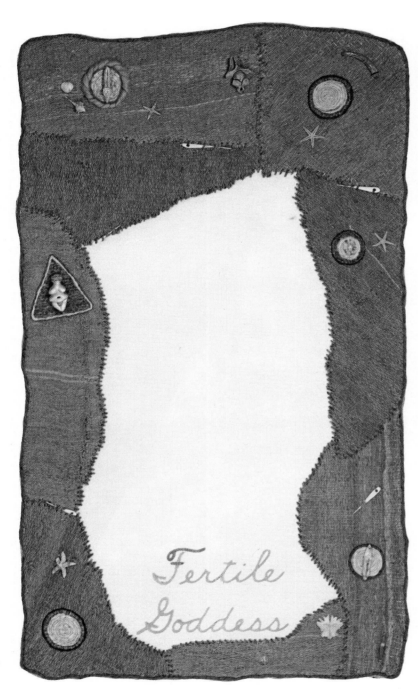

Full runner.

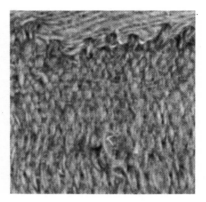

Detail of weaving.

Porcelain figurine.

Fertile Goddess plate.

Illuminated capital.

Ishtar plate.

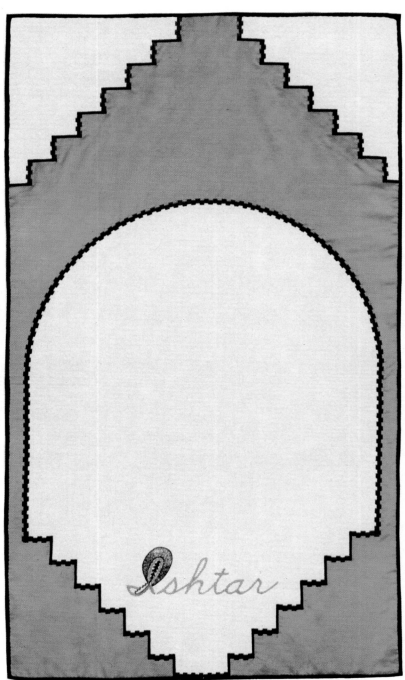

Full runner.

with teaching women the textile arts.

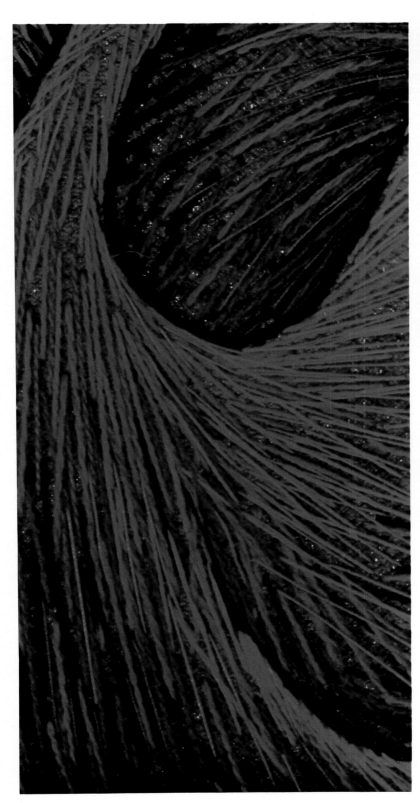

Detail of stitching.

Full runner.

Kali plate.

Full runner.

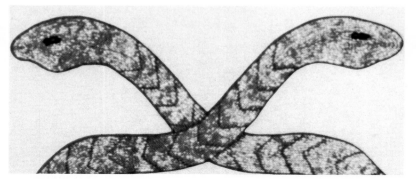

Detail: couched snakes.

Snake Goddess plate.

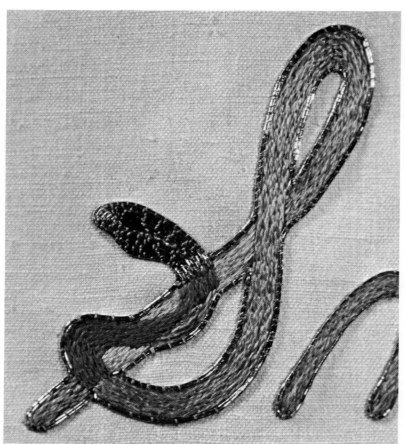

Illuminated capital.

Detail: petals.

Sophia plate.

Full runner.

Full runner.

Detail: runner back.

Amazon plate.

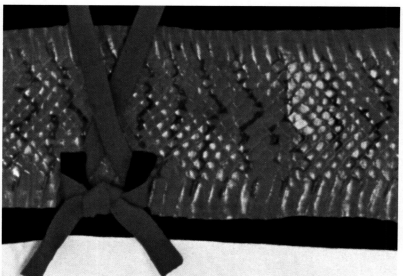

Detail: snakeskin and lacing.

Section of back of runner.

Great, great woman hath done things

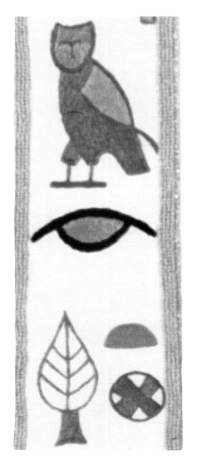

Detail: side band.

Hatshepsut plate.

Full runner.

of all kinds precious.

Roundlet and back border.

Embroidered figure on runner front.

Ankh symbol on runner front.

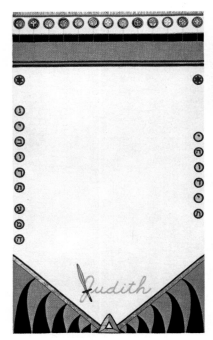

Full runner.

Detail: back of runner.

Judith plate.

Belt buckle.

Embroidered Star of David.

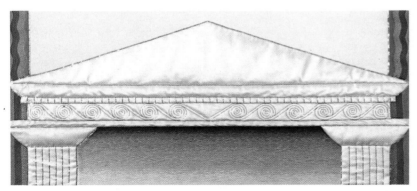

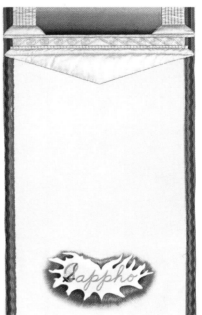

Back of runner.

Full runner.

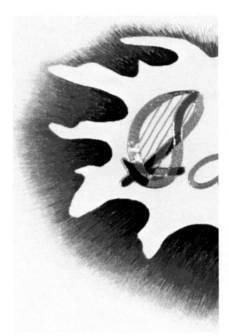

Detail: side band.

Detail: front of runner.

Sappho plate.

Full runner.

Palmette from back band.

Aspasia plate.

Detail: front of runner.

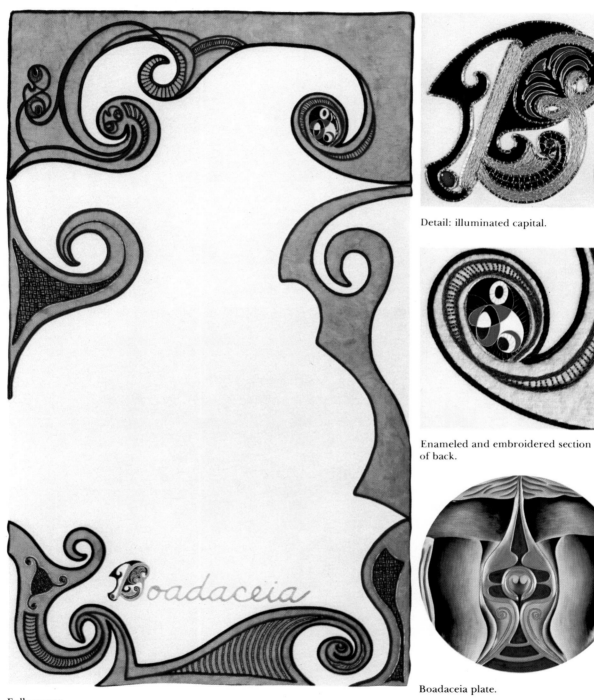

Full runner.

Detail: illuminated capital.

Enameled and embroidered section
of back.

Boadaceia plate.

Boadaceia

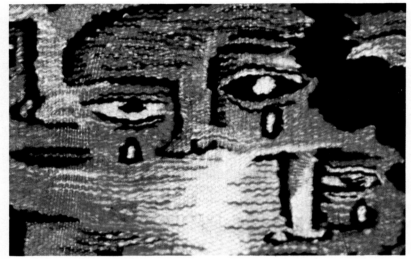

Section of woven runner back.

Full runner.

Hypatia plate.

Detail: illuminated capital.

The first Millennium runner marks the entryway to *The Dinner Party*. Positioned between place settings for the Primordial Goddess and Georgia O'Keeffe, it links the past and present and signifies the future.

The black spiral of the capital letter – a reference to the spiral forms carved and painted on rocks as symbols of the Goddess – was painted on the linen with heat-set fabric paint.

Primordial Goddess

The first runner represents the paleolithic period, which was characterized by primitive needlework techniques. Women punched holes in animal skins and – with needles made of bone and animal ligament or hair for thread – sewed them into clothing. Sometimes these garments were adorned with shells, particularly those of the cowry, which were thought to have magical properties and were associated with female fertility.

In the first mockup we painted a border which matched the dark, earth-red color of the plate. This border was to be made of leather, decorated with bone needles and cowry shells, and then stitched to the linen runner. We chose a piece of commercially produced leather with a deep burgundy tone, and Kathleen Schneider did the translation from the painted mockup. When the runner was almost complete, however, we knew it wasn't working. The leather surface looked machine-made; the clean cuts, made with a matte knife, looked slick and phony; the cowries and beads looked contrived. The simple, spontaneous quality of the mockup was lost, and the appearance of the runner was completely inconsistent with the historical model upon which it was based. In paleolithic times, the whole skin of the animal was trimmed with a flint scraper and used almost intact. It took us many months and several attempts before we could make a runner as simple as the Primordial Goddess required.

The spiral form is frequently found in art dating from paleolithic times. This block with spiral decorations is outside the entrance to New Grange, the site of a megalithic tomb.

The Primordial Goddess was the first runner designed and one of the very last finished. It went through many transformations, from the original painted mockup to the finished runner, which is covered by soft fur hides.

Primordial Goddess place setting.

Most early societies were matriarchal, and in almost all ancient religions the feminine principle was seen as the fundamental cosmic force. This female creative energy is embodied in the Primordial Goddess, who symbolized the universal female principle from which all life emerged.

Finally we found some small, supple skins of an unborn calf, which had a beautiful shape and a wonderfully soft brown-and-white color. We overlapped the two skins on the linen runner, much as our foremothers might have done, working with them until we found a shape we liked. We attached the skins to the linen with strong thread from the underside and placed cowry shells (later to be attached with leather strips) around the edge of the hides. We then added a short string of cowries and stone beads to the front of the runner, to enhance the beautiful lines of the hides, and placed the plate directly on top of the skins.

Schneider and Hill scraping hides.

I had studied the crafts of the North American Indians at the University of Wisconsin during my undergraduate schooling. There I learned the Native American techniques of tanning deerskin, beading moccasins, carving bone needles, doing willow wicker work, and making rawhide and sinew – a wonderfully interesting collection of skills which I thought would never be put to practical use outside the classroom. Four years later I found myself in Los Angeles, trying to convince Judy Chicago that tanning our own deerskin was a symbolic act that couldn't be passed up, especially since I possessed the knowledge and the deep desire to perform this ancient craft – traditional women's work.

During a trip to Idaho in September, I made arrangements with the Department of Natural Resources in Pocatello to ship me three or four hides of deers killed accidentally. (This solved the problem of needlessly killing an animal, something which we all opposed.) Two months later I received two boxes of fresh deerskins. The next day Susan and I set to work with sharp knives and determination, attempting to deflesh the hairy skins (the first step in the tanning process). After a few hours and little progress, we decided that the number of maggots found on the skins made them unsatisfactory for our purposes, and we threw them in the trash bin, wondering what the garbage collectors would think of this rather grisly mess.

—*Kathleen Schneider*

We made several mockups for the Primordial Goddess. In the second version, we worked with an irregularly shaped piece of thick, tan leather which was laid out over most of the surface of the runner. I had an idea about positioning the plate in an opening in the center of the leather-covered runner – an opening that would appear forcibly pulled apart. Since the plate represented the feminine as the source of all life, I wanted to place it in an environment that would suggest the violence which accompanied the creation of the universe.

We cut jagged pieces in the middle of the leather and pulled them back upon themselves, stretching and tearing the leather as we did so. After securing these pieces with roughly stitched cowry shells, we tried flax and fleece wrapped in coils inside the opening under the plate. I didn't like this version any more than the first and felt unequipped to pretend I was a prehistoric woman.

Working on early mockup.

Second mockup.

Despite the enormous amount of work that went into the translation of the second mockup, it still ended up looking as if it had been made at the local craft shop.

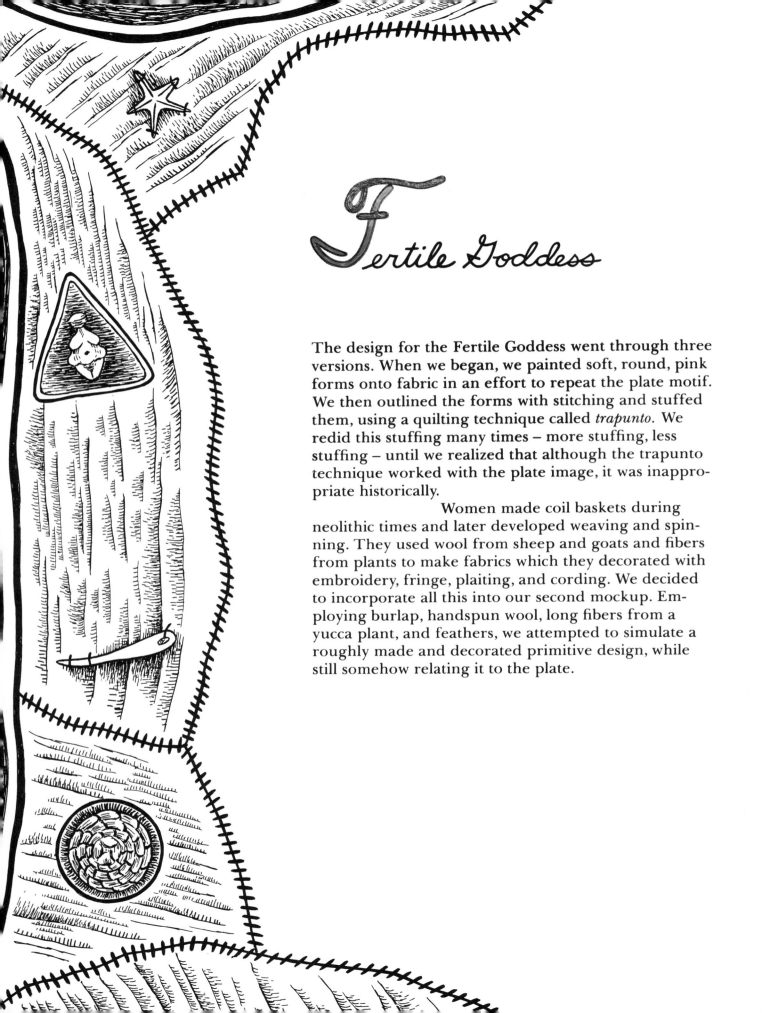

ℱertile Goddess

The design for the Fertile Goddess went through three versions. When we began, we painted soft, round, pink forms onto fabric in an effort to repeat the plate motif. We then outlined the forms with stitching and stuffed them, using a quilting technique called *trapunto*. We redid this stuffing many times – more stuffing, less stuffing – until we realized that although the trapunto technique worked with the plate image, it was inappropriate historically.

Women made coil baskets during neolithic times and later developed weaving and spinning. They used wool from sheep and goats and fibers from plants to make fabrics which they decorated with embroidery, fringe, plaiting, and cording. We decided to incorporate all this into our second mockup. Employing burlap, handspun wool, long fibers from a yucca plant, and feathers, we attempted to simulate a roughly made and decorated primitive design, while still somehow relating it to the plate.

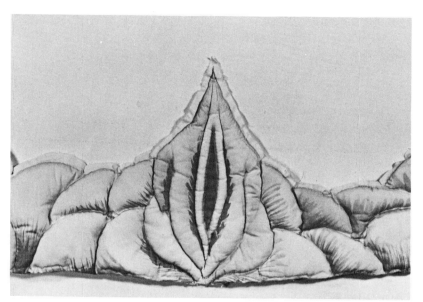

When I began designing the needlework, I tended to simply try to extend the image on the plate onto the
front and back of the runner. At
first I didn't pay very much attention to the historical period we were
representing with the runner or to
the textile technique appropriate to
that period. But gradually I came to
see the runner as the context or environment in which each woman
lived, and I wanted it to reflect her
context through both the design and
the technique.

Section of trapunto mockup.

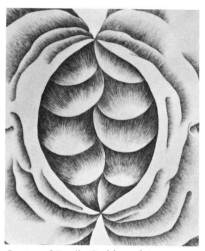

Center of Fertile Goddess plate.

Fertile Goddess place setting.

The generalized concept
of the universe as amor-
phous and feminine gave
way to the idea of the
female human being as
magical and holy. Woman
herself – whose body was
the symbol of birth and
rebirth and the source of
nourishment, protection,
and warmth – was wor-
shiped as a "Fertile
Goddess."

We made coils out of the handspun wool and molded a group of small clay figurines like the amulets created in tribute to early goddesses from which the plate image was derived. Attaching both the coils and the fetishes to the runner, we added feather borders, a band of carefully dyed and woven flax, and additional fleece wrapped with pale green yucca fibers. The runner matched the plate in color perfectly, yet it looked as if it belonged in a contemporary craft fair. We discarded it and did not resolve the design of this runner until much later in the Project.

We tried many versions of small coils for the Fertile Goddess runner. Coils were used in both early women's basketry and pottery, and we wanted our coiled forms to suggest the rich tradition to which they referred.

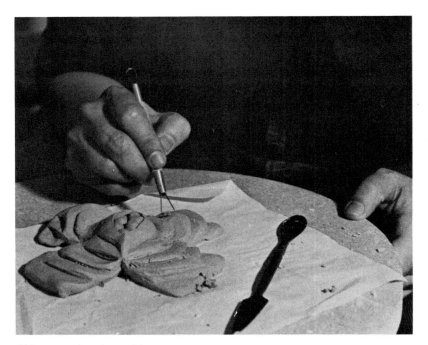

Chicago carving clay goddess.

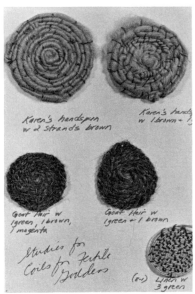

Coil tests by Hesterman.

It was wonderful making the small clay goddesses for the Fertile Goddess. A number of us worked on them for several days. Those we didn't use ended up as necklaces or positioned over the doorways in the studio.

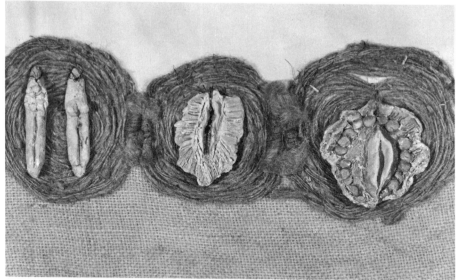

Detail: Back of early mockup.

Spinning fleece with a drop spindle.

Eventually we were able to create a simpler, more direct design, although the tendency to make these early runners too complex remained a problem. In the final runner, we wove rough fabric in pieces and crudely stitched it to the linen. We placed the coils, clay figurines, and bone needles on the woven surface, but the addition of shells, rocks, and beads soon made the runner look cluttered again. Then one night, about eleven o'clock, we stripped the Fertile Goddess of all her adornments. Selecting just a few of the original pieces, we carefully arranged them on the fabric and pronounced the runner complete.

Arla Hesterman learned to use a drop spindle – a tool developed thousands of years ago and traditionally associated with the Goddess and symbolic of the transitory nature of life. Hesterman spun fleece into long strands of wool which were wound into coils of different sizes, then stitched in a variety of patterns until we found one we liked.

"Mistress Sun sat on a bare stone
And spun on her golden distaff
For three hours before the sun rose."

41

"In the beginning, there was the Earth Goddess; the Sky-God married the Earth Goddess, and she wove the whole world as a big mantle and spread it over an oak. The world is actually a huge coat, which is spread over an enormous world tree, the oak; in it are the ocean and the earth and everything else. The sum of it is reality."

Detail: final runner.

The drop spindle was one of the earliest tools invented by women.

"Life built herself a myriad of
    forms,
And flashing her electric spark,
Flew shuttlewise above, beneath,
Weaving the web of life and
    death."
        —Source unknown

"The warp was woven at noon,
The woof in the house of dawn,
The rest in the hall of the
    sun..."

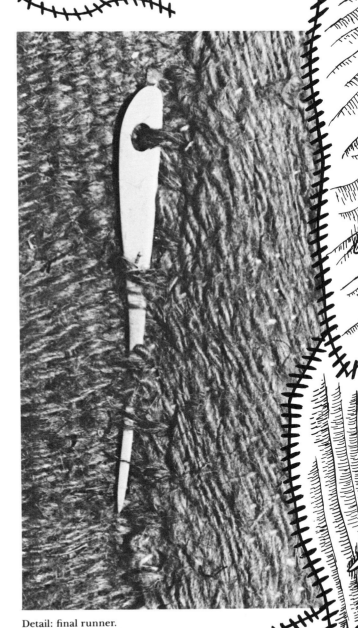

Adrienne Weiss wove the pieces for the final runner on a simple loom. Her warp was flax and her weft was wool and hair, hand-spun in the studio. When the woven pieces had been sewn in place on the runner with cotton thread, long, straight, even stitches were used to bind the fragments to the linen. The stitches were made with plied wool equal in weight to the weft threads.

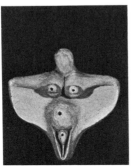

Chicago's prototype for figurines.

The bone needles were made from the femur of a cow. The bone was stewed, cleaned, and cut into small pieces. Kathleen Schneider chose the strongest of the pieces, avoiding the fragile ones nearest the marrow. Each piece was shaped with a file and then polished by hand until smooth.

Detail: final runner.

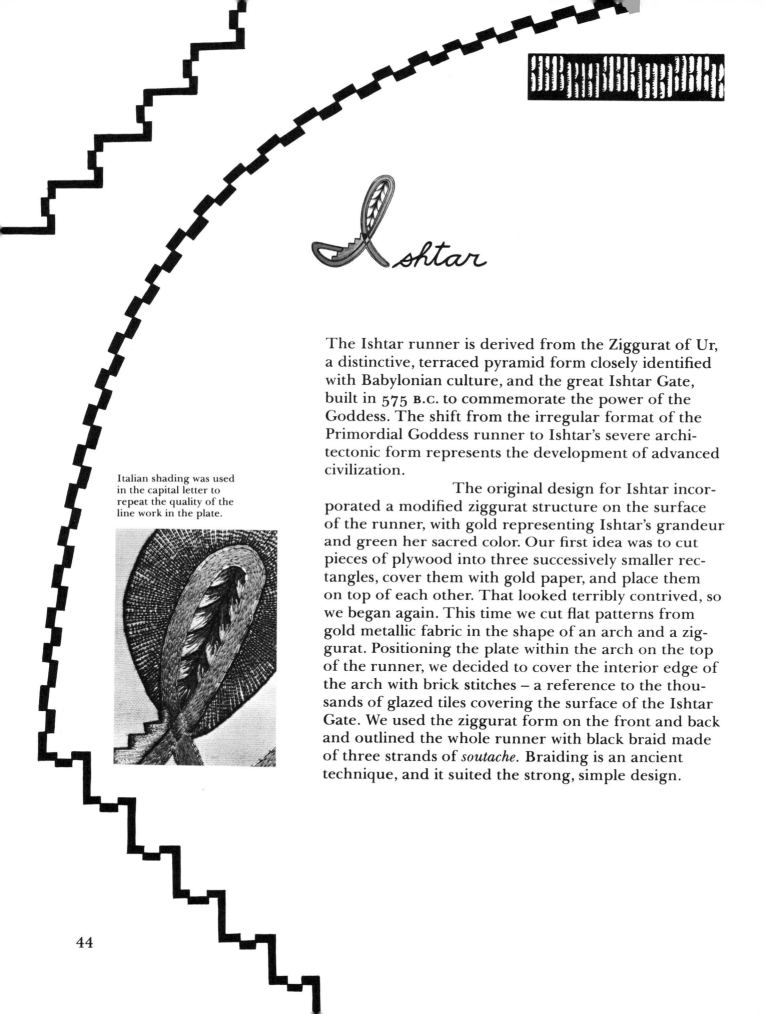

Ishtar

Italian shading was used
in the capital letter to
repeat the quality of the
line work in the plate.

The Ishtar runner is derived from the Ziggurat of Ur,
a distinctive, terraced pyramid form closely identified
with Babylonian culture, and the great Ishtar Gate,
built in 575 B.C. to commemorate the power of the
Goddess. The shift from the irregular format of the
Primordial Goddess runner to Ishtar's severe archi-
tectonic form represents the development of advanced
civilization.

The original design for Ishtar incorporated a modified ziggurat structure on the surface
of the runner, with gold representing Ishtar's grandeur
and green her sacred color. Our first idea was to cut
pieces of plywood into three successively smaller rec-
tangles, cover them with gold paper, and place them
on top of each other. That looked terribly contrived, so
we began again. This time we cut flat patterns from
gold metallic fabric in the shape of an arch and a ziggurat. Positioning the plate within the arch on the top
of the runner, we decided to cover the interior edge of
the arch with brick stitches – a reference to the thousands of glazed tiles covering the surface of the Ishtar
Gate. We used the ziggurat form on the front and back
and outlined the whole runner with black braid made
of three strands of *soutache*. Braiding is an ancient
technique, and it suited the strong, simple design.

Brick stitch.

Once the design was drawn on the linen, we chose satin for the appliquéd form. Since satin moves as you sew, creating puckers, we lined it with flannel, which helped – but not enough. The long basting stitches used to hold the flannel in place made lines in the surface of the satin when the Ishtar runner was ironed. We removed these with steaming, blocked the linen to bring it back into a rectangle, steamed the satin to ease the puckers, and added areas of felt to the lining to make the surface smooth.

Simich plotting Ishtar Gate.

Ishtar Gate.

Making the technical drawing for Ishtar was one of the most difficult problems our technical illustrator, Helene Simich, encountered. She worked for at least three days plotting the curve, dividing it into equal parts for the tiny green brick border, making a template, and finally drawing the pattern onto the linen. She was determined to make all the steps equal and even, but – because the linen moved as she worked – she had to do the drawing several times.

Ishtar place setting.

Ishtar, the Great Goddess of Mesopotamia, "the giver and taker of life," was believed by those who worshiped her to be a being whose power was infinite. Revered for thousands of years, she expressed the power of the female principle as lifegiving, protecting, and nourishing, and reflected women's social and political power in early history.

45

$\mathcal{K}$ali

After the design for Kali was painted onto the fabric incorporating colors from the plate, Connie von Briesen – an accomplished needleworker and painter – translated the mockup using an original technique. Her intention was to match the lusters in the plate. Overlaying gorgeously colored, sheer, iridescent fabric called "luminaire," she built the deep purples with as many as ten layers of color. She reproduced the shimmering whites by using pale fabrics over each other, creating a pearlescent effect. To unify the tones, she covered the colors with a fine net. The fabrics were then invisibly tacked in place, and the outlines of the forms were embroidered in the stem stitch through the fabric layer. With tiny scissors, slowly taking one stroke at a time, Von Briesen cut away the excess fabric. Using individual threads to create line work similar to the pen work on the Kali plate, Von Briesen embroidered the surface with Appleton wool, Ver au Soie silk, cotton embroidery floss, and strands of sewing cotton.

Hill and Chicago working with Connie von Briesen, who transformed the traditional stem stitch and the long-and-short stitch so that the threads give the illusion of shaded strokes of a pencil.

Stitching the arms of the Goddess.

The back of the runner represents the gaping maw traditionally associated with Kali. But instead of symbolizing destruction, as this image has in the past, the forms express the beauty of feminine strength.

In Kali, an ancient Indian goddess, the death aspect of the Goddess ceased to be part of a unified and venerated concept and became instead a separate and terrifying entity. The traditionally positive view of female power was misrepresented as a destructive force, coinciding with the loss of women's authority and the diminishment of women's status.

The reaching forms on the front of the runner are derived from the many-armed representations of Kali.

Kali place setting.

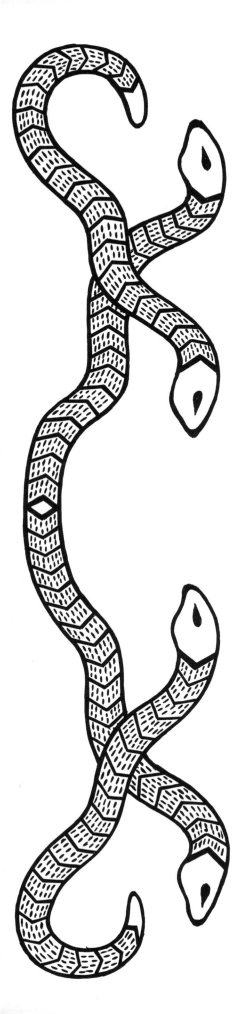

Snake Goddess

The runner for the Snake Goddess relates directly to small Minoan figurines called "snake goddesses." These were found in shrines or buried with the dead and identify Crete as a goddess-worshiping society. Depicted with snakes in their headdresses or around their arms, these goddess figures were carved from ivory, banded in gold, and usually represented as wearing bell-shaped skirts with tiers or flounces.

The color and iconography of these sculptures are reflected in the runner, which is done primarily in yellows, browns, and golds. The snake motif is incorporated into the illuminated letter as well as the entwined snakes on the back. These shimmering serpents are couched in Japanese gold with threads of contrasting colors. The runner is bordered by inkle-loom woven strips embroidered in a pattern similar to that found on Minoan garments. The ruffles on the front and back of the runner refer, of course, to the costumes of the original snake goddesses. After many frustrating attempts to make these ruffles, Pearl Krause – an experienced fashion designer – showed us that instead of gathering fabric to produce a flounce as we had been doing, we could cut a semicircular strip on the fabric bias that would produce beautiful, undulating curves.

Detail: couched snakes on back of runner.

The snakes, made of strands of Japanese gold and couched with Maltese silk thread, were also couched with two strands of DMC cotton floss to create the snakeskin pattern. Pam Checkie worked meticulously on these snakes for months – first in our Santa Monica studio, then at her home.

Sculpture of Cretan Snake Goddess which was the source for the runner design.

"Once upon a time, long long ago, when there were no poisonous snakes and the python was the king of the reptiles, there lived a woman called Aunt Eve. One day the python, who was snow white, met Eve, and she asked the snake to live with her. After much persuasion, the python consented on condition that Eve knit a pattern on his back in order to make him beautiful. Eve began and knit the most beautiful pattern on the snake's back, commencing from his tail."
—Malayan myth

The relationship between the snake and the female has its origins in the goddess religions of earliest history. The snake was the embodiment of psychic vision and oracular divination – both of which were traditionally considered to be among women's magical powers.

Detail: front band.

Jan Marie DuBois used an inkle loom to weave the runner borders with six strands of DMC cotton embroidery floss for both warp and weft. (The word "inkle" refers to a band, belt, tape, or any other long, narrow strip; inkles have been woven for thousands of years.) The herringbone stitch was used to simulate patterns from Cretan costumes.

Snake Goddess place setting.

Sophia

The flower/petal image for Sophia's runner is consistent with the imagery on the plate. The iconography of both the runner and the plate is derived from traditional representations of Sophia, who symbolizes the highest form of feminine wisdom and takes her form as a flower. The petal shapes were cut from sheer fabrics in colors that matched those of the plate. These were overlapped on the runner to create both gradual color fades and a strong interior white area.

Because working with silk chiffon was so difficult, we had to devise a special method for making the petal forms. Stephanie Martin and Karen Valentine made patterns of each shape, consisting of two or more layers and different colors of chiffon. The edges were carefully sewn with a French seam and the petals were turned inside out, gently pressed, and tacked in place with silk thread.

When the runner was finished, its brilliant color was too intense for the pale plate and it had to be muted. This muting also represented the waning of female power. We used some white chiffon to shroud the colors, but it was not quite right; then Valentine offered her wedding veil, which created a perfect visual effect and emphasized the symbolic aspect of the runner.

The muting of feminine wisdom.

The muting of Sophia's runner with Karen Valentine's bridal veil saddened me. Watching those wonderful colors being subdued was difficult. Then I realized how fitting it was, as Chicago had intended it to be – as a metaphor speaking softly, reminding us again of our subdued history.

—*Stephanie Martin*

Valentine and her wedding veil.

The strangest part of giving my veil for Sophia's runner was that everyone in the studio insisted that I put it on before we cut into it. It was made of the softest netting and had completely covered me and trailed behind me on the floor on my wedding day. Now the fairytale was over, and here I was prancing around an art studio in my wedding veil and jeans.

—*Karen Valentine*

The Sophia runner started to become special on the first day we all sat down at the table to begin the design. We had a pile of multi-colored scraps, and we began to cut petals and arrange them in color sequence. Chicago asked if any of us knew who Sophia was; no one did. While we were working, she read to us about Sophia and what she represented.

—*Karen Valentine*

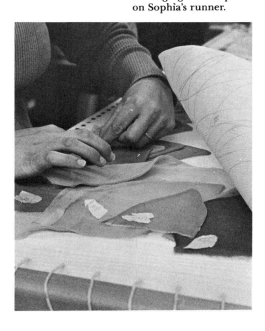

Arranging chiffon petals on Sophia's runner.

Sophia place setting.

The concept of Sophia developed in the centuries after Christ, when early Gnostic religions believed in her as an incorporeal reality – the active thought of God – who created the world. Conceived as the highest form of feminine wisdom, her power was diluted and she became a purely spiritual image. Through this transformation, the gradual contraction of women's position in society can be observed.

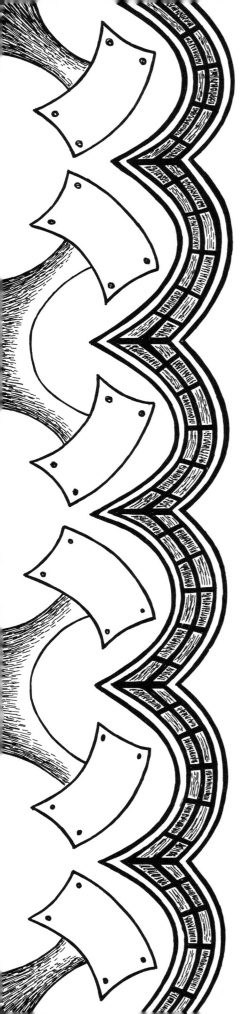

Amazon

The symbols of the egg, the crescent, the breastplates, and the double axe which had been used in the Amazon plate were repeated in the runner. The simplicity of the design belies the difficulty of its construction. The white satin egg was slightly padded with felt, appliquéd, and outlined with couched black silk threads. The crescents were executed in a padded satin stitch and edged with the same black cotton floss used to embroider the triangle. In the breastplates, we tried to simulate – with silk thread – the metallic quality of the lusters used in the plate; eventually we found beautiful copper and silver fibers, which were carefully couched by Elfie Schwitkis. The axe handles were stitched in DMC perle cotton using a modified long-and-short stitch to shade from black to white. After lengthy experimentation with nickel, chrome-plated metal, and then plastic, the final axe blades were made of titanium, a silvery metal that will not tarnish or discolor but is strong and light. The blades are attached to the runner with French knots made of copper fibers.

These copper French knots, derived from the studs on the laced boots Amazons wore in battle, are repeated on the lacing that appears on the top of the runner. The red snakeskin strip bordering the front of the runner refers to the material used by the Amazons for their boots and shields. The black, red, and white colors were traditionally associated with these great warrior women of antiquity.

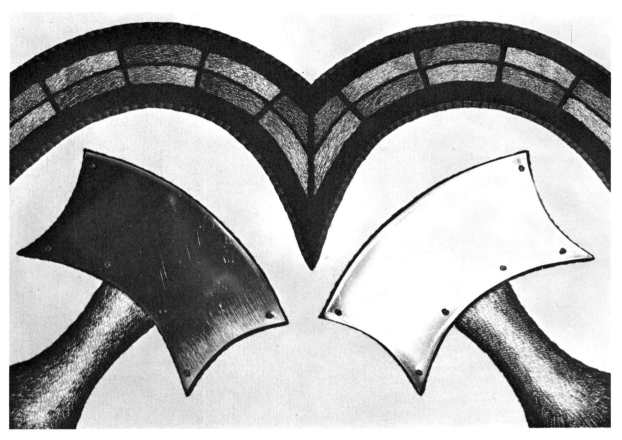

Detail: back of runner.

The Amazons were reputed to
wear breastplates into battle
and to carry a double axe in
each hand. This "labyris" was a
traditional part of the worship
of the Mother Goddess and was
also used to cut down trees.

Amazon place setting.

Amazon societies are
thought to have existed
during the third and sec-
ond millennia B.C., one on
a lost island off the coast
of North Africa and
others on the southern
shore of the Black Sea.
They were communal,
clan-based cultures and
were egalitarian, demo-
cratic, and generally
peaceable. There is evi-
dence that some of the
women in these societies
fought in battles against
the encroaching patriar-
chal forces.

Detail: back of runner.

The white egg symbolized fertility; the red crescent referred to the moon, traditionally associated with women; and the triangle was the sign of the Goddess.

The Amazon runner seemed to have a willful life of its own. Inexplicably and repeatedly, the linen stretched on the frame, making the runner too big for our format. When I tried to bring it back to shape, the runner – like the legendary Amazon warriors – resisted every attempt to be controlled.
—*S. H.*

Detail: side lacing.

54

The most common way in which Greek art depicted the Amazon was as dying or wounded, as shown in this classical relief. The vanquishing of these warrior women seemed to be of singular importance to the Greeks.

"What more can I say to you about these Amazons? They have done so much, by the force of their bodies, these women of Amazonia who were throughout all countries feared and respected. And even into the land of Greece, which was rather remote from them, the news traveled about them and how these women did not cease invading and conquering lands, and how they went everywhere laying countries and territories to waste unless all was given over to them, and how there was no force which could resist them. And because of this, Greece was terrified, fearing as it did that the force of these women would be extended into their very own country."
—Christine de Pisan

The lacing on the front of the runner is derived from this detail of the Pergammon Altar, depicting Amazons in battle.

Hatshepsut

1503–1482 B.C., Egypt

Hatshepsut's capital letter combines the eye of justice with the life-giving symbol of the Pharaoh.

The design for Hatshepsut's runner combines elements from the frescoes of her tomb, details of pharaonic costume, and motifs from the plate. The blue roundlets on the back of the runner evolved from the collars traditionally worn by the Pharaohs and also repeat the blue forms on the plate. (In the New Kingdom, blue-green was a color associated with gods and goddesses, and worn by rulers.) We determined the design for the patterned border below the roundlets by studying photographs of Hatshepsut's tomb. The walls of her tomb contained bands with geometric motifs and hieroglyphic panels separated by pink or green lines. We repeated these colors in the thin borders and divisions of the runner design, which are done in the tent stitch.

Chicago painting mockup.

Marilyn Akers translating
Chicago's design into
needlweork.

Hatshepsut's runner was
the first put into production. Marilyn Akers, a
university student, began
work on the roundlets in
October 1976. She had
Helene Simich divide each
semicircle into narrow
bands parallel to the edge,
which provided her with a
precise guide for the rows
of color. Using the long-
and-short stitch and working with six strands of silk
thread, Akers gradually
decreased the number of
strands as she shaded to
the lightest colors. This
heightened the visual illusion of the form.

Hatshepsut place setting.

Hatshepsut, the mighty
ruler of the XVIII
dynasty, was one of four
female Pharaohs in
Egypt. She bolstered
Egypt's economy through
trade, strengthened her
country's defense, initi-
ated many building proj-
ects, and achieved peace
and prosperity during
her reign. There is evi-
dence that she also introduced embroidery into
Egypt.

Carved portrait of Hat-
shepsut on fragment of
obelisk at Karnak (wear-
ing the kind of collar
which inspired the round-
lets on the back of the
runner).

*The design of both Hatshepsut's
plate and runner incorporates art-
historical themes in a more direct
way than any of the previous images. After the earlier runners were
designed, I decided to use more
specific historical iconography. This
both expanded my imagery and presented an increased esthetic challenge: how to create a synthesis between my personal imagery and
varying artistic styles.*

Detail: roundlet on back of runner embroidered by M. Akers.

Detail: back border.

Before designing the border pattern for the runner, we researched the Egyptians' method of making the colored bands that were embroidered on their garments. We came upon a description of stitches that "went over and over a specific number of threads," which seemed similar to the needlepoint technique called tent stitching. Deciding to use it, we experimented and found that we could stitch over canvas with just the right tension and then withdraw the warp of the canvas, leaving the even rows of "over-and-over" stitches. We used a 22-mesh canvas because we wanted the scale of the stitching to be as fine as the linen thread count.

The oldest known form of writing is the hieroglyphic, in which various objects – both animate and inanimate – are depicted as accurately as possible by descriptive characters. The hieroglyphic system was probably brought from northeast or central Asia to Egypt, where it was carved into tomb walls; painted on stone, wood, and later paper; and embroidered onto garments.

Fragment of Egyptian fabric.

The hieroglyphic characters represent a roughly translated narrative praising Hatshepsut's reign. These were embroidered in split stitch using one or two strands of DMC thread. The stitching was done on appliquéd bands of fine, closely woven linen that approximates the high-quality linen cloth made in Egypt at least 4000 years ago. (Linen was thought to be a gift from the goddess Isis.) We chose the whitest fabric we could find, as Egyptians dressed almost entirely in white – their sacred color and a symbol of truth. When these bands were finished, the edges were embroidered in the tent stitch and then couched with two strands of Japanese gold. It required almost two years of work to complete this runner.

![top hieroglyphic band]

These traditional hieroglyphic characters were combined to create a series of phrases about Hatshepsut and her reign.

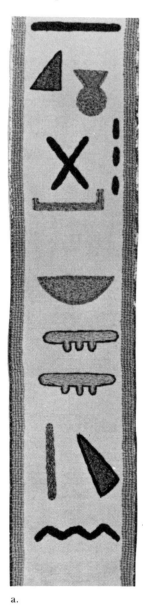

a.

b.

Embroidered hieroglyphs for runner.

a. Egypt under the majesty of the ever-living Queen; beloved daughter of Isis; mighty lady of two lands.

b. Mighty one of strength; Great great woman hath done things of all kinds precious; Well-doing Queen of the Eighteenth Dynasty.

c. The Queen, the lady of the two lands.

d. Beloved goddess rising like the moon over Egypt.

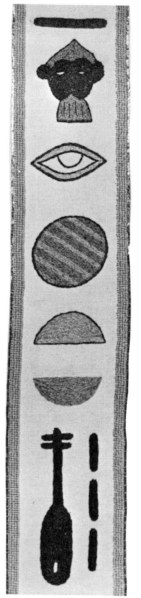

c.

d.

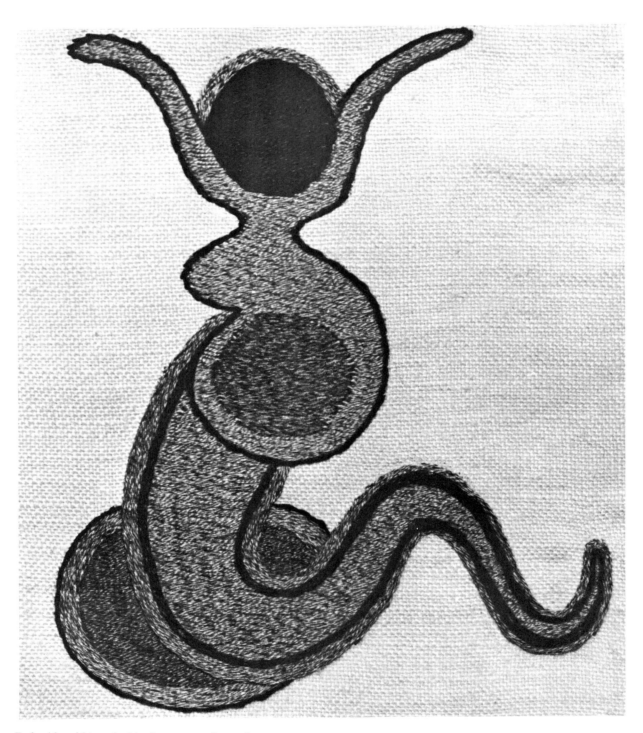

Embroidered hieroglyphic character on front of runner.

The front band of the
runner includes five sym-
bols suggesting the
phrase, "Well-doing God-
dess, Just Pharaoh of
Egypt." A female Pharaoh
was considered the earthly
representative of Isis and
symbolized the continuing
female vitality inherent
in the throne. This embroidered character is the
symbol for the Goddess.

Representation of Neith.

In Egyptian mythology, weaving represented the creation of
life, and Neith and Isis were
both associated with weaving.
Neith was referred to as "the
great weaver" who wove the
world on her loom. She was
often represented standing
with a shuttle on her head. The
shuttle, which is connected to
the magical power of the Goddess, is in the shape of the
mandorla – symbol of the inter-
section of heaven and earth.
The invention of weaving is attributed to Isis, and she is also
credited with teaching this art
to women.

Judith

6th century B.C., Hebrew

The design for the illuminated capital letter was prompted by the image of Judith beheading Holofernes with a sword, by the seventeenth-century Italian painter Artemisia Gentileschi.

Our conception for the Judith runner was influenced by a Yemenite dowry headdress which relates to traditional Middle Eastern bridal headcoverings. Jewish needlework was generally patterned on the prevalent style or technique of the country in which the Jews settled. In this case the headdress, which combines different fabrics and forms of ornamentation, reflects the Middle Eastern custom of displaying the dowry money as a symbol of both the bride's wealth and her position as chattel.

The runner – translated from the mockup by Terry Blecher – is a rich mixture of wool, velvet, and linen, embellished with embroidery, beading, silk and metal cording, gold fringe, and dangling coins. The front of the runner contains appliquéd forms of wool and velvet that repeat the shapes in the plate. In the center there is a bold beaded and corded triangular belt buckle, which suggests Judith's strength as well as the ornamentation used on ancient Hebrew clothing. The triangle, symbol of the female, attests to Judith's allegiance to women.

The top of the runner contains a series of Hebrew letters, carefully satin-stitched inside beaded circles. These letters form phrases identifying Judith as the heroine of her people. Two Jewish stars appear in similarly beaded circles on the back of the runner. Below these there is a band of wool like that on the front, edged with beading and cording, from which hang thirteen specially made coins.

Detail: buckle on front of runner.

The belt buckle and the ribbed bands on the front of the runner were made from a combination of gold cord, strands of Japanese gold, and bronze beads.

Judith place setting.

Judith, a Jewish heroine, is a legendary figure whose story is told in the *Book of Judith,* written to inspire the Jews to acts of heroism. Savior of her people, she is representative of the strength and courage of early biblical women.

Embroidered phrase on top of runner.

An antique Jewish bridal headdress covered with dowry coins – a reminder of women's position as chattel.

The design for these coins, which were made by Juliet Myers (a printmaker, photographer, and former member of the research team), was derived from ancient Jewish coinage. During nearly every period in which Jewish coins were struck, the pomegranate appeared on the reverse side of the coins. Rich in symbol and metaphor, the pomegranate – characteristically depicted as three fruits on a single stem – represented blessing and fertility and also connoted piety, good deeds, and knowledge. Our coins incorporate this triple image and depict the pomegranate at the moment of transition from flower to fruit.

The heroine of her people.

Detail: back of runner.

Three pomegranates on a single stem are a characteristic symbol on Jewish coins. This traditional coin was the source for Juliet Myers' design for the coins on Judith's runner.

Juliet Myers had fourteen-gauge sheet metal cut into discs at a machine shop, made a stencil from her drawing, and cut masks for each of the discs. Using transparent contact paper to mask the pomegranate forms and rust-proof spray paint to cover the surrounding area, she coated the edges and backs of the coins with asphaltum, an acid-resistant blockout. The coins were placed in a solution of one part nitric acid to ten parts water, and this chemical bath etched only the paint-treated area. This allowed the pomegranates and the edges of each coin to remain smooth and highly polished while the background acquired an etched texture which became dark and dull after sulfur oxidation. The thirteen coins were attached to the runner with gold cords through small holes drilled into the coins.

Ancient Jewish coin.

Myers' drawing for Judith's coins.

Sappho

b. 612 B.C, Greece

The illuminated capital for Sappho suggests a gold lyre, the instrument played by this great lyric poet. Couched with Japanese gold, the tiny intersections – embroidered, like the capital, in split stitch – repeat the colors of the runner borders.

Sappho's runner combines the colors from the plate with motifs from Greek art and architecture. The front of the runner contains a great eruption of color around Sappho's name, a reference to the burst of female creativity she represents. The graduated colors – embroidered in silk thread – closely parallel the painted fades on the plate.

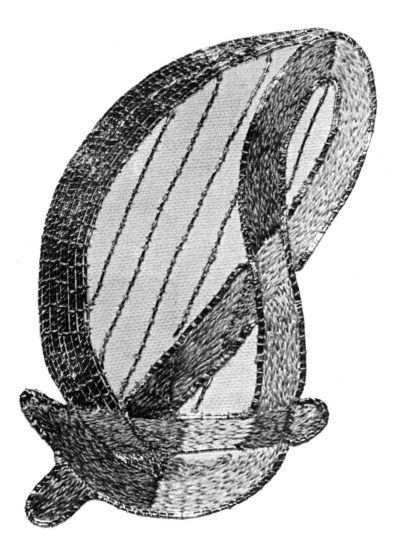

Watching the design for Sappho's runner evolve from paint to thread was a turning point in my development in making images with needlework. I painted the burst around Sappho's name on the mockup in the same way I had painted the plate – with blended brushstrokes. Terry Blecher evolved a method of translating my painting technique into embroidery: Using long, straight stitches that corresponded to my brushstrokes, she was able to achieve an intense field of subtly graduated color. Moreover, the light play on the silk thread animated the color and made it even more dazzling than the effects achieved through china-painting. After seeing the mockup translated into this splendidly stitched "painting," I felt much more comfortable about my capacities as a needlework designer, and I started taking more artistic risks.

Front of runner.

"Don't ask me what to wear

I have no embroidered
headband from Sardis to
give you, Cleis, such as
I wore
        and my mother
always said that in her
day a purple ribbon
looped in the hair was thought
to be high style indeed

but we were dark:
                a girl
whose hair is yellower than
torchlight should wear no
headdress but fresh flowers."

—*Sappho*
(Mary Barnard translation)

Sappho place setting.

Born on the island of Lesbos, Sappho was one of the greatest lyric poets of Western civilization. She became a renowned teacher, and many women gathered around her to learn the arts of poetry, music, and dancing. She was known for poems expressing her love of women, often in openly erotic terms. Because Sappho came from Lesbos, the word "lesbian" has come to mean a woman who loves women.

The undulating side borders on the top and front of the runner extend this same burst of color and refer to the long, curly tresses found on statues of women from this period. The back of the runner contains an image of a Doric temple. Elfie Schwitkis appliquéd the padded white satin forming the temple shape to the runner surface, then couched the architectural details and the decorative frieze on the temple pediment with gold thread. The expanse of airy blue Aegean sky that appears between the columns of the temple was worked in running stitch. Using single strands of Zwicky silk, Schwitkis slowly built the 5½-inch-high sky, laying three-quarters of an inch of colored thread a week.

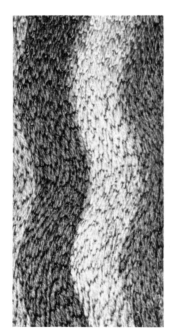

Detail: side band.

Using three strands of silk, the bands were embroidered in chain stitch. The rhythmic quality of this type of stitching was particularly suited to the bands' curvilinear pattern.

Needlework Loft, 1977. L. to r.: Blecher, Leverton, and Schneider.

The curly hair on this statue provided the basis for the wavy bands that border the runner.

Greek statue.

There weren't many needleworkers when we began work on the Sappho runner, and I have a clear picture in my mind of those early days: an empty loft; Ruth Leverton sitting at the runner frame with a great expanse of white linen in front of her, embroidering the side borders; the stitching progressing maybe an inch a day. I asked Kathleen Schneider to help with the work on Sappho, and she learned Leverton's method of making long, closed chain stitches for the solid-colored bands. Schneider and Leverton then divided the bands by color – one doing all the green and lavender and the other doing all the pink and blue – so that both sides would match in style. Even with two workers, the color stitching hardly seemed to move along. To complicate the situation, the studio was undergoing major renovations to accommodate the growth of the Project. All the runners, frames, stands, and supplies were moved to Schneider's small house, where we continued to work. By day we worked in the pleasant backyard, and at night we set up in the living room and both bedrooms. I stitched the name on Sappho's runner; it was my first effort at embroidery. I was upset and compulsive. Schneider was tired and irritable. We worked side-by-side like that for days, both deeply involved in the intense effort to finish.

—S.H.

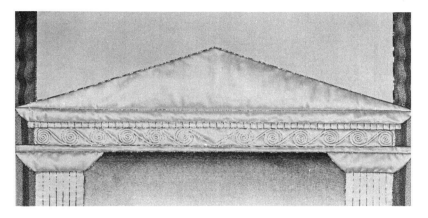

Back of the runner with image of a temple and the Aegean sky, embroidered by Elfie Schwitkis.

In order to work on the runner full-time, Schwitkis took it to her home in San Diego. The runner returned beautifully stitched, but the color fade in the sky did not blend properly. The thread dye lots had varied, and when Schwitkis used them in order, as we planned, streaks resulted. Instead of using each skein separately, all the threads of each color should have been mixed together. We set the runner up at one end of the loft and looked at the embroidered sky for a long time, trying to solve the problem. It would have been unthinkable and heartbreaking to take out all those weeks of stitches. So Terry Blecher worked over the surface of Schwitkis' embroidery, breaking up the streaks with long stitches of blending color.

Detail: back of sky.

Aspasia

470–410 B.C., Greece

Aspasia's runner incorporates Greek costume styles with ornamentation and motifs from vase paintings. The colors relate to the plate, which is painted in muted tones of the bright colors that were used on classical Greek sculpture. (These sculptures were not originally white.) The linen drapery on the front and back of the runner is derived from Greek togas. Green polished cotton lines the end folds of the drapery, and the front drape is held in place by embroidered palmettes. A reference to the pins or buckles used to hold the long *chiton* (toga) in place, these palmettes were embroidered in Ver au Soie silk using the split stitch. They were stiffened, backed with linen, edged in Japanese gold, and sewn in place.

The frieze bands on the side of the runner – embroidered in the stem stitch, split stitch, and satin stitch – are derived from traditional Greek ornamentation. The palmette form, which appears frequently in Greek art, is repeated on the back of the runner on a panel completely embroidered in stem stitch in the colors and style of Greek vase painting.

The specific iconographic references in Aspasia's runner were particularly important because the plate is a rather generalized image that relates to Aspasia's period only through color. By placing the plate in the context of classical Greek imagery, we clarified Aspasia's identity.

Our first idea for the drapery involved using colored fabrics that would pick up the blended tones in the plate. Stevie Martin tried working with green satin overlaid with pink silk chiffon, but neither the satin nor the silk reacted well to being treated with paste. In addition, she found it impossible to sew the two fabrics together to form the complex double-sided drapery we wanted.

We were, however, reluctant to abandon the idea of using colored fabrics. They looked wonderful with the plate and also were historically consistent with the colors on Greek statues. Finally it became apparent that we couldn't have elegant folds and color too. So we used our own linen, which Martin learned to cut and drape on the bias.

Section of mockup.

Aspasia place setting.

Aspasia, a scholar and philosopher, came to Athens from another part of Greece and was not subject to the same restrictions as Athenian women, who were generally uneducated and sequestered in "women's quarters." The companion of the orator and statesman Pericles, Aspasia established the first known salon and urged her male guests to bring their wives. For the first time, Athenian women were exposed to the intellectual dialogue of this "golden age of democracy." For her heretical behavior, Aspasia was eventually charged with and tried for "impiety." Only Pericles' intervention on her behalf saved her life.

Back of runner.

The drapery was a major technical problem. We wanted a softly colored fabric in tones of green and mauve that would match the plate. And for soft, elegant folds we needed a permanently stiff, nearly weightless drape. In the mockup we used fabric dipped in plaster to create the stiff, sculptural form, but it chipped and crumbled easily. Stephanie Martin undertook the solving of the technical problems – how to get the right colors and what to use for a hardening agent. The process took well over a year.

Martin first investigated hardening agents. She experimented with many kinds of fiberglass and resin, but they didn't work. She began to research fabric stiffeners and talked to museum personnel and textile experts. From one of them, she got a recipe for a paste the Chinese have used on fabrics for centuries; we used this not only on the Aspasia drapery and palmettes, but also on all the other fabrics that needed stiffening.

Recipe for "Stevie's Paste":

Mix together ¼ lb rice flour and 1 qt cold water
Add 1 tsp alum powder
    1 tsp formaldehyde
Boil the mixture in a heavy pot or double boiler 4 or 5 minutes, stirring constantly with a wooden spoon or stick.
Store in a closed container, in a cool place.

Once made, the paste can be diluted with water. The rice flour and water provide the consistency; the alum and formaldehyde prevent insects from eating the rice flour (and destroying the fabric). Fabrics impregnated with this paste are stiff and light, will not crack, and can be re-formed if necessary. Additionally, "Stevie's Paste" is useful for stiffening appliquéd pieces, preventing raw edges from fraying, adhering fabrics together, and securing fragile stitching.

Detail: palmette on back of runner.

Traditional Greek ornamental design.

The palmette form on the back band (as well as that used for the pin in front) relates directly to Greek ornamentation and vase painting.

Embroidered palmette simulating Greek pins traditionally used to hold toga in place on shoulder.

The association between female deities, women, and the fiber arts can easily be seen in the fact goddesses were traditionally pictured as teaching textile skills to women and taking pride in the things they spun, wove, or embroidered. As reflected in myths, women's work was seen as important to society, but by the time of the Athene/Arachne myth, there was a significant change.

Arachne was a skilled spinner and weaver. When it was suggested that she must have been taught by Athene, the goddess of textiles, she rejected this idea, stating that she was more skilled than the goddess herself. Athene, who considered the textile arts peculiarly her own, became enraged by Arachne's claim and arranged a weaving competition between herself and the young woman. When Arachne's weaving surpassed that of the goddess, Athene destroyed her work, transformed her into a spider–the insect Athene hated most–and condemned her to spin eternally.

The runner progressed gradually as workers began to come in to the studio regularly. The embroidered bands were a group effort, with many different people responsible for various areas. This sometimes caused a problem because the stitching didn't always match. Slowly the bands were filled, but it took months to fill the solid areas with stem stitching.

and uneducated.

Athene is pictured here wearing the traditional chiton, which served as the inspiration for the drapery and clasp on the Aspasia runner.

This is one of the first myths in which a goddess turns against a woman, punishing her for her skill and power by changing her into an insect she detests. Spiders were originally associated with women and spinning (the word "spider" is derived from the root "to spin"), and Athene's hatred of spiders is a symbol of her hatred of women, an inversion of all earlier relationships between the Goddess and her daughters. Arachne's condemnation to eternal and useless spinning, an activity previously considered not only meaningful but magical, is an apt metaphor for the lives of most Greek women of this period; it also demonstrates how myths reflect cultural realities: In the "golden age of democracy," women were kept uneducated, sequestered in their houses, and prohibited from doing meaningful work.

Another myth that demonstrates the inversion of women's traditional relationship with textiles is that of Penelope, who wove daily and tore out her work every night.

Boadaceia

1st century A.D., Britain

Designing Boadaceia's runner presented very different
problems from those we encountered for Aspasia. The
plate was much more specific in its iconography and
therefore did not need to be clarified by the imagery of
the runner. But the events of Boadaceia's life suggested
very literal images. The people of her country had
been humiliated and oppressed by the Roman legion-
naires, and Boadaceia's property had been seized.
Moreover, as had happened to many women, particularly during military invasions, her daughters had been
brutally raped. In the design session, we discussed
how to symbolize her experiences visually – particularly
how to create an image of rape.

By the time we worked on the runner
for Boadaceia, we had expanded our design process
to include some of the needleworkers who had embroidered the first group of runners. Instead of partici-
pating only in the translation of the design, they began
to be involved in the preliminary research on historic
iconography, needlework techniques, and materials.
The information they found on Celtic imagery made
it obvious that we could not portray such graphic
subject matter while still honoring the historic patterns
and techniques.

Several small, enameled pieces are stitched into Boadaceia's capital letter. These and the other jeweled objects on the runner were made by Shirley Bierman, a professional enameler.

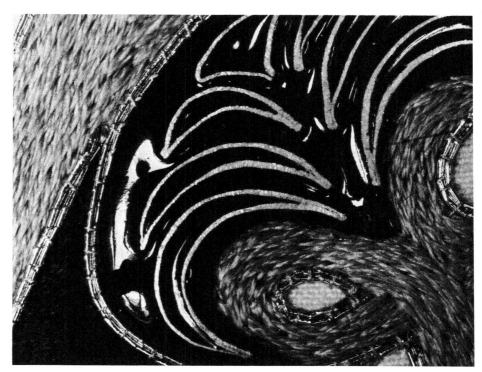

Detail: capital letter.

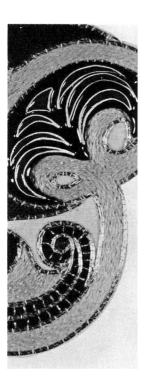

Boadaceia place setting.

Boadaceia represents the tradition of warrior-queens extending back into legendary times. Living during a period when the Romans were spreading their empire into the British Isles, Boadaceia's people – the Iceni – were conquered, then exploited, by the Romans. Boadaceia, enraged by the Romans' unjust treatment and their brutal rape of her daughters, organized and led an army of 70,000 in an attack upon the Roman oppressors. They were vanquished by the highly skilled Roman legions, but Boadaceia died a heroine, her story a continuing symbol of courage to the British people.

Reviewing the artifacts, armaments, incised objects, and enameled jewelry typical of early Celtic art suggested another design approach. We used the curvilinear forms of much of this art to express a less literal, but equally powerful, idea. Boadaceia's runner incorporates curved forms cut from thick hand-made felt with rhythmic lines of cording and complex patterns that are stitched to imitate decorative motifs of the time. These encircle Boadaceia's plate and signify both her personal strength and the Roman encroachment upon her autonomy and power.

The runner was executed by Terry Blecher, who used Appleton wool in the large areas and Ver au Soie silk for the fine lines. The felt, which had been made in one large piece, was cut into the approximate shapes of the design. The areas to be stitched were marked by basting thread through paper patterns pinned to the felt. The needlework techniques used included couching, stem stitching, running stitch, and cording. Once the felt pieces were embroidered, the shapes were cut exactly and appliquéd to the runner, then outlined with handmade wool cords. Small enameled copper pieces simulating Celtic jewelry were set into the felt to enrich the runner and repeat the curvilinear motifs.

The flowing, curvilinear lines of the famous Battersea shield were incorporated into the rhythmic forms of the Boadaceia runner.

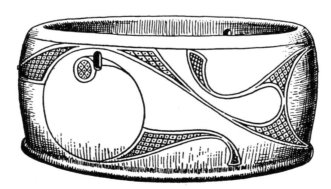

This Celtic ornament provided the basis for some of the embroidered patterns on the runner.

The incised patterns on this mirror were reproduced in the stitched and enameled motifs.

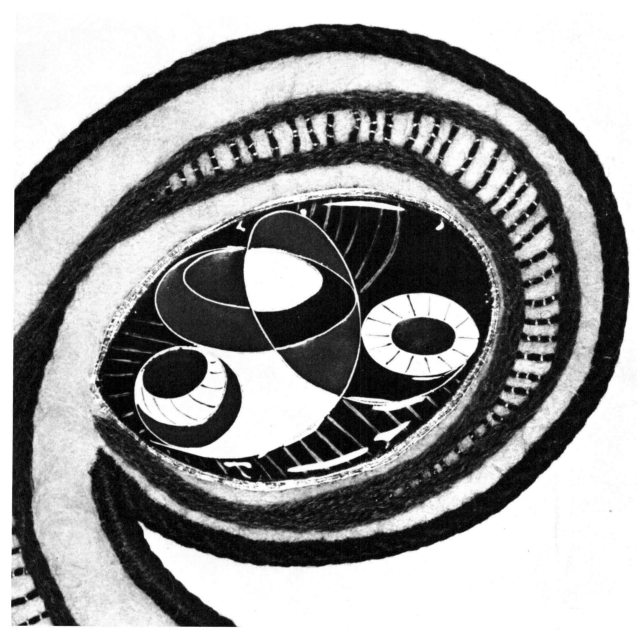

Detail: enameled piece on back of runner.

The designs for the jeweled pieces are based on jewelry typical of this period, which is famous for the quality and beauty of its enameling.

At the meeting to discuss Boadaceia's runner, Ruth Leverton brought up the conflicting descriptions she had read about this British queen. Some books presented Boadaceia as a great warrior, valiantly leading her troops; others presented her as a harsh and bloodthirsty woman. We knew from the intensive research for the Heritage Floor that strong and powerful women in history had systematically been presented from a negative point of view. We all agreed that one of the goals of *The Dinner Party* was to redress that historic bias by emphasizing the positive contributions of women.

Sculpture of Boadaceia.

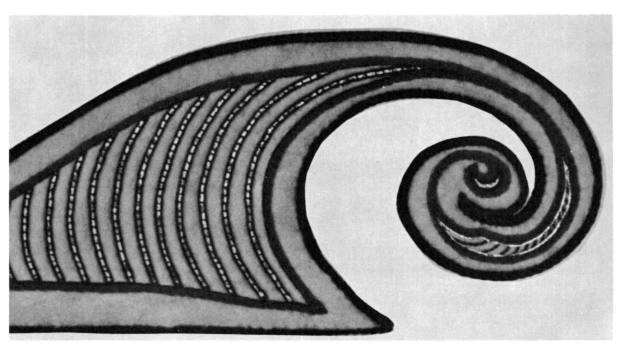

Felted piece on front of runner.

The felt was made by Susan Leverton using the traditional method. Felt is the oldest form of fiber, predating weaving. It is a thick, compact fabric made by matting wool fleece, and the name has its root in a word meaning "to grow or join together." It was used extensively by many ancient peoples, including nomadic tribes of Central Asia and civilizations of the Mediterranean. When the Roman army invaded Britain in 55 B.C., they reported finding garments of sheepskin and felted wool, and legends tell of Boadaceia, splendid in a fur-lined, embroidered cape and woolen tunic.

Fragment of ancient felted hanging.

Felt is made by the application of pressure, water, and heat to wool. Loose, carded wool is spread layer by layer on a long reed mat. When the desired thickness of fleece is reached, the mat is rolled up and secured. Next the wool is shocked or hardened with hot water and pressure, causing the fibers to contract or bond. Then the mat is unrolled and the felt is ready for use.

ypatia

370–415, Alexandria

This Coptic weaving of a goddess indicated both the imagery and the fine work associated with the Copts and the continued existence of goddess worship even after the advent of Christianity.

Detail: illuminated capital.

Coptic weaving of a goddess.

Susan Hill stitching capital letter from Chicago's drawing.

Hypatia's runner repeats the strong colors of the plate and combines abstract and figurative imagery with traditional Coptic iconography and weaving techniques. The Copts were early Christians who embellished their clothing with appliquéd bands and medallions that identified them to one another as Christians. Their weaving – which was an innovative style of tapestry that developed and flourished in Alexandria from the third to the seventh centuries A.D. – was typified by plant and animal motifs, abstract interlacings, and – despite the fact that the Copts were Christians – images of goddesses.

The woven bands of wool containing a heart motif and appliquéd onto the runner are patterned on the woven pieces used on Coptic tunics, as is the interlaced band in front. These strips were woven by Elizabeth Eakins on an upright loom. The naturally uneven edges of the woven bands were covered by narrow strips of embroidery. We used the raised stem stitch to simulate the texture of the weaving and to effect a transition between the thickness of the weaving and the flat surface of the linen. In addition, the use of two thin bands of orange and green unites the color of the borders with that of the plate, and the raised circles on the woven bands repeat the raised center form of the plate.

Detail: front band.

The interlacing in this woven band on the front of the runner is directly related to Coptic patterns.

Hypatia place setting.

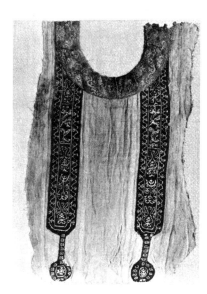

These Coptic tunics demonstrate the use of appliquéd woven bands on clothing.

Hypatia, a Roman scholar and philosopher who lived in Alexandria, is the last representative at the table of female genius and culture in the classical world. Appointed the head of the University of Alexandria, Hypatia became an advisor to the government and an important political force in the city. The misogynist Christian archbishop – who despised her because she advocated a reawakening of reverence for earlier deities and because her stature incensed him – organized a horrible plot against her, and she died an agonizing death.

85

Detail: left front corner of runner.

The raised edges around the woven green circles were embroidered in satin stitch over hard rubber rings.

86

DuBois weaving runner back.

The intense feeling in the weaving that expresses Hypatia's destruction is conveyed largely by the intensity of the color. Although Jan Marie DuBois, who wove the back tapestry, was an experienced weaver, she had no training in color theory and had a great deal of difficulty producing the color shifts. Judy worked closely with her, often sitting on the floor beside her, teaching her to "see."

—S. H.

Back of runner.

Detail: back of runner.

This tapestry was executed from a cartoon painted by Judy. Jan Marie DuBois did extensive research into the weaving techniques of the Copts. To recreate their methods, DuBois worked at an upright loom, using a fine, bleached linen warp and a weft of tightly spun, single-strand wool dyed in a wide range of brilliant color.

—S.H.

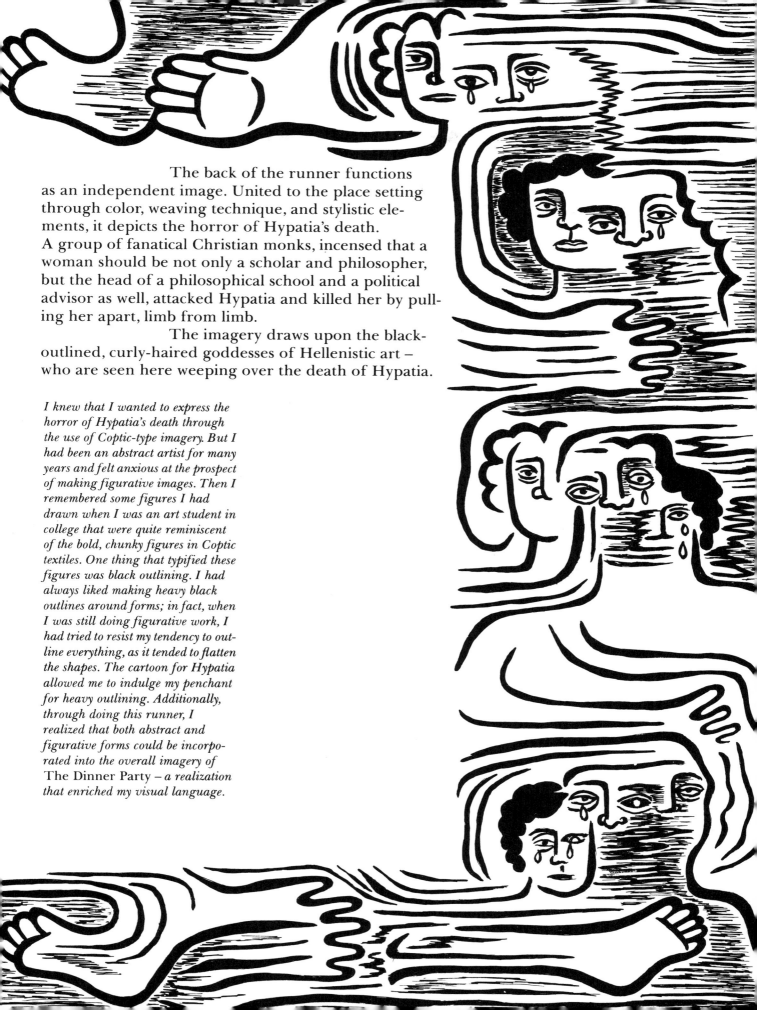

The back of the runner functions as an independent image. United to the place setting through color, weaving technique, and stylistic elements, it depicts the horror of Hypatia's death. A group of fanatical Christian monks, incensed that a woman should be not only a scholar and philosopher, but the head of a philosophical school and a political advisor as well, attacked Hypatia and killed her by pulling her apart, limb from limb.

The imagery draws upon the black-outlined, curly-haired goddesses of Hellenistic art – who are seen here weeping over the death of Hypatia.

I knew that I wanted to express the horror of Hypatia's death through the use of Coptic-type imagery. But I had been an abstract artist for many years and felt anxious at the prospect of making figurative images. Then I remembered some figures I had drawn when I was an art student in college that were quite reminiscent of the bold, chunky figures in Coptic textiles. One thing that typified these figures was black outlining. I had always liked making heavy black outlines around forms; in fact, when I was still doing figurative work, I had tried to resist my tendency to outline everything, as it tended to flatten the shapes. The cartoon for Hypatia allowed me to indulge my penchant for heavy outlining. Additionally, through doing this runner, I realized that both abstract and figurative forms could be incorporated into the overall imagery of The Dinner Party *– a realization that enriched my visual language.*

Embroidering Our Heritage

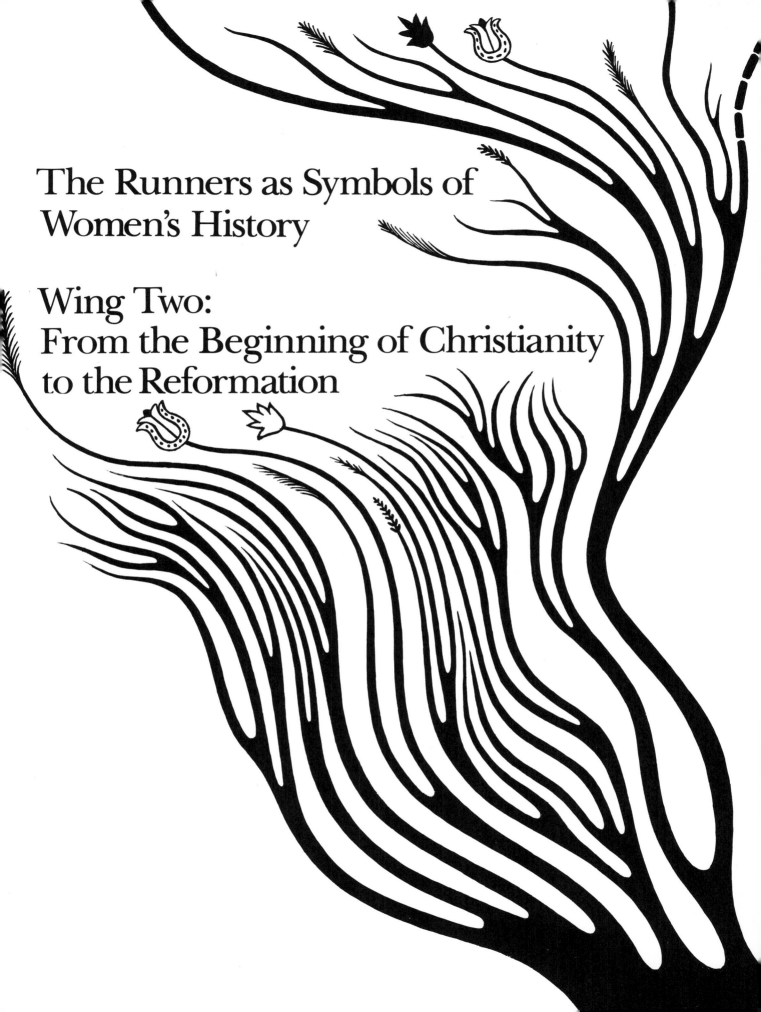

The Runners as Symbols of Women's History

Wing Two:
From the Beginning of Christianity to the Reformation

The second wing of the table chronicles the fluctuations in the position of women from the early days of Christianity – when in many religious communities women enjoyed equal rights or, at least, respect for their persons – to the Reformation, which brought about the dissolution of the convents and the end of the education and independence they had provided women for centuries.

During the Middle Ages, it was the religious houses which were centers of culture throughout Europe. The needlework produced in these communities was a major art industry. Both nuns and monks wove fabric and made garments for themselves and for neighboring peasants, and both participated in the making of vestments – the ritual garments worn during certain services. In the early Western church, this sacramental attire was quite simple, as there were few distinctions between the clothing of the clergy and that of the laity. In the Eastern church of Byzantium, however, vestments quickly became elaborate, and their influence soon spread West.

As the Christian hierarchy developed, so did the ornate embellishment of churches, ecclesiastical garments, and furnishings. Nuns, in particular, designed and embroidered narrative hangings for decorating basilica walls. The development of the Gothic style of architecture rendered them superfluous, however, as wide expanses of wall space were eliminated. Although some convents continued making tapestries, the emphasis shifted to the adornment of altar cloths and frontals, church furniture, and vestments.

Special masses required white liturgical garments, white being considered by the Christians – like the Egyptians before them – a sacred color. Whitework embroidery was done extensively in the German convents, where the nuns developed a style called *opus teutonicum,* typified by drawn and counted-thread work on a linen ground. Another kind of

Altar frontal.

The most common form of medieval German whitework was opus teutonicum, done on a natural or bleached linen ground. The altar frontal shown here is a good example of this type of convent work, in which drawn-thread and counted-thread work were combined.

Detail: altar frontal.

Frequent images of Mary occur throughout medieval needlework, as the ancient reverence for a nurturing female deity found its expression in the veneration of the "Mother of God." Sometimes, as in this image, Mary is presented in typical Christian attitudes. At other times she is seen with some of the attributes of pre-Christian goddesses, particularly the skills of weaving and spinning.

whitework, called cutwork – an early form of lace –
was practiced by the Italian nuns. This technique was a
jealously guarded church secret, and the nuns were
continually exhorted to confine it to ecclesiastical use.

A recurring theme in books detailing
the history of church hangings, embroidery, and lace is
the conflict between the high-ranking male clergy and
the religious women about both the subject matter and
use of their needlework. The large medieval hangings,
intended to educate the populace in religious themes,
frequently contained decidedly non-Christian motifs,
which were introduced by the nuns themselves despite
church prohibitions. This is a reflection of how long
indigenous religious beliefs and myths lingered on
after countries were Christianized, and of women's desire to determine the content of their own work.

Göss chasuble

The back of this chasuble
from the Göss vestments –
which contain five in-
scribed references to the
Abbess Kunigard, who
supervised their produc-
tion – is a good example
of the elaborate embroi-
dery done by medieval
nuns on garments the use
of which was restricted
to the male clergy. The
vestment shown, done in
another form of opus
teutonicum, was embroi-
dered on linen with the
satin, brick, long-armed
cross, and stem stitches in
colored threads.

It is interesting to spec-
ulate on whether women
ever wore the ecclesiastical vestments they pro-
duced. As this seal suggests,
there is evidence that
medieval abbesses, who
were extremely power-
ful, celebrated Mass and
performed the Eucharist
at the convents they
administered.

Medieval seal.

considered a high art.

In French convents, as a result of the nuns' insistence on adorning themselves with hand-embroidered silk robes, the clergy actually discouraged them from doing all needlework. In England, there was also dissension about the nuns' inclination to decorate their clothes – particularly with *lacis,* a patterned darning on net that was another form of early lace. Despite church restrictions on lace for ecclesiastical use, nuns – especially those in Italy – began to teach lacemaking to their lay students, and knowledge of it spread quickly. Italy soon became a great lacemaking center, and, in addition to lace for vestments and altar cloths, elaborate laces for royal garments were produced there.

By the seventh century, a rudimentary form of *opus anglicanum* – the work for which England became famous – began developing in English religious houses. This technique is characterized by illustrated biblical scenes done in highly refined stitching, using colored silk floss combined with gold and silver thread, pearls, and gems on a silk, linen, or velvet ground. Although opus anglicanum was used almost exclusively for ecclesiastical purposes, by the thirteenth century it had become an extremely lucrative business.

The famous Syon Cope, a magnificent example of opus anglicanum, depicts the Coronation of the Virgin and the Crucifixion. This vestment exemplifies the way embroidery was used by the church expressly to identify and aggrandize the priesthood. The struggle between the clergy and religious women about the latter's personal use of their embroidery makes clear the hierarchal distinction between the sexes that developed as Christianity became more established. Christ taught that in the eyes of God there was no male or female; in the eyes of the medieval Christian church, however, women's needlework was meant to confer power on the church fathers, never on the women themselves. The very nature of the vestments reflected power, which was implicitly understood in the church's instruction to Bishops that they must always wear all of the trappings of rank attendant upon their station.

Syon cope.

Opus anglicanum was produced not only by nuns and monks, but also by noblewomen in their domestic workshops, which were common throughout medieval times. Just as abbesses often designed and directed the needlework of the nuns, so noblewomen supervised the production and determined the embellishment of many secular and religious textiles. In most feudal castles, there were special workrooms where the royal women, their attendants, and some professional women spent their time doing needlework.

This glove – part of the insignia of the Holy Roman Empire, and made in Palermo, Sicily, before 1220 – was worked in red silk with gold couching and embellished with pearls, rubies, sapphires, and enameled plaques. It provides a good example of ecclesiastical embroidery and indicates how far vestments had developed since the fifth century, when Pope Celestine said, "We should be distinguished from the common people, or from all others, by our learning, not by our dress; by our habit of life, not by our clothing; by the purity of our minds, not by the cut of our garments."

This mitre – which contains an image of the Pietà – was made in Paris at the beginning of the fourteenth century and illustrates another type of ecclesiastical embroidery. Although not all ornate vestments were in the opus anglicanum style, the purpose of most of these vestments was, according to St. John Chrystostom, to cause the members of the congregation to "tremble with awe."

Although medieval artists rarely signed their work, there are records of some of the early needlework produced in convents. In the sixth century, Scholastica, founder of the first formal religious order for women, presided over a community which became famous for its textile work. Her nuns – who spun, wove, and manufactured clothing which they distributed to the peasants – also created elaborate hangings for the church.

Two sisters, Harlind and Reinhild, founded a religious settlement in Germany in the eighth century. There the sisters and twelve other women, both *religeuse* and lay, devoted themselves primarily to spinning, weaving, designing, and embroidering. The oldest known Anglo-Saxon vestment was made by them and later found with other textiles in the sisters' shrine.

The Abbess Kunigard, who ruled the Benedictine nunnery of Göss from 1239 to 1269, commissioned and supervised a set of vestments that remained at the convent for 600 years – important examples of the counted-thread needlework tradition among German nuns. In the same century, Agnes, the Abbess of Quedlinburg, devoted her life to the manufacture of enormous wall hangings which she and her nuns produced. The subject matter of these hangings combined religious and non-Christian themes.

The story of the Syon Cope illustrates the commitment religious women felt to both their needlework and their choice of a religious life. The Cope – probably created by English nuns in the late fourteenth century – was, at the time of the dissolution of the convents, in the possession of the nuns of Syon. These nuns fled England together, taking the Cope with them on their wanderings. It was kept within the order until the community finally returned in the nineteenth century and donated the vestment to a museum.

When the nuns were dispersed after the convents had been dissolved, some, like those from Syon, tried to keep their communities intact by reestablishing themselves elsewhere. Some joined convents in other countries or returned to their families. But most wandered aimlessly, desperately trying to deal with the loss of their homes and livelihood and the total disruption of their dedicated and protected existence.

From early medieval times, Englishwomen were known for their skill with the needle, which probably accounts in part for the high quality of opus anglicanum. Another reason for its excellence was that as the demand for opus anglicanum increased, there was an accompanying proliferation of professional embroiderers, both female and male. After serving a seven-year apprenticeship, they worked independently and, later, in organized workshops. These workshops developed in response to the increasing profitability of ecclesiastical embroidery – particularly opus anglicanum – throughout Europe.

Within the religious houses, needlework, like all medieval art, had been done in the service of the church. And for noblewomen the making and donating of vestments and furnishings had been part of their class responsibility and role. As long as the monasteries and feudal castles were the centers of production and culture, women – by their very presence and importance – were virtually assured of a major role. But as needlework production moved into secular workshops and the spiritual or social rewards were replaced by financial gain, the number of male embroiderers increased and women were gradually eliminated from work that had traditionally been theirs.

In addition to doing ecclesiastical embroidery, medieval noblewomen were involved in many textile-related tasks. Noble dwellings frequently had special spinning and weaving workshops supervised by the lady of the castle or manor, who was responsible for the production of cloth and garments for the entire household. As towns developed, the fabric industry, which had been quite primitive, expanded. Trade increased, and high-quality cloth became more accessible. Noblewomen therefore began to spend less time on functional textiles and more on refined needlework, pictorial tapestries, and narrative embroideries.

women embroidered tales of heroic exploits

It became customary for royal women to embroider bands to enrich clothing, which, during the Middle Ages, was rather plain. They also designed and stitched large banners for use in military battles and at tournaments. During warfare, these banners identified the leaders of the troops and also helped to distinguish one side's armored soldiers from those of the enemy. In addition, insignias, badges, shields, and even blankets for horses were embroidered with heraldic motifs.

At the tournaments – where noblewomen acted as the umpires – the knights carried embellished pennants made by the noblewomen to whom they were pledged. Sometimes the women carried their own standards, which they embroidered with representations of the Virgin and, often, with portraits of themselves.

One of the most significant forms of needlework done by medieval noblewomen was narrative hangings. These were used for warmth and comfort in the cold and draughty manors and also as temporary partitions which served as walls. The narrative tradition in women's embroidery dates back to Babylonian times, and there are references throughout Greek and Roman literature to women working tapestries filled with religious, military, and domestic scenes. The most famous of these was made by Helen, who, according to Homer, recorded the events of the Trojan War with needle and thread.

There is evidence of European noblewomen creating narrative hangings as early as the sixth century. Norse sagas from the eighth and ninth centuries include accounts of hangings that might have been the precursors of the Bayeux Tapestry, produced in England in the eleventh century. In Germany, there was a strong tradition of narrative tapestries made by nuns – exemplified by Agnes of Quedlinburg, an abbess whose wall hangings were her lifetime work.

Many medieval royal women, particularly in England, are known to have been involved in the textile arts – some on a small scale, others as major figures.

In the tenth century, Aethelwynn and her needlewomen embroidered an ecclesiastical stole that is one of the great treasures of the period.

In the eleventh century, Queen Emma embroidered altar cloths, hangings, and other furnishings for the church at Ely, as well as a banner that many consider the most exquisitely crafted piece of needlework in England. Queen Ethylwyn had a workshop in her quarters where she and her assistants did ecclesiastical embroidery that became widely celebrated, and Queen Margaret of Scotland established a gynaceum in her chambers where elaborate vestments and church ornaments were produced.

Another English queen, Edith, was both a patron and a designer, collaborating with the Archbishop and her needleworkers in the design of vestments. A scholastic writer of the twelfth century, describing the gynacea where most royal needlework was done, stated that the ladies of the castles and their attendants apparently spent the better part of their days working in these large chambers, which were equipped with looms as well as needlework equipment.

and embellished vestments for the church.

In fact, convent hangings – those used both on church walls and as altar frontals – probably derived from this secular narrative tradition. This is understandable in the light of the fact that ruling abbesses were members of the royal class and noblewomen, educated at convents, often retired there, bringing their design and needlework skills – as well as their skilled needlewomen – with them.

❧✦❧✦❧✦❧✦❧✦❧ ✦❧✦❧✦❧✦❧✦❧

Many of the narrative hangings of the Middle Ages – which were often referred to as tapestries – were, like the Bayeux Tapestry, actually embroideries. Others were either knotted pile carpets or real woven tapestries. The art of weaving figured and narrative tapestries, which dates back to Egyptian times, was continued during the Middle Ages in religious houses, where weaving was done by nuns and monks. They faced increasing competition, however, from secular weavers in both cloth production and tapestry-weaving.

Throughout the early Middle Ages, itinerant weavers of both sexes emigrated into Europe from the great Sicilian workshops, particularly after the Iconoclastic Controversy made image-making suspect in areas under Byzantine rule. The Moorish invasions of Europe were followed by an influx of Saracenic weavers, who brought weaving techniques with them that were derived from the highly skilled Egyptians. These weavers traveled around the countryside weaving patterned cloth from yarns produced in households. They also began to develop weaving centers: In 732, Aubusson, an important early secular center, was established by either the Sicilians or the Saracens, who also settled in areas that had been textile centers since Roman days. As towns developed, many weavers went there to live, setting up small shops where, in most instances, whole families worked at the weaving trade.

There are few extant embroideries from Britain before the Norman Conquest, and the only surviving large, complete piece of early Norman embroideries is the famed Bayeux Tapestry from the late eleventh century. Over 230 feet long, it was worked on linen with colored wools in laid and couched work and outline stitch. The narrative scenes tell the story of the Norman invasion of England from the point of view of the conquerors. Although the authorship of this hanging has been disputed, its relationship to the tradition of narrative hangings by royal women seems to support the idea that it was done by Matilda and her needlewomen in a castle workshop – particularly since these gynacea were a marked feature of the life of English noblewomen.

Detail: Bayeux Tapestry.

Detail: painting by Giotto.

One of the needlework tasks of noblewomen was the weaving of ribbons and braids like those seen on the gown of the center figure in this painting.

Detail: hanging.

Needlework in which colored wool covered the entire ground was another important type of work done by German nuns. Some of these – like this large (7 by 14 feet) hanging featuring the legend of Tristan and Isolde – can still be found in German convents. The dark blue background of this hanging, which was made in the fourteenth century, is worked in a form of couching. It is a good example of the type of narrative tapestries produced in the convents.

In many parts of Europe between the fifth and tenth centuries, peasant women – like the one pictured in this sculpture – lived in houses below the castles and noble estates. In addition to gathering and cleaning flax, they did the carding, spinning, and weaving of the coarse wool and linen that were used for the rough clothing most people wore.

Despite the fact that religious women were continually enjoined to restrict their work to ecclesiastical subject matter, this hanging – created by the Abbess Agnes of Quedlinburg and her nuns – contains distinctly secular as well as religious themes. A monumental carpet measuring 26 by 20 feet, it depicts scenes from classical mythology, including one section which portrays Cyprus, the ancient Germanic Mother Goddess. On Cyprus' right there are three female figures representing the seasons, and on her left a sea nymph pours water from a jar. This image relates to the vegetation rites and spring festivals which continued to be held in honor of the Goddess even after the imposition of Christianity upon Europe. The Abbess' point of view can be construed not only from her representation of the Goddess in a supposedly Christian work, but also from the inscribed border of another of her hangings.

In this latter work, male classical and Christian philosophers were depicted along with Agnes' remark about their ideas: "Man may long seek a rational explanation but he will scarcely find it much less prove it."

Detail: knotted carpet.

The development of the drawn loom (thought to have been invented in Syria) into the complex and elaborate high-warp, vertical loom of the later Middle Ages resulted in the possibility of making larger and more finely woven and intricately patterned tapestries. As a result, a more organized secular industry evolved, first in France and then in Flanders, partly in response to the popularity of tapestries among the new royal families of the early Renaissance.

The noble classes quickly adopted these high-warp tapestries, hanging the colorful weavings of epic and romantic scenes in their dark and draughty castles. Tapestries soon became symbols of power and status; they were collected, given as gifts, and used in trade. Although the industry flourished, women, who had been involved in weaving throughout the Middle Ages, were virtually forced out by the restrictive regulations of the developing guilds. In France, for example, they were expressly forbidden to use the high-warp looms on the pretext that they were dangerous to pregnant women.

These historical developments resulted in the virtual exclusion of women not only from the act of weaving tapestries, but also from any participation in their design. The evolution of the naturalistic art style of the Renaissance – after the development of oil-painting – required a degree of art training that could be obtained only through the new atelier and apprenticeship system, which excluded women. The sophisticated style of high-warp pictorial tapestry, increasingly being designed by the major painters of the day, made the symbolic religious iconography of the Middle Ages – which women had been as qualified as men to create – appear more and more naïve.

The continued tradition of weaving among noblewomen can be seen in these historic examples, which span almost 2,000 years. Both cloth production and tapestry weavings were commonly done in household workshops by individual women or groups.

Greek woman with tapestry loom from vase painting.

Anglo-Saxon women at work on loom in early Middle Ages.

Noblewoman and her attendants.

French high-warp
tapestry loom.

Although the French
tapestry industry em-
ployed high-warp vertical
looms exclusively, low-
warp horizontal looms
were used in Flanders,
which became the center
for tapestry production by
1500. This picture indi-
cates that the weavers
there were men.

After French law prohibited
women from practicing their
traditional craft, many female
tapestry weavers became vagabonds, wandering about the
countryside looking for work.
Some, unable to earn a living,
turned to prostitution, while
others, angry at being dis-
placed, became involved in the
political turmoil and religious
dissent that plagued Europe in
the thirteenth century.

There seems to have been
persecution of weavers
throughout the Middle Ages, in
part because their independent
status (before the formal organizations of the tapestry industry) made them prone to
free and sometimes heretical
thought. In addition, many of
the weavers who emigrated
from Sicily were Jews and thus
were natural targets for Christian zealots. Both Christian and
Jewish weavers had settled
primarily in Italy and France.
In Italy, their presence contributed to the development of a
silk industry that produced fabrics that were as fabulous as
those from the weaver's original
homeland.

In France, however, the
weavers encountered a different fate. During the Crusades
against the Albigensians, the
number of looms in southern
France was reduced from 3000
to 30 when the members of the
Cathari – including those who
were weavers by trade – were
massacred. Many of those killed
were women; not only were
there many female weavers
generally, but because the
Cathari practiced complete
equality between the sexes, they
attracted a large number of
women to their cause.

This engraving by Durer –
which depicts a witch
holding a spindle and a
distaff – indicates that
the association between
female weavers and heresy
expanded to include
witchcraft. In addition
to the weavers who were
killed during the Albigen-
sian Crusades, there is evidence that other weavers,
especially women, were
tried and burned in the
witch hunts.

Embroidery, like tapestry, was affected by the artistic and political changes brought about by the Renaissance. In a vain effort to imitate painting, embroiderers tried to duplicate Renaissance pictorial space by introducing perspective and raised work to create dimension and depth. Because of the impossibility of competing with the new realism, embroidery became increasingly ornamental, and both its importance and its quality declined.

Women continued to do domestic needlework, but the bulk of the work done in guilds and workshops by the time of the late Renaissance was probably made by men. As women were gradually eliminated from commercial textile work, they also were either forced out of the professional embroidery workshops or their numbers drastically reduced. The few known embroiderers from the seventh to the thirteenth century were primarily women, but by the fourteenth century most of the references are to men.

Answitha was an extremely successful English embroiderer in the early ninth century. The Anglo-Saxon needlewoman Edelprym, in the tenth century, and the English embroiderer Ethylwyn, in the eleventh, were both well known for their ecclesiastical embroidery. A famous thirteenth-century English needlewoman, Mabel of Bury St. Edmonds, may have been embroiderer to Henry III.

The changes that were taking place as a result of the decline of feudal society and the rise of the Renaissance affected all classes of women. Although those in the lower classes had shared a rough equality with men throughout the Middle Ages, all workers were dominated by the church and the feudal lords. In the face of this situation, guilds developed from associations of workers who grouped together for mutual assistance and support. The earliest organized guilds were in textile-related fields. At first, family units were the association members. Jobbers would bring fleece to a family, who would produce cloth and then sell it back to the merchant. Sometimes a family would perform one step of the clothmaking process and pass the work along to another family. As this was obviously more efficient, specialization began to emerge, thus leading to organized household workshops. As long as the guild workshops were connected with the home, however, it was still easy for women to participate.

Early craft-guild workshops were like extended families; even if a woman wasn't allowed to be a guild member, her presence in the house virtually guaranteed her involvement. Wives of guild masters supervised the apprentices and sold the products of the workshop. If the husbands died the wives assumed their roles, if not their status, losing the right to membership only if they married out of the guild.

In some of the textile guilds, women had equal positions, which meant that they could attend meetings, vote, serve apprenticeships, and become *maestras* (female masters). However, becoming a guild master sometimes required government and military service, and, since female guild members were excluded from such duties, they would obviously be denied full guild rights. The spinning, carding, yarn and lacemaking, gold-spinning, dressmaking, millinery, and some embroidery guilds were, for a long time, composed exclusively of women.

As the size of the mixed guilds increased and most of the home workshops disappeared, more quotas and regulations restricting women began to appear. Although women had always been at a certain disadvantage in the guild structure, their real marginality did not become obvious until it was too late.

In the same century, Rose de Burford and her husband had an embroidery workshop where they made royal and probably ecclesiastical garments. As late as the fifteenth century in Spain, three needlewomen were associated with the Seville workshop: Isabel Fernandez, Joana Gonzalez, and Isabel Valdes. In mixed guild workshops, women generally did the silk embroidery while men did the goldwork.

Silk workers.

The silk industry, which developed in Italy, was established in other parts of Europe by the Florentines. From the beginning, the bulk of the workers were women who were organized in guilds. The only way a man could be admitted to a guild was by marrying one of its members. But the conditions under which the workers produced the silk were deplorable. By the end of the fifteenth century, there were 16,000 underpaid and overworked women in the industry. As early as the fifteenth century, records document the exploitation of silk workers, as expressed in this song:

We shall always work the
  silk – but never will this
  improve our clothing;
We shall always be poor
  and naked;
We shall always suffer
  hunger and thirst,
As the bread is given par-
  simoniously to us –
A little in the morning
  and still less in the
  evening.

These manuscript illuminations indicate the continued identification of the spider with women and the textile arts.

Although women continued to work in the textile industry throughout the Middle Ages, they were gradually excluded from all aspects of commercial weaving. One of the earliest recorded craft guilds was that of the English weavers, which was a mixed guild.

By the thirteenth century, only the wives and daughters of male weavers could be trained, and, by the 1500's, in many parts of England women were not allowed to be trained in weaving at all.

Wool workers.

Women textile workers were better off in France than in England, as many of the French guilds remained available to them. Even after the weavers' guild closed, women continued to do all the cleaning, carding, and spinning of wool. Yet, during periods of low employment, these jobs – which had previously belonged only to women's guilds – were given to men.

an early sign of the Goddess.

By the fourteenth century, the character of the guilds had changed. Instead of being protective organizations of workers, they began to employ thousands of laborers who were not guild members and had no rights. Work was done in warehouses and factories, and workers lived in slums. Those women who could find textile work put their children in "baby farms," gave them opiates to keep them quiet, and sometimes committed infanticide. Others, forced out of their professions, became vagabonds, criminals, or prostitutes.

The Goddess' magical womb of regeneration – from which the life process was spun – had become inseminated with the poison of exploitation and misery. This is all reflected in the runners of the second wing, as the embroidery moves up onto the table surface and begins to encroach upon the plates.

As evidenced by late medieval images of women using their spindles and distaffs as weapons, women did not willingly accept the changes that were taking place. These figures, found in manuscript illuminations and in the marginalia, may have been painted by nuns, who are documented as having worked as both illuminators and scribes.

Manuscript illumination.

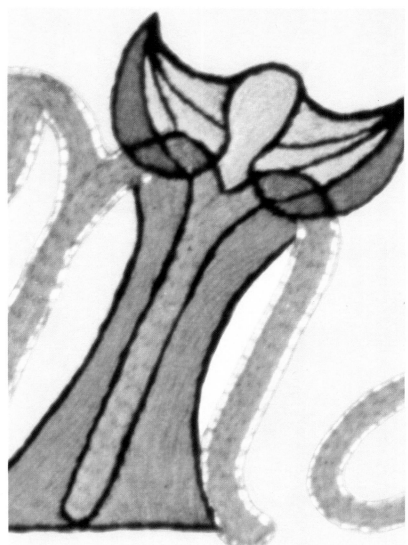

Detail: illuminated capital.

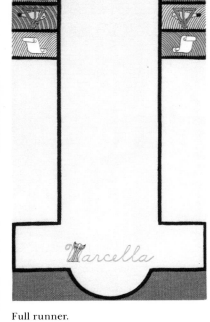

Full runner.

Marcella plate.

Detail: back of runner.

Full runner.

Saint Bridget plate.

Detail: carved and embroidered front band.

Embroidered shell form.

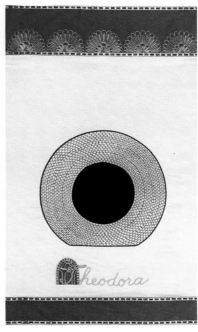

Full runner.

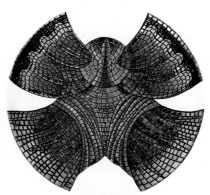

Theodora plate.

Detail: illuminated capital.

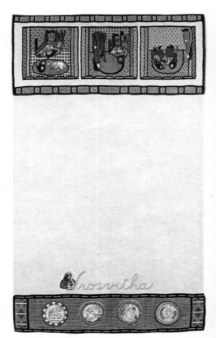

Full runner.

Hrosvitha plate.

Detail: back of runner, panel 2.

Roundlet from front of runner.

Illuminated capital

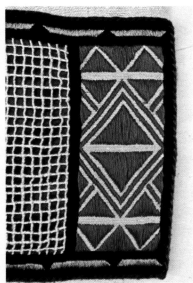

Front right corner.

Detail: panel 3.

Full runner.

Trotula plate.

Detail: illuminated capital.

Full runner.

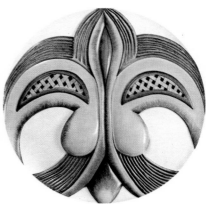

Eleanor of Aquitaine plate.

Tapestry detail.

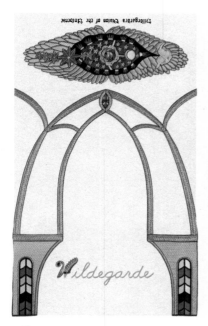

Full runner.

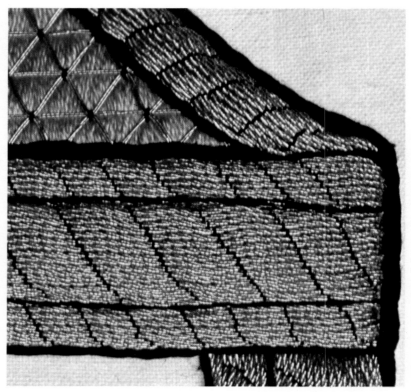

Detail: raised goldwork.

Hildegarde of Bingen plate.

Center of image on runner back.

Top and front of runner.

Full runner.

Petronilla de Meath plate.

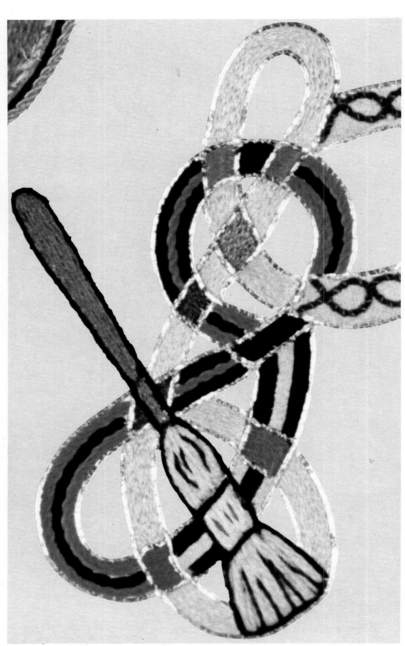

Illuminated capital.

were weavers.

Front of runner.

Section of back interlacing.

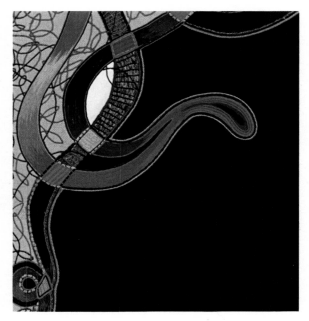

Section of front interlacing.

Full runner.

Christine de Pisan plate.

Detail: Bargello work.

Illuminated capital.

Center image, front band.

Full runner.

Isabella d'Este plate.

Full runner.

Elizabeth R plate

Embroidered pomegranate on runner front.

Blackworked feather.

Illuminated capital.

Full runner.

Illuminated capital.

Artemisia Gentileschi plate.

Full runner.

The runner text reads:

WOMAN HAS THE SAME WISH FOR SELF-DEVELOPMENT AS MAN, THE SAME IDEALS, YET SHE IS TO BE IMPRISONED IN AN EMPTY SOUL OF WHICH THE VERY WINDOWS ARE SHUTTERED.

Anna van Schurman

Anna van Schurman plate.

Stitched house on runner back.

Embroidered angel on front.

of female role.

This second altar cloth
– executed in traditional ecclesiastical embroidery techniques
– was placed at the second
corner of the *Dinner Party*
table and marks the transition
from classical to Christian
times. Although ornate embroidery was not used during
early Christian services, whitework, which was to become
an important part of church
needlework, was already being
practiced.

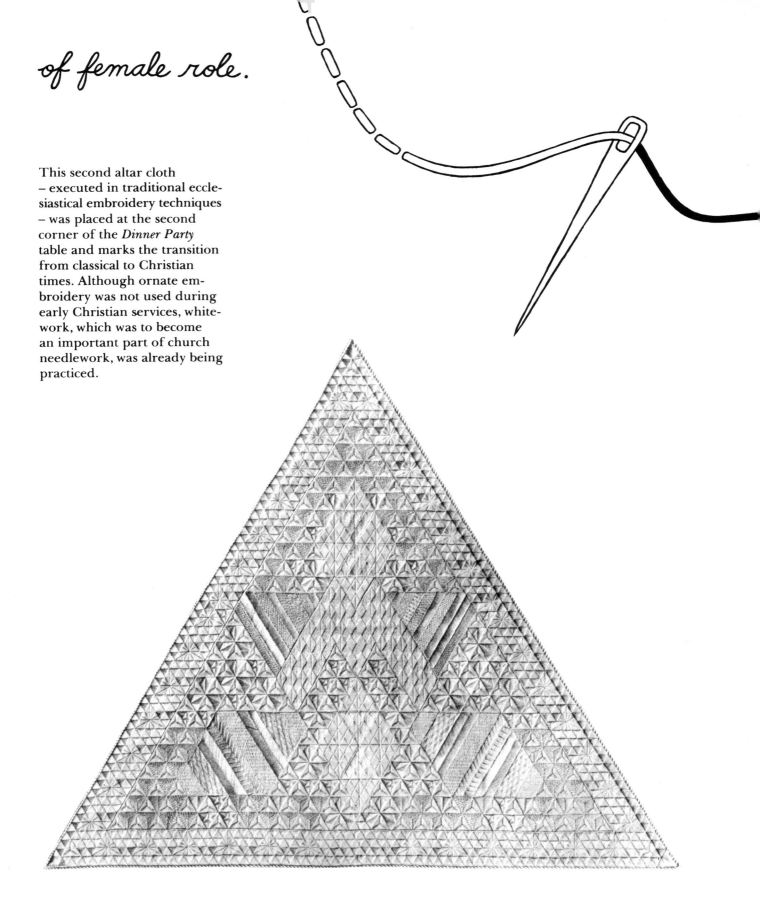

Marcella

325–410, Rome

The runner for Marcella – who helped establish the basis for the Christian monastic system – has its source in Christian iconography and architecture. A simple basilica structure is embroidered across the runner surface in raised stem stitch with three strands of black Appleton wool. The plate sits in the center of the nave (or great aisle) of this simple architectural form.

The capital letter for Marcella is derived from the Christian *orans* figure from the Catacomb of Priscilla.

Female figure in attitude of prayer from Catacomb of Priscilla.

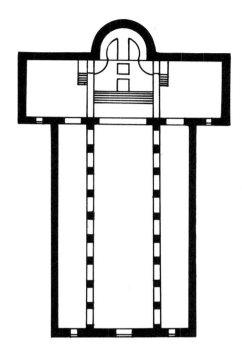

 Christianity

The orans figure of a praying woman can be traced back to early representations of the Goddess with upraised arms. Later, Christian female saints were represented in this pose, and eventually portraits of Christ in an attitude of benediction evolved from the original image of the Goddess. This transformation is an apt demonstration of the changeover from matriarchy to patriarchy that occurred in Western civilization and is symbolized by the drawn heading for this runner.

The basilica plan for the early church of Saints Petrus and Marcellinius (ca. 820–830) upon which the runner design for Marcella was based.

Representation of the goddess Astarte.

Marcella place setting.

Born of a noble and wealthy family, Marcella dedicated herself to a religious life at a time when many Christians advocated equality between the sexes. She made her palace a center for women interested in a simpler, more purposeful life. In her "Little Church of the Household," women studied religion and the Scriptures and, under her guidance, were educated in the Christian way of life. They traveled and preached, set up religious houses and schools for women, established hospitals, ministered to the sick and the needy, and helped lay the groundwork for the great monastic system of Christianity.

107

was both a curse and a blessing for women.

Thecla, a Byzantine ruler and saint, in the traditional pose of both the Goddess and the orans figure.

Detail of woven hair shirt on Marcella's runner.

In this painting, Christ's posture is directly related to earlier images of female figures and demonstrates the way Christianity, like many religions, incorporated previous deities and images into iconography.

The apse and the bays interlock with the modified shape of a hair shirt to form the front of the runner. These shirts were traditionally woven of goat or camel hair, and, when worn close to the skin, caused considerable irritation. Marcella and the other ascetic women involved in her order, like many early Christians, wore hair shirts under their clothing as an act of mortification and penance. The tabby weaving on the runner was done by Jan Marie DuBois in a style reminiscent of historic sackcloth, using a linen warp and a weft of wool and camel hair to create a thick, rough surface.

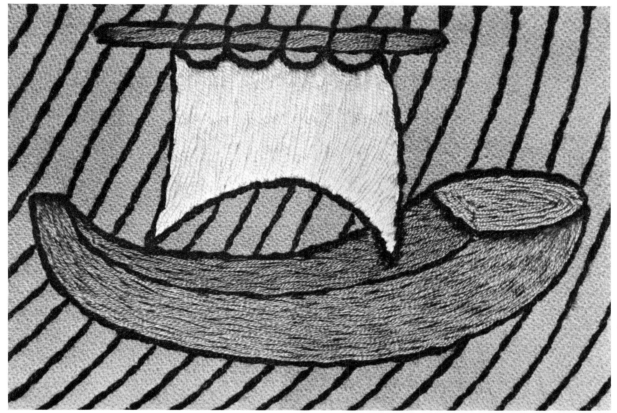

The images on the back of the runner – a scroll, a ship, and a combined image of a fish, a staff, and a triangle – are related to Marcella's life and work. The scroll is a symbol of learning, for Marcella was proficient in scriptural analysis; the ship is an emblem of the early Church; and the fish was a secret symbol during the days of the Roman persecutions of the Christians. (Each of the letters in the Greek word "fish" is the first letter of one of a series of words which form a phrase praising Christ as the Savior and son of God.) We combined the fish with a shepherd's staff, a reference to Christ leading his flock of disciples. Enclosing these two symbols in a triangle, the traditional sign of the Goddess, creates an association between Christ and Marcella, who was a "savior of women."

Detail of the ship, an emblem of the early church. The main part of a church is still called the "nave," from the Latin word for ship.

Detail of the fish, staff,
and triangle – represent-
ing Christ, leadership, and
female power.

Each of the symbols on the back of the runner was embroidered on a piece of soft, colored wool by Terry Blecher, who used four strands of Ver au Soie silk in the stem stitch. The images are set against a field of stripes and were worked in chalky colors to resemble the frescoes in Christian catacombs. The embroidered wool squares were vigorously blocked to release the puckers caused by the density of the stitching, then appliquéd to the runner and outlined in the same black wool used for the basilica form.

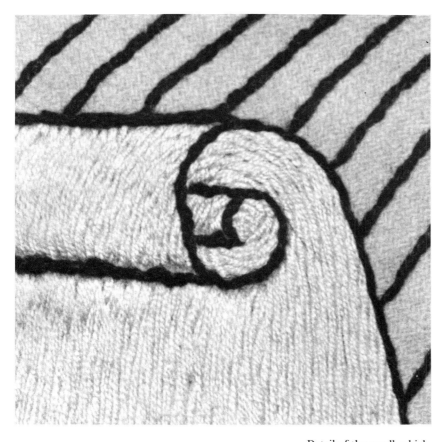

Detail of the scroll, which symbolizes learning.

Saint Bridget

453–523, Ireland

While Christianity was developing in Rome, the Celts were still worshiping goddesses such as the one represented on this silver cauldron. Cauldrons were a traditional part of Mother Goddess worship.

Detail: cauldron with goddess figure.

Mother Goddess worship still existed in Ireland when the early Christian missionaries first arrived, and the overlay between indigenous Celtic female deities and later Christian saints is reflected in Saint Bridget's runner. Its iconography combines Celtic motifs with Christian symbolism. The early Celtic religion, like other ancient religions, revered trees as symbols of the Goddess and believed that Her lifegiving spirit dwelt in the tree trunk. Saint Bridget established her first religious cell in a giant oak tree which had formerly been the shrine of the goddess Brigid. It was upon this same site that Bridget later founded her great monastery.

The runner surface is a colored, textured silk linen, the appearance of which suggests the bark of an oak tree. Using colored fabric for the runners had been considered before, but we were afraid that the long tables would appear fragmented if there were too many color blocks along their lengths. Now, having established a certain visual continuity among the runners, we felt that gradually altering their color and surface would allow us to express more about each woman's environment or circumstances.

Detail of carved hardwood band.

Detail of the Cross of Muiredach. This "Scripture Cross," carved in the early tenth century, is one of the best examples of Irish monuments that blend Celtic and Christian styles.

Saint Bridget place setting.

The Celts maintained their traditional religious ties to Mother Goddess worship through Bridget, who became associated with all the symbols that had formerly belonged to the Celtic goddess Brigid. The patron saint of Ireland, Bridget founded the first convent there, which eventually grew to be a great monastery and center of learning. She was one of the earliest Christians to make the monastery a kind of settlement house to which all the neighboring peasants could come for help, advice, and education. She traveled extensively, established educational opportunities for women, and was extremely influential in both political and church affairs.

The wooden cross on the back of the runner is related to the Cross of Muiredach, an elaborately carved stone cross that is one of the monuments of Irish Christianity. The wooden carving is repeated on the front of the runner using interlaced motifs typical of Celtic patterns. At first, we thought of knitting both the cross and the front band. We wanted to combine authentic religious iconography with traditional Irish handwork, particularly because the intertwined forms of cable knitting closely resembled the Celtic motifs carved in stone.

This drawing for the carved cross on Saint Bridget's runner is derived from authentic "Scripture Crosses."

Detail of back of runner, with carved cross and appliquéd and embroidered flames.

Many knitting samples were made to test wools for their color, weight, and texture. We tried several cable patterns and experimented with scale, using larger and smaller configurations. The knitted strips, however, seemed cumbersome in relation to the luminous runner fabric and the delicately painted forms on Saint Bridget's plate. We could achieve finer details in wood and also continue the oak-tree symbolism. Sharon Kagan and Connie von Briesen made the cross and the band, carving each shape from single pieces of thin hardwood. They worked with dremels and fine carving tools to produce the intricately pierced and reliefed pieces.

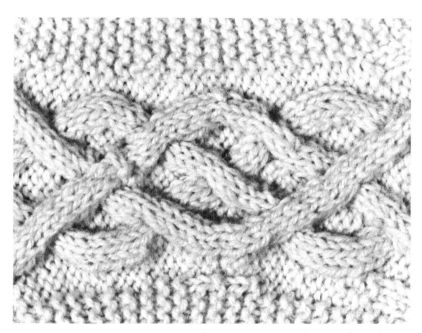

Knitting sample by Sally Turner.

Knitting is basically a continuous series of knots, which were once thought to have magical properties.

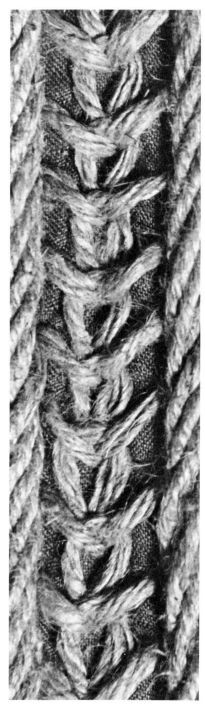

Detail of wheat ear stitch from runner border, embroidered by Linda Preuss.

There was much on-the-job training in the *Dinner Party* Project. For example, neither Sharon Kagan nor Connie von Briesen was an experienced woodcarver, although Von Briesen had been a sculptor and Kagan was an art student and had done some carving. They did extensive tests with different woods and practiced using the carving tools. Each brought to the work an acute visual sensibility and an understanding of the meaning of the imagery. This proved – as happened over and over in the Project – to be more important than technical skill.

Corner detail: carved wooden band.

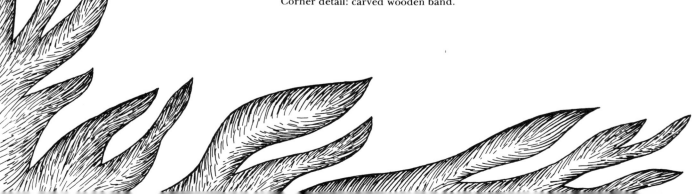

On the back of the runner, flames extend from the wooden cross and Saint Bridget's name is illuminated by similar embroidered flames. These are a reference to the sacred fire of the goddess Brigid that was kept burning by Vestal Virgins and to the continuation of this custom by nuns who maintained this fire in honor of Saint Bridget for seven hundred years. A pattern was made for each flame, and then the shapes were cut from pieces of fine silk. These were appliquéd to the runner, leaving the edges raw. To both bind their edges and intensify their color, the flames were embroidered with one strand of DMC cotton floss, as was the illuminated letter, using the shading technique Von Briesen had developed for Kali.

We added a decorative border along the sides of the runner in the wheat-ear stitch, which is similar to the Celtic pattern that edges the front band. This stitch was done over narrow strips of appliquéd green silk which repeat the color of the plate. Strands of both green and blue Appleton wool were blended and used to create a vibrant field of matching color behind the pierced areas of the carved wooden pieces.

Detail: stitched flames on back of runner.

 *Theodora*

508–548 Byzantine Empire

The elaborately embroidered runner for Theodora reflects both the imperial majesty of the Byzantine Church and Theodora's personal power as a ruler. The vast empire of Byzantium, founded by Constantine and dedicated to the Virgin Mary, had a distinct artistic style. Byzantine iconography is highly formalized and symmetrical and is characterized by brilliant mosaic surfaces and the lavish use of gold. The gold halo that surrounds Theodora's plate is a reference to the mosaic image of the Empress in the Church of San Vitale, Ravenna. Established by Theodora and Justinian, the churches of Ravenna contain some of the greatest examples of Byzantine art.

Mosaic of Theodora and her retinue from San Vitale, Ravenna.

The splendor of Byzantium

Satin stitch, long-and-short stitch, split stitch, couching, and appliqué were used for Theodora's capital letter. The image represents the Hagia Sophia – the great basilica of Constantinople which was built in 530 A.D. in honor of the Virgin Mary.

Theodora, the famed Byzantine Empress, ruled equally with her husband Justinian. She initiated many reforms on behalf of women, never forgetting the suffering and humiliation she saw women endure during her youth, when she was an actress. She broke down the legal barriers that kept actresses in a socially inferior role, made procuring punishable by death (many women had been virtually forced into prostitution), established the death penalty for rape, improved divorce laws in women's favor, prevented physical abuse of women by their husbands, made it possible for women to inherit property, and generally improved women's position in society. Moreover, Theodora personally enforced these measures and left a legacy that enhanced women's lives for centuries.

Theodora place setting.

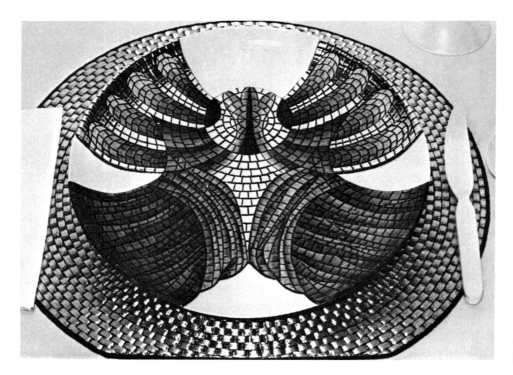

Theodora plate on embroidered halo.

Detail of head, halo, and collar of Theodora from Ravenna mosaic.

For the embroidered halo, Marjorie Biggs – who translated the painted design into needlework – used a raised basketwork technique. Biggs first built a foundation for the couched goldwork with heavy cord, tacking the lines of cord close together to create a circular form with radiating spokes. She then couched Japanese gold over this foundation, using strands of red and purple Zwicky silk thread to create the mosaic-like design. This blended color intensified the pattern and also duplicated the colors on the plate.

Chicago working with
Marjorie Biggs.

I have always loved Byzantine art, and it delighted me to simulate its iconography with porcelain, china-paint, and needlework and thereby expand the art-historical references in The Dinner Party. *The mosaic image on the plate is derived from the representation of Theodora that appears in the fabulous church in Ravenna. The halo behind her head on the cathedral wall suggested positioning the plate on an embroidered gold halo. I wanted the runner to provide a splendid context for Theodora's plate in the same way the Byzantine mosaics surrounded her with opulence. But it was extremely important to me that the nature of the stitching in the halo and the color of the gold be consistent with the quality of the plate. When I first saw Marjorie Biggs' gold-work, I was impressed by the way she had translated the luminous color and incised surface of the plate into stitching. It was both extraordinary and consistent with Byzantine art and my images.*

Back of runner.

The purple silk strips on the front and back of the runner relate to the fabric and color associated with Byzantine royalty. In 550 A.D. the techniques of silk production were brought from China and introduced into Byzantium. Looms were installed in the women's quarters of the imperial palace, where female slaves wove the purple silk that was worn exclusively by the aristocracy.

Shell worked in Italian shading.

The rich red, purple, and gold – colors associated with royalty – are repeated on the front and back of the runner. Purple silk was appliquéd to the pale gold satin runner surface and then edged with a traditional Byzantine motif. The imperial costume often included collars embroidered with gold and set with precious stones. In imitation of these collars, the edges of the purple silk on the runner were couched in gold and the "jewels" worked with the padded satin stitch and then outlined with black silk thread. For the shell motif on the back, Biggs used a technique known as Italian shading. The strands of gold were couched with green and purple silk thread in a pattern that causes the surface to shimmer as light glances across it.

Detail of shell on back of runner.

The shell is historically related to the moon and to women and, as a symbol of the vulva, represents the female principle. The shell form used on Theodora's runner is derived from a silver Byzantine book cover from the collection at Dumbarton Oaks in Washington, D.C. This artifact contains a scallop-shell motif, which was commonly used in mosaics and niches. In antiquity, the scallop shell was associated with the goddess Venus, who was born from the sea. Later it was connected to Mary and the virgin birth.

rosvitha

935–1002, Germany

The runner for Hrosvitha was done on an unbleached, loosely woven linen cloth in an embroidery technique based on the needlework style *opus teutonicum.* Opus teutonicum involves complex geometric patterning and counted thread work. We modified these slightly to accommodate the imagery, but the geometric patterning on the runner is closely tied to traditional German needlework motifs. A grid was developed for each pattern that was consistent with both the thread count of the linen and the pattern desired. Once the counted pattern was worked out to scale, it was embroidered in the satin stitch.

The illuminated capital, embroidered in split stitch, represents Hrosvitha writing one of her plays.

When I saw this wonderful example of the homely Germanic opus teutonicum, *I knew it was perfectly suited to the period in which Hrosvitha lived. I could imagine the nuns at work stitching these almost obsessive patterns while they practiced their "plain song." The pictorial quality of this style lent itself to my idea of telling the story of Hrosvitha's life — and a little German history — through needlework.*

Hrosvitha place setting.

Hrosvitha, Germany's earliest poet and dramatist, occupies a unique place in literary history as the first playwright in medieval Europe. She was educated at the Abbey of Gandersheim, in Saxony, at a time when convents offered women the chance to participate in artistic and intellectual life. With the support of her abbess, Hrosvitha wrote sacred legends in verse, historical poems, and the history of the Ottonian dynasty, as well as plays that focused on spiritual aspiration and the plight of women.

Drawn thread work, which is characteristic of opus teutonicum, was used on both the front and the back of the runner. The area to be worked was outlined with back stitches, and satin stitches were used to create a strong, bound edge. Warp and weft threads were cut and withdrawn in a systematic pattern of counted threads, creating open areas. The remaining threads were bound with white cotton floss, which contrasted with the beige linen. The scale of the drawn thread work had to be large enough to be proportionate to the weave of the linen. A dark green fabric was placed behind the open areas to emphasize the negative spaces and also to repeat the tones in the plate.

Marny Elliot working on drawn thread pattern on front of runner.

I learned the technique of drawn thread work in 1966, when I lived on the island of Crete, from Sister Marina – an eighty-year-old Orthodox nun who taught embroidery at the Girl's Technical School run by the Bishop of Kissamos and Selivos.

—*Marny Elliott*

A fine beige linen was stretched over these padded discs, and the forms were outlined in brown stem stitching. When the roundels were complete, a bottom layer of felt was added and the circles appliquéd to the runner. Additional stitching was used to embellish the images, which were then edged in cord. Marny Elliott embroidered the runner using DMC cotton floss.

Four padded circular forms adorn the drawn thread work on the front of the runner. Modeled on the coins minted by medieval abbesses, these roundels contain images from Teutonic mythology. They were made by first stretching muslin onto an embroidery hoop, then tacking felt circles to the muslin and placing felt wherever greater relief was desired.

During the Middle Ages, a ruling abbess had considerable power. Many times she was a member of the royal family and acted as the representative of the king in his absence. She often administered large estates, exercised political as well as ecclesiastical influence, and had the right of coinage. The coins shown are typical of those belonging to a medieval ruling abbess.

Abbess' coins.

The Valkyries, thirteen legendary warrior women, were associated with weaving as well as warfare. They were attributed with the weaving of a web which would ensnare their enemies and were represented at the spectral loom singing, "Weave, weave, the web of spears" (from *The Song of the Valkyrie*).

Chicago's drawing for roundlet.

The four roundlets on the front of the runner relate to German history and folklore. The first disc represents a typical medieval baronial household where a servant woman might tell old Germanic tales to the small daughter of the lord and lady, as she is pictured doing in the second seal. The third roundlet depicts a scene from one of these tales: A Cimbrian princess holds the head of an enemy soldier over a cauldron (legends recount that Teutonic warriors, sometimes led by women, customarily drank the blood of their adversaries). The last seal contains a rather Wagnerian image of a Valkyrie.

Cimbrian princess.

Servant woman and child.

When I was working on the roundlets for the front of the runner, I realized that Judy's drawing of the fireplace was historically inaccurate. I am a stickler for minute historical detail and knew that fireplaces had not existed in Hrosvitha's time. Judy redrew the scene so that a few pans hung on the wall where the chimney had been, and an open fire replaced the original design.
—*Marny Elliott*

The panels on the back of the runner provided a brief narrative of Hrosvitha's life. In the first scene, Hrosvitha enters the convent at Gandersheim, in Saxony, as a young girl. There she sees the nuns playing and singing music. Many women entered religious orders or lived under the protection of the church in order to participate in music, the arts, and general intellectual activity. With the support of her abbess – who ensured that Hrosvitha's writing became known outside the convent – Hrosvitha was able to produce plays, poems, and a history of the Ottonian dynasty. Hers was the first voice in Germany to emerge from the darkness of the early Middle Ages.

In the last scene, Hrosvitha, pictured as an old woman, has dozed off at her writing table. She is dreaming about the recent visit of a royal emissary. In recognition of her historic work on the reign of the Ottos, the king sent her a saint's relic considered a treasure in the Middle Ages. Hrosvitha accepted the honor tearfully, for when she entered the convent she had never imagined she would become the most famous woman writer in Germany.

Panel #1.

Panel #2.

Panel #3.

130

Nuns were active in textile
production and competed
with guilds by working for
lower wages and offering
cheaper products. Com-
plaints lodged by guild
members resulted in taxa-
tion of the convents, limitations on the numbers of
looms, and the establish-
ment of a maximum in-
come for nuns. These
measures, enacted in the
mid-fifteenth century,
totally underminded the
convents' economy and
contributed to their eventual demise.

Detail: floor pattern of Panel #1.

Detail: Panel #3.

rotula

d. 1097, Italy

The runner design for Trotula is based on a Tree-of-Life image, which we selected because it seemed appropriate to her occupation as a gynecologist and midwife, a "bringer of life." The Tree-of-Life motif originated in ancient myths and iconography and was incorporated into needlework during a very early period of history. Originally, it represented the cosmic tree – i.e., the Goddess or the Great Earth Mother – and was the symbol of the world in a continual process of regeneration. This theme, however, underwent a gradual transformation from the time it first appeared to its later manifestations in samplers, quilts, and crewel work.

A bird encircles the illuminated letter for Trotula's name, and other birds perch on the branches of the Tree of Life that is depicted in the runner design.

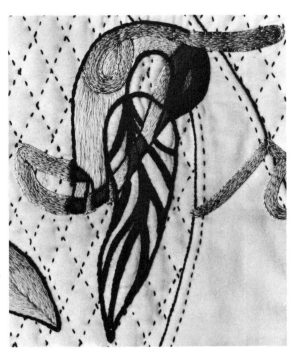

This Indian hanging, called a "palampore," was one source for the Tree-of-Life design.

Our design was derived from an eighteenth-century Indian cloth hanging. Indian fabrics – many incorporating the Tree-of-Life motif – were imported into Europe in the mid-sixteenth century and immediately became popular with domestic needlewomen. We decided to interpret the design in a quilting technique called *trapunto,* the same technique we had tried to use in the earlier Fertile Goddess runner. Our discovery of a trapunto quilt made in Sicily in the eleventh century provided us with a historic foundation for our choice.

The drawing for the runner was traced onto a soft, white fabric that recalls swaddling cloths. The material was backed with a piece of muslin and stretched on one of our embroidery frames that had been modified to allow the runner to function as a traditional quilting frame. This allowed us to roll and unroll the runner for each process: embroidery, trapunto, and quilting.

Trotula place setting.

While most of Europe was still relying on saint's relics, prayers, and ineffective and dangerous remedies for curing sickness, Salerno doctors were employing advanced forms of medical healing in southern Italy. Among them was a group of women doctors, the most prominent of whom was Trotula, who taught at the university in Salerno. She wrote prolifically on gynecology and obstetrics, and her book, *Diseases of Women,* was consulted for 700 years after her death. The first doctor to give advice on the care of the newborn infant, Trotula stressed hygiene, cleanliness, and exercise throughout her writings. Despite her fame and importance, several centuries after her death she was dismissed as a witch by male doctors – who then attempted to prove that her book had been written by a man.

133

We had wanted to use trapunto – a method of quilting in which the design is worked through two or more layers of fabric and then selectively stuffed – from the time we first learned about it from our textile consultant, Pearl Krause. Judy Mathieson, an expert quilter, provided valuable technical information and helped Kathy Miller establish high standards for her quilting team. Miller did extensive work with Chicago in translating the flat design into a reliefed surface.

The tree was outlined with DMC cotton floss in the stem stitch. A running stitch was added on the interior edge of the tree to make a narrow channel for cord. After the cord was inserted, additional relief was created by stuffing the flowers and the birds. The background was then quilted in a diamond pattern. Next, the flower petals and the veins of the leaves were worked in both the stem and running stitches. The elaborate embroidery on the birds was developed last and was used to visually strengthen the image and tie the color of the runner more closely to that of the plate. Trotula's runner was completed by appliquéing an undulating, multicolored border that repeated a motif from the plate.

This historic quilt, which originally measured 17′x 17′, is one of the earliest known examples of trapunto. It was probably executed during the time Trotula lived near southern Italy.

Dinner Party quilting team.

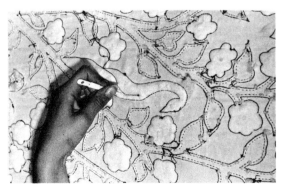

Doing trapunto for runner.

The frequent use of the Tree-of-Life motif and its various transformations can be easily perceived in rites, images, and myths from different countries. In Egypt, the goddess Nut was represented as the Tree of Life. In Mesopotamian cylinder seals, the tree was often flanked by a king and queen in postures of worship. The Jewish menorah was derived from Mesopotamian Tree-of-Life symbols, and the pomegranate, also related to this symbol, was very common in Jewish iconography. Assyrian versions embellished woven hangings, and similar patterns existed on Greek garments. In Roman rites, gifts and offerings to the Goddess were attached to the branches of trees. There are fragments of tapestries from the fourth century A.D., woven in the eastern Mediterranean area, that reflect the Tree-of-Life design, and the Persians developed many distinctive renditions of this theme. (Their fabrics had a tremendous influence on subsequent textile history.)

This picture, as well as those that follow, and the Siberian creation myth illustrate the consistency of the Tree-of-Life motif as it appears in the myths and iconography of almost all societies.

In this image, the goddess Nut is depicted as the Tree of Life.

Mesopotamian cylinder seal.

Jewish menorah.

Roman tree tied with gifts.

The Tree of Life is also evident in early Christian and Byzantine embroidery and later became an important element in Christian symbolism. By then, it had divided into numerous forms: the tree of paradise, the tree of Jesse, the tree of knowledge, the tree of good, the tree of evil, and the tree of death.

By the late Middle Ages, the Tree-of-Life motif had changed dramatically from its representation in Egyptian times. The cosmic tree that was once identified with the Goddess and which symbolized the regeneration of life had become associated with Christ. Christian mythology asserted that it was Christ's sacrifice upon the Tree of Life (the Cross) which perpetually renewed the world. Moreover, the Virgin Mary, who embodied many of the attributes of the Goddess found in ancient symbolism, had been reduced to being the Mother of God instead of the paramount deity.

The coronation mantle made for Roger II of Sicily in the twelfth century also shows Byzantine influence. In addition, the flanking of the Tree of Life by animals in this image is reminiscent of other inconography (such as the Mesopotamian cylinder seal) in which people or animals are represented around the Tree.

"In a wonderful place a White Youth (or Lonely Man) sees a mighty hill, and on the hill an immense tree. The resin of this tree is transparent and sweetly perfumed; its bark never dries or cracks, its leaves never wither, and liquid light flows through all its branches. These branches pierce the sky, penetrating the nine spheres and seven stories of heaven. Its roots penetrate into the underworld, where they become pillars of strange mythical beings. Through the rustling of its leaves the tree converses with the spirits of the sky-world.

As the Youth looks at the tree, the leaves begin to rustle, a fine white rain falls from them, and a warm breeze blows. The tree begins to shrink, creaking and groaning in the process. From within, there appears a spirit, an ancient white-haired goddess, gaily colored as a partridge, and with breasts as large as leather bags. The Youth addresses this tree divinity: "High Honored Mistress. Spirit of the tree and of the dwelling place, everything living moves in couples, and gives birth to descendants, but I am alone. I wish to travel and seek a partner. Do not refuse my blessing, I pray thee, with humbled, bowed head and bent knee."

The White Youth learns that his mother is Kubaichotum, the mother of all things, and his father the celestial god Ai-Toyon. They lowered him from heaven that he might become the ancestor of mankind. The tree goddess takes water from under the root of the tree and blesses him. Then the goddess offers him milk from her ample breasts, as he drinks he feels his strength grow nine-fold."

—Siberian creation myth

136

In this painting, *The Dream of the Virgin,* Mary – the Christian version of the Goddess – is pictured as a prone and passive figure. Instead of being represented *as* the Tree of Life, she is only there to provide sustenance for a male deity. It is Jesus who is now associated with this sacred tree, replacing the Goddess as the source of regeneration.

Eleanor of Aquitaine

1122–1204, France

The Unicorn Tapestries at the Cloisters in New York were the inspiration for the runner design for Eleanor of Aquitaine. The caged creature – the unicorn held captive inside a circular corral – provided a perfect metaphor for the imprisonment of this strong and powerful queen.

In the design session, we painted a very simple mockup that went through a series of transformations, including a rendered pencil drawing, a colored study, and extensive weaving tests. The tapestry, woven by Audrey Cowan, took a year and a half to complete. It was blocked flat and then sewn to the runner, its edges held by bands of silk embroidery.

Satin strips had been embroidered with a simplified version of the *fleur-de-lis* image that appeared on the plate. These were attached to the tapestry but allowed to hang free over the front and back of the runner. The fleur-de-lis, which was a symbol of Mary as the Queen of Heaven and was also associated with the French monarchy, was often embroidered on the opulent banners used in royal tournaments.

Detail: back of runner.

We used a fleur-de-lis motif in the satin borders and the illuminated letter for Eleanor's runner. The fleur-de-lis is derived from the iris, which was sacred to the Virgin Mary. It frequently appeared in the *mille fleurs* tapestries that were a source for the runner design. Worship of Mary reached a high point in the Middle Ages and was intimately connected with courtly love – the "religion of the gentle heart."

Eleanor of Aquitaine place setting.

Born to the ruling family of southern France, Eleanor of Aquitaine was raised in a court where women had considerable power. She brought her rich properties and the liberal ideas of her childhood to both her marriages, the first to the King of France and the second to Henry of England, whom she helped gain the throne. Her efforts to retain her power, however, resulted in her being imprisoned by Henry for sixteen years.

Before her imprisonment, Eleanor had established the Courts of Love, through which women in the feudal castles were able to improve their status in society. Women heard cases concerning relationships between the sexes, and their judgments and values were communicated by traveling troubadors. By supporting these troubadors, noblewomen were able to make their courts major cultural and social centers and help shape the mores and values of their class.

139

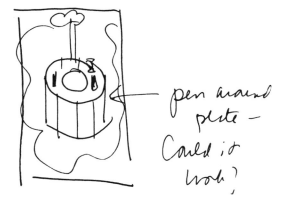

Unicorn tapestry.

Long after the tapestry for the runner was in progress, I realized that my initial sketch, which was actually just a notation, had become the basis for a rich, complex image. When I saw the caged unicorn, it conjured up visions of the romantic Courts of Love which Eleanor had instituted, the whole quality of medieval society, and the tragedy of Eleanor's life.

The Unicorn Tapestries and most of the other great weavings associated with medieval activities, particularly chivalry, were made long after Eleanor of Aquitaine's lifetime. But the mille fleurs backgrounds that typify many of these tapestries were derived from earlier customs of women hanging sheets decorated with flowers in the streets during the feast of Corpus Christi. There is evidence that the tapestry industry developed as early as the twelfth or thirteenth century, yet the oldest surviving French weaving is from the fourteenth century.

The Unicorn Tapestries were probably woven on low-warp looms. The cartoons were divided into sections and placed under the warp to be copied by the weaver. Wool was the predominant material used for both the warp and the weft; linen was used occasionally for details in the weft, silk threads were used for highlights, and gold or silver threads were woven into certain areas to enrich the design. The shading of the Unicorn Tapestries was achieved through *hachure*, a technique of hatching in which light tones are introduced into darker areas and vice versa. The origin of these tapestries is unknown.

Wounded, penned Unicorn —

What about translating it!

pen around plate — Could it work?

Chicago's notebook study for runner.

140

The mockup for Eleanor's runner was very crude. I felt awkward trying to match the gorgeous quality of the Unicorn Tapestries on a piece of cheap white fabric with acrylic paints. The general idea was there – the corral, the flowers, and the fleur-de-lis motif – and I knew that the runner process we had developed would ultimately transform this crude mockup into a rich tapestry. In the meantime, however, I didn't want anyone outside the Project to see it.

The first transformative step was to do a careful black-and-white rendering for the weaving. The fleur-de-lis pattern could best be done by the technical illustrators who would grid it out and make sure that it was symmetrical and that the intervals between the forms were equal. I did the drawing for the top of the runner after Elaine Ireland had made some preparatory sketches of the flowers we were going to include – roses, irises, and violets. I also consulted studies I had done for my "Through The Flower" series in 1973. As I began to render the cartoon for the tapestry with pencil, all my years of classical art training came up through my fingers. I discovered that I could still draw not only figures, as in Hypatia, but flowers as well.

Then Audrey Cowan asked me for a color rendering to aid her in weaving. I had thought that once we chose all the wools and did the translation work, the black-and-white study would be enough. But I was glad she needed a full-color version because I always loved to color.

Painted mockup.

Audrey Cowan cutting finished tapestry from loom.

The technical problems to be solved in order to properly interpret Chicago's cartoon were sobering. The cartoon was incredibly detailed, and Chicago wanted the beauty and delicacy of those details translated into tapestry. I had never worked in such fine detail before and found the slowness of the work frightening at first. I was concerned that I might not be able to complete the piece on time. As the weaving progressed, however, and I saw that it was just as gorgeous as Chicago and I had hoped, my excitement grew.

I used linen warp – fifteen warp threads to the inch – and wool for the weft; I worked on a studio-built upright loom. Often as many as six shades were used in each flower petal, and the weaving was done with one thread per shot.
—*Audrey Cowan*

Chicago's technical drawing.

Chicago's color rendering.

"The Queen sings softly
Her voice blends with the
   harp:
Her hands are lovely, her
   songs good
Sweet the voice and gentle
   the tones."

—Refrain from
medieval song

Songs like this were sung in feudal castles while the women embroidered. The "housework" of ladies consisted primarily of needlework, and when they worked together the women would take turns giving the verse while the others would answer with the refrain. Most medieval embroidery was for ecclesiastic use, but some was intended for secular purposes. Like the women in the convents, noblewomen produced gorgeous vestments which were given as gifts to prominent clergymen. They also embroidered pennants, banners, badges, shields, and streamers for the royal tournaments. They acted as umpires in these tournaments and carried banners which depicted the Virgin Mary, and often their own portraits.

As early as the sixth century, women of high rank embroidered large hangings sometimes referred to as tapestries. These narrative hangings, like the Bayeux Tapestry, often portrayed epic tales and were in constant use throughout Western Europe. In the church these hangings provided scriptural lessons, and in the castles they were used for warmth and to create partitions in the large, draughty halls; they were also hung in the streets during festivals.

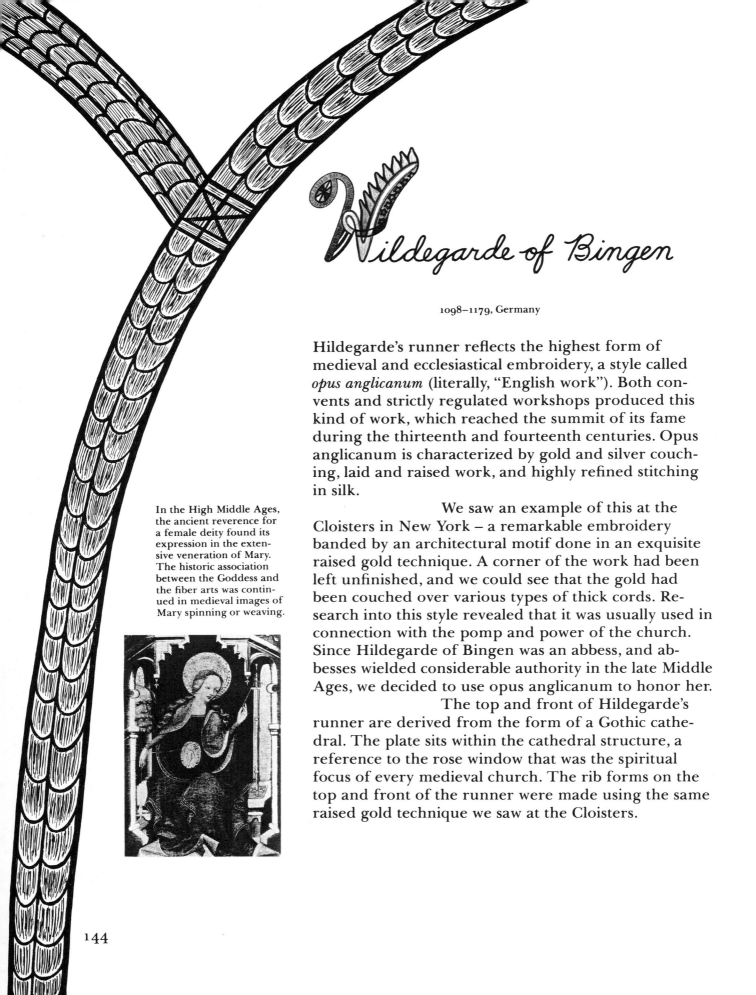

Hildegarde of Bingen

1098–1179, Germany

Hildegarde's runner reflects the highest form of medieval and ecclesiastical embroidery, a style called *opus anglicanum* (literally, "English work"). Both convents and strictly regulated workshops produced this kind of work, which reached the summit of its fame during the thirteenth and fourteenth centuries. Opus anglicanum is characterized by gold and silver couching, laid and raised work, and highly refined stitching in silk.

We saw an example of this at the Cloisters in New York – a remarkable embroidery banded by an architectural motif done in an exquisite raised gold technique. A corner of the work had been left unfinished, and we could see that the gold had been couched over various types of thick cords. Research into this style revealed that it was usually used in connection with the pomp and power of the church. Since Hildegarde of Bingen was an abbess, and abbesses wielded considerable authority in the late Middle Ages, we decided to use opus anglicanum to honor her.

The top and front of Hildegarde's runner are derived from the form of a Gothic cathedral. The plate sits within the cathedral structure, a reference to the rose window that was the spiritual focus of every medieval church. The rib forms on the top and front of the runner were made using the same raised gold technique we saw at the Cloisters.

In the High Middle Ages, the ancient reverence for a female deity found its expression in the extensive veneration of Mary. The historic association between the Goddess and the fiber arts was continued in medieval images of Mary spinning or weaving.

144

Hildegarde's illuminated capital was stitched by L. A. Olson with exquisite attention to detail. Each star was embroidered in the split stitch, using one strand of silk thread, and then outlined with strands of gold. The columnar left stroke of the "H" was padded to match the raised goldwork on the runner.

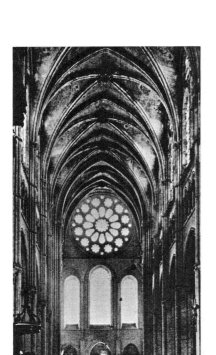

The nave of Chartres Cathedral, built 1194–1220, showing the intersections of a vaulted arch and the rose window.

Hildegarde of Bingen place setting.

Hildegarde of Bingen was one of the greatest and most original thinkers of medieval Europe. She was an abbess, a scientist, a leading medical woman, a musician and prolific composer, an artist, a political and religious figure, and a visionary. Her writings are among the earliest important mystic works of the Middle Ages. She maintained a voluminous correspondence with leading medieval thinkers and became increasingly involved with the political and religious issues of the day. In her later years, she concentrated on developing a theory of the universe which stressed the relationship between the human and the divine.

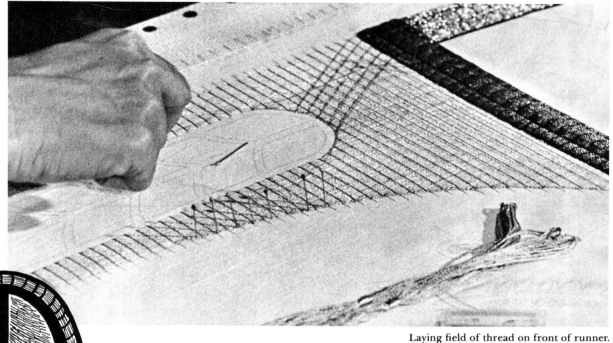

Laying field of thread on front of runner.

Part of the quality of laid-work comes from the precision with which the stitching is executed. The threads are laid one at a time to create a smooth field of stitching; a trellis-like pattern is then worked diagonally across the field of thread, and the intersections are tacked down. Dorothy Goodwill, who researched the style of opus anglicanum and did most of the goldwork on the runner, used Zwicky gold silk for the laid surface. For the minute triangles that form the grid she used fine metallic gold, couching each junction with one strand of black silk thread.

Detail: raised goldwork.

The front of the runner represents the facade of a Gothic cathedral, its surface done in laidwork. The facade includes two stained-glass windows embroidered in the split stitch using two strands of Zwicky silk. The colors of the windows had to match the plate, which contained areas of iridescent lusters. To achieve the same kind of shimmering effect, we mixed several pale colors of thread, using two and three strands in the needle at once. The other sections of the windows were embroidered in solid colors, and the direction and scale of the stitching created visual depth.

Heavy cotton cords of different weights padded with narrow strips of white felt are the foundation for this work. Gold threads were couched one at a time, using black silk carefully worked in a spiral pattern that repeats the architectural details of a Gothic cathedral.

Detail showing raised goldwork and stained glass window on top of runner.

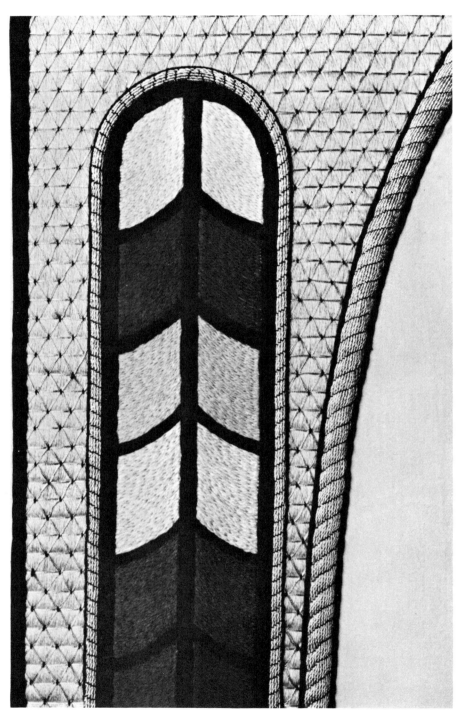

Detail: front of runner.

The visual shifts that occur on the embroidered windows are a result of blended threads and directional stitching.

Each line of the couched pattern over the laidwork had to be exactly parallel to the last. Any imperfectly laid thread would be glaringly evident because it would throw the whole pattern off. I had been a needleworker for many years, but I was not sure I could meet the exacting standards of the opus anglicanum style. As I was finishing the laidwork, my hands were visibly shaking —I felt that I had accomplished the impossible.
—*Dorothy Goodwill*

Opus anglicanum influenced embroidery throughout Europe. This example, produced in Flanders, also demonstrates the close relationship that existed between needlework designs and painting.

Example of opus anglicanum.

"Then I saw a huge image round and shadowy. It was pointed at the top, like an egg... Its outermost layer was of bright fire. Within lay a dark membrane. Suspended in the bright flames was a burning ball of fire, so large that the entire image received its light. Three more lights burned in a row above it. They gave it support through their glow, so that the light would never be extinguished."
—*Hildegarde of Bingen*

Illumination by Hildegarde of Bingen.

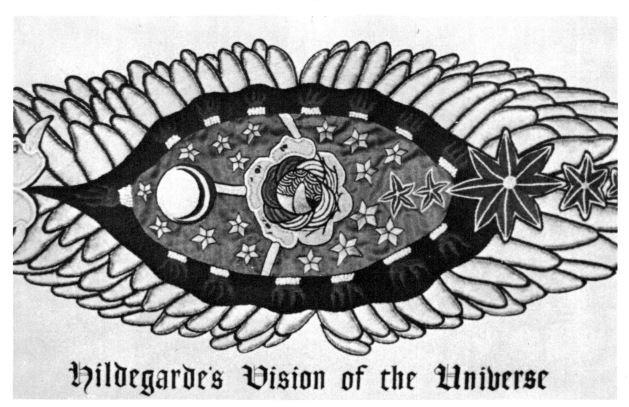

Center back of runner.

The design for the back of the runner evolved from an illumination by Hildegarde of her vision of the universe. The embroidery was done primarily by Marilyn Akers, using silk thread on a blue satin ground. The central image is worked in stem stitch, split stitch, and satin stitch. The flame-like forms surrounding the image of the universe are done in padded satin stitch edged in red and gold cords. The embroidery on the flames was done over successively raised pieces of felt to create a sense of dimension which corresponds to that of the Gothic arch.

Detail from Chicago's drawing for back of runner.

I was studying the history of medieval abbesses at UCLA in early 1977 when I stumbled upon a facsimile of a work by Hildegarde — a drawing of an image that had appeared to her during one of her visionary trances. Her illumination bore an amazing resemblance to my own work, partly because we both used centered images. Discovering that Hildegarde was an artist, in addition to being a scientist, a leading medical woman, a scholar, a musician and composer, and one of the greatest and most original thinkers of her time, intensified my deep admiration for her. As I incorporated her work into the design for her runner, I felt as if our visions were united.

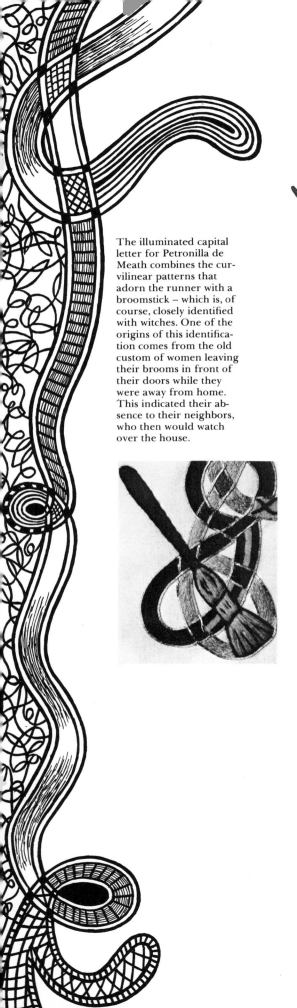

The illuminated capital letter for Petronilla de Meath combines the curvilinear patterns that adorn the runner with a broomstick – which is, of course, closely identified with witches. One of the origins of this identification comes from the old custom of women leaving their brooms in front of their doors while they were away from home. This indicated their absence to their neighbors, who then would watch over the house.

etronilla de Meath

d. 1324, Ireland

The imagery on Petronilla de Meath's runner is directly related to both Celtic motifs and witch symbolism. The famous ninth-century Irish manuscript *The Book of Kells* – one of the most extraordinary works of the medieval period – was the source for the convoluted forms and interlaced patterns. The mockup went through several stages; the first included the animal imagery often found in Celtic iconography, where animals are intertwined with letters and shapes. We used only the types of animals associated with witches, primarily the hare and the cat.

Chicago discussing work with Elaine Ireland, who – with Adrienne Weiss – executed this runner.

 *During the witch hunts,*

This drawing, adapted from *The Book of Kells,* shows the interlaced forms and complex surface that typified Christian Celtic art and inspired the runner design.

Petronilla de Meath place setting.

The extent of witch-hunting during the Middle Ages was much wider than is commonly thought. Eighty-five percent of those executed were women, and, although they were tried and burned on countless pretexts, their real crime was their attempt to preserve the traditions of the past and to resist the destruction of female power. Burned as a witch, Petronilla de Meath is a symbol of the terrible persecution of these women that occurred from the thirteenth to the seventeenth century.

Back of runner.

When the mockup was finished, we decided it was too complicated and simplified it, eliminating the animals and incorporating a single large form in the back of the runner that resembled a horned head – a reference to the horned god worshiped by some of the witch cults. The horns were easily integrated with the rhythmic bands that undulated across the runner surface and appeared to engulf the plate.

Petronilla's runner has a rich surface of wool, silk, cotton, and fleece, which was made by first appliquéing the ground fabrics to the linen and then padding some of the forms with felt. Other raised areas were fashioned by couching heavy cotton cord wrapped with plied wool. We used this same technique for heavy outlines. For thinner edges, we made finer cords of DMC floss, Appleton wool, and Zwicky silk. Some sections of the interlaced forms were made of soft fleece and couched with a lattice pattern; others were made with rows of rough wool. All were couched with cotton floss.

many of whom were weavers.

We were determined to incorporate the red garter of the witches, which was an insignia of rank in the covens, yet we couldn't find a way to accomplish this until the runner was almost complete. By then a year and a half had elapsed, and everyone breathed a sigh of relief at the prospect of the runner finally being done. But when we looked at the plate with the runner, it was obvious that they didn't work together. We finally added a piece of black fabric which helped to unite the forms, and, in a flash of inspiration, we couched three red cords on the front black edge. Without quite realizing what we were doing, but knowing that it was right, we had finally made the garter we had wanted to include all along.

Manuscript illumination showing witch on broomstick.

The complexity of the forms of the runner, which involved diverse materials, patterns, and stitches, presented some interesting esthetic problems. The various parts could easily have looked fragmented and disconnected, particularly since Ireland and Weiss approached the stitching of the same motifs differently. To integrate the disparate parts, I used color to emphasize the intersections between the interlacing and the edges of the curvilinear forms.

Detail of back of runner.

When we began work on the needlework book, we knew that there were legends, folk tales, and fairy stories that included references to the magical properties of weaving and spinning and their connection to women. The research team from *The Dinner Party* had previously unearthed a great deal of information on the mythical and positive relationship between goddesses and the fiber arts. We wanted to see if there were differences between these ancient myths and more recent material. Continued research revealed that the later mythical female creatures – like fairies and enchantresses – were also associated with weaving and spinning and – like the goddesses – interceded in human activities. But many of these later stories depicted the weavers and spinners negatively. Old women (hags or crones) were attributed with supernatural powers and represented as evil or as having become disfigured because of spinning or weaving. In fact, they began to be associated with witchcraft.

Witch hunts occurred during a period of European history in which women's status was undergoing a profound transformation. The traditional occupations of women, including textile production, were being steadily usurped by men; the guilds and the tapestry factories began to systematically exclude women; and the weavers – most of whom were women – became increasingly persecuted as witches.

In this tale, Habitrot, a patroness of spinning, is represented as a kindly old woman, but she and the other spinners who work with her have become ugly as a result of their work. In many other fairy tales, like *Sleeping Beauty*, the wise woman/spinner uses her magical powers to "weave" an evil spell.

There was once a girl so idle that she would never learn to spin. Her mother scolded her and punished her and at length she gave her seven heads of lint and promised her a beating she would not forget unless she spun them up in three days. The girl was frightened, and for a whole day she worked hard but made no headway. On the second day she left the work in despair and went out into the fields. Seated by the stream on a self-bored stone she saw a woman spinning, twisting her spindle like lightning. She had a lip so long that it hung down over her chin. The girl went up to her with a friendly greeting and asked her what made her so long-lipped.

"Spinning thread, my bonnie," said the old woman.

"I should be spinning too," said the girl, and told her all the story.

"Fetch me your lint," said the old wife, "and I'll spin it for you."

Women being hanged as witches.

156

The girl ran for the lint, and no sooner had the old wife received it than she disappeared. The girl sat down by the stone to wait for her return and fell asleep. When she woke it was twilight, and a light and the sound of voices came from the self-bored stone. She put her eye to the hole and saw a great company of spinners, all with their lips twisted to a strange deformity, and her friend was walking among them, directing their work. It was her voice the girl had heard saying: "Little kens the wee lassie at the brae heid that my name is Habitrot."

As the girl watched, Habitrot walked up to one who sat apart reeling yarn and said: "Hurry wi' yir yarn, Scantlie Mab, my wee lassie's wanting it to give tae her mither."

Pleased at the news, the girl made for home, and as she reached the door Habitrot gave her the yarn and, in reply to her thanks, only said: "Tell nane wha spinned it."

Overjoyed, the girl went into the house. It was dark, and her mother was asleep; but hanging up to dry in the chimney were seven black puddings she had just made. The girl had been fasting all day, so she took the puddings down, fired them, and ate them all seven. In the morning her mother came downstairs and found the seven skeins laid neatly out and the seven puddings gone. Frantic with surprise, she ran to the door, crying:

Ma dochter's span
se'en, se'en, se'en,
Ma dochter's eaten
se'en, se'en, se'en,
And a' afore daylicht.

The laird was riding by and enquired the meaning of her song. She led him into the house and showed him the shining skeins and the empty pan. The pretty girl was there too, and the laird, who desired a notable wife, asked her to marry him. So far all was well, but the girl was

afraid that he would expect her to live up to her reputation; so, soon after her marriage, she ran down to the self-bored stone and asked Habitrot's advice.

"Bring your bonnie man here, my dawtie," said the fairy, "and I'se warrant he'll no ask ye tae spin again."

And so it befell. When the laird saw the muckle-mou'd company and learned the cause of their deformity, he forbade his pretty bride to touch a spinning-wheel; and she was very ready to obey him.

Habitrot.

The illuminated letter for Christine de Pisan, embroidered by L. A. Olson, is derived from a medieval manuscript illumination which depicts De Pisan presenting one of her books to her patroness, the Queen of France.

Christine de Pisan

1363–1431, France

"Beyond Bargello" is the term we jokingly used to describe the work we did on the runner for Christine de Pisan. *Bargello,* which is also called "flame stitch" or "Florentine stitch," is an old form of counted-thread embroidery similar to needlepoint. Although Bargello has rarely been used for anything but the upholstery of chairs or for rugs, curtains, and bed valances, the pointed and undulating patterns that characterize it suggested an unexplored potential – the creation of a series of jagged forms which, if placed with their points toward the center of the runner, would appear threatening to the plate. This seemed an appropriate image for De Pisan, who felt so threatened by the anti-female tone of French literature that she devoted much of her writing to defending women.

In order to create these menacing forms, we designed shapes that thrust toward the center of the runner at different angles. This caused the first of many problems in the translation of our design into needlepoint. Bargello is normally constructed on a horizontal/vertical axis using a single piece of canvas. Our design required that each of the shapes be stitched separately on canvas, applied to the runner, and then somehow integrated into a visually unified image.

Bargello chair.

Studying the difference between the traditional Bargello stitching and our Bargello pattern makes clear the way we extended an old technique into a new dimension.

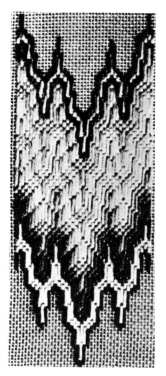

Traditional Bargello pattern.

Connie von Briesen, an experienced needlepoint worker who – with the aid of Betty Van Atta and Thelma Brenner – executed the runner, believed that it was possible to extend the Bargello technique to accommodate our needs. Working on thirteen-mesh canvas with Paternaya wools, she made tests for several weeks. It became clear that making and applying the separate pieces was actually going to be less of a problem than working out the internal design of each shape. The patterns we had created on the mockup (which related to the plate) were not consistent with the natural patterning established by counted-thread work. Eventually Von Briesen, although reluctant to lose the originally conceived configuration, had to let the progression of colors take over, with the colors making their own design in the traditional Bargello shading. Because the thread closely matched the tones in the plate, however, the runner and the plate remained closely tied together despite the change in the runner design. This was accomplished partly by Von Briesen's using the same color progression in each of the individual shapes, the interior edges of which were consistently dark green.

Christine de Pisan place setting.

Christine de Pisan – the first female professional author in France – was educated by her father, a humanist from Italy. Widowed at 25, she supported herself and her children by writing, first gaining prominence when she defended women against the misogyny of a famous French book, *Le Roman de la Rose*. She argued for the equality of women and initiated one of the earliest dialogues on women's rights in Europe.

The anti-female literature that developed during and after the Renaissance may be looked upon as a tool in driving women out of their longstanding occupations as spinners and carders, workers in wool, linen, and silk, and weavers. In England women played an important part in the production of textiles; in France six of the one hundred craft guilds were composed entirely of women, and women participated in many of the others; in Germany women enjoyed independent membership in guilds (without fathers or husbands), could undergo apprenticeships, and also had their own all-female guilds. By the sixteenth century, however, women's professional participation in textile work had been profoundly reduced and their energies devoted increasingly to unpaid domestic needlework. Christine de Pisan's famous book *The City of Women* was written against not only this background, but also growing diatribes against women by male writers.

The symbol heading relates to this famous book and depicts the signs of Reason, Justice, and Virtue and the city they encouraged Christine to build.

Detail: back of runner.

160

The colors came from the plate. To match them, Connie von Briesen worked out a sequence that used thirty-two colors in a progression of tonal bands, shaded from green to neutral beige, which became brighter in hue as they approached the core of the form. The small front shapes could only accommodate thirteen colors, but the larger, bulging shapes on the back of the runner glow with the whole range of vibrant colors that Chicago had used in shading the plate.

Connie von Briesen working on Bargello, matching colors to the Christine de Pisan plate.

This contemporary waste-basket, like the historic chair, shown on p. 159, demonstrates a typical use to which Bargello is put.

An additional row of dark green stitches was added to unify the different pieces after they were applied to the runner. When the canvas pieces were securely in place, the canvas was cut away and the edges cleaned up with additional stitching. The outside edges were finished the same way, using each color of wool as it occurred in the design. When we looked at the plate with the finished runner, we were ecstatic. We had accomplished our purpose – going "beyond Bargello" and transforming both the technique and the style into an expressive rather than decorative form.

sabella d'Este

1474–1539, Italy

The runner design for Isabella d'Este is closely related to the color and imagery on the plate, which simulates an Italian lusterware called *Urbino majolica*. The blue, yellow, and white colors of early majolica also appeared in Assisi work, a counted-thread embroidery technique that was quite popular during the Italian Renaissance. Assisi embroidery, customarily done in silk over a white linen ground, employs two stitches – the long-armed cross stitch for the background and the double running stitch for outlining. The design motifs are left unworked except for small interior detailing, while the negative space is entirely filled with densely worked, precise stitches.

In the D'Este runner, the semicircles on the side bands repeat one of the motifs on the plate. These bands, like the front border, are done in Assisi work using Ver au Soie silk. Stylized flower and fruit forms, like those that distinguished the sumptuous embossed velvet and silk brocades typical of fifteenth-century Italian weaving, are incorporated into the embroidered front piece.

Study for pomegranate image on front of runner by Chicago.

We first saw examples of Assisi work at the New York Metropolitan and Cooper-Hewitt Museums. Incorporating this reverse technique (filling in the background while leaving the image unstitched) provided a visual change from the rest of the runners. Moreover, its popularity at the time D'Este lived and its color relationship to majolica made Assisi work particularly suitable for this runner. This example, which contains a Tree-of-Life motif, is another indication of the historic significance of this image.

Isabella d'Este place setting.

Isabella d'Este, a perfect example of a Renaissance noblewoman – a scholar, a linguist, a musician, and a stateswoman – was best known as a patron who assembled one of the finest collections of art in her small gallery in Mantua. She played a crucial role in Italian history, not only through her voluminous correspondence with the leading scholars and statesmen of her day, but because of her importance in protecting and consolidating the political and social interests of the prominent D'Este family.

Back of runner showing
embroidered crest and
Cavandoli work.

The back of the runner relates to the great hanging heraldic flags used by the noble classes of the Renaissance. The center of this satin banner form contains a simplified insignia in honor of D'Este and derived from her family crest. A series of tassels ornaments the runner back and is duplicated in the front. These tassels emanate from a length of Cavandoli work, which is a type of macramé created by an Italian woman, Valentina Cavandoli, as an amusement for her children. The use of the tassels was suggested by a painting of a Renaissance woman wearing a dress with rows of delicate knotting and dangling tassels.

This painting of a Renaissance woman represents her wearing an elaborate gown with rows of knotting and tassels on the sleeves. The Cavandoli work on the runner was modeled on this costume and is the only example of macramé in The Dinner Party. *Although I was able to make innovative use of many relatively limited needlework techniques, macramé eluded me until Susan pointed out the existence of earlier forms of knotted work (among which was Cavandoli) that were quite beautiful.*

This piece of Italian velvet, with stylized pomegranates, is typical of the way Italian weavers enlarged motifs to unusual dimensions. Because the pomegranate image reappears throughout textile history, we used it repeatedly in our runner designs.

The D'Este runner was executed primarily by Elfie Schwitkis, Judy Mulford, and L. A. Olson. The Cavandoli work was done by Schwitkis' young son Kent – a fitting note considering the development of this technique.

The imagery of the two illuminated capitals for Elizabeth I combines the blackwork feathers from the runner surface with the flourish Elizabeth used in signing the R after her name to signify Regina or Queen. This flourish is accentuated by a small crown capped with pearls.

Elizabeth R

1533–1605, England

Seeing paintings of Queen Elizabeth in her gorgeous costumes and wide, elaborate ruffs inspired not only the runner design, but a modification of the plate as well. White satin was used for the runner surface, which was embroidered primarily by Kacy Treadway, Susan Hill, and Audrey Wallace, who worked with extraordinarily fine shaded stem stitching, split stitching, running stitches, couching, and French knots. Traditional blackwork designs and patterns were combined with Elizabethan floral motifs, which – when stitched in the purple and red shades of Zwicky silk (chosen to match the plate) and embellished with gold thread, cord, and pearls – made a regal environment for the great queen's plate.

The plate itself was transformed by the addition of a simulated ruff produced by Ellen Dinerman. At first, we tried to make a white silk organza ruff edged with lace like the ones worn during Elizabeth's time. Dinerman worked several weeks to devise a method of forming a pleated ruff with the organza. She constructed a fine mockup, but the ruff, although historically authentic, did not suit the plate.

A book of prayers handwritten by Elizabeth I as a child, with a cover embroidered by her.

This portrait of Elizabeth I was the basis for both the runner design and the ruff that surrounds the plate.

Not only was Queen Elizabeth a skilled needle-woman herself, but she was responsible for the reestablishment of the Embroidery Guild in England. After a period of decline in needlework, Elizabeth incorporated the Borderer's Company in 1561, three years after her accession to the throne. Fashion played a significant role during Elizabethan times, and court dress was very important. Royal costumes were incredibly ornate and richly embellished with embroidery in silk, gold, and silver thread as well as jewels and lace. The resurgence of professional needleworkers and the implementation of high standards contributed to the production of beautiful garments, but, unfortunately, under Elizabeth membership in the Embroidery Guild was restricted to men.

Elizabeth R place setting.

A woman whose birth had been cursed by her father, Henry VIII, because he wanted a male heir, Elizabeth became one of the greatest rulers of the Western world and one of the most erudite women of the sixteenth century. Never married, she was determined to retain her autonomy and rule England in her own way. During her reign there was an increase in the economic power of England, a decrease in religious strife, and establishment of the right to a fair trial.

167

Blackwork is embroidery in black silk on white fabric, which became fashionable during the reign of Henry VIII in England and continued in popularity until after the death of Elizabeth I. Catherine of Aragon is reputed to have been responsible for introducing blackwork into England when she came there from Spain, but counted-thread embroidery in black and white was certainly known there previously. Blackwork was principally used for dress embroidery, although during Elizabeth's reign both its scope and its design expanded. More patterns were developed, and blackwork began to be used on bed hangings and other household articles as well as on clothing and royal garb.

Blackwork test for feathers on Queen Elizabeth's runner. In the final work, gold French knots were placed inside the blackwork diamond pattern – an extremely difficult needlework task.

We decided to make a symbolic rather than literal reference to Elizabethan costume, and, instead of using white, we incorporated colors that would unify the plate and the ruff. We had a flat, smoke-colored, transparent ring fabricated to fit around the foot of the plate. A continuous line of tiny holes was drilled into the edge of this ring to accommodate the fabric, the embroidery, and the lace edging we had chosen. We first placed an iridescent, sheer fabric, woven with fine gold thread and purple silk, over the plastic ring. This "cloth of gold" was a contemporary analogue to one of the fabrics which was particularly associated with Elizabeth's father, Henry VIII. Over this silk surface, we positioned a layer of sheer blue chiffon which had been embroidered with a blackwork pattern, using two strands of Zwicky silk and highlighting the black lattice work with crosses of fine gold. The chiffon – like the cloth of gold – was cut to fit the ring and attached through the small holes, and the edges were protected against fraying with Stevie's Paste.

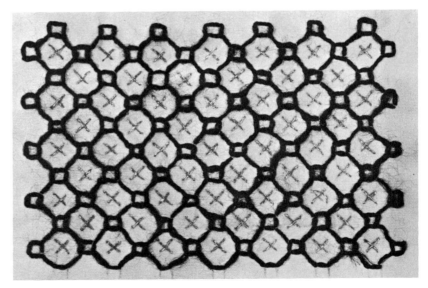

Blackwork test from *Dinner Party Sampler Book.*

168

The lace edging was also attached through the drilled holes, and rows of black silk and gold couching were added to antique lace that had been dyed black. The addition of pearls to the scalloped edge of the ruff created a strong visual connection to the runner surface, which had already been studded with pearls.

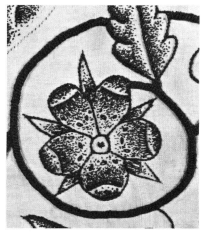

Detail of jacket.

Despite the exclusion of women from the professional embroidery workshops during Elizabethan times, women contributed significantly to the vast amount of English domestic needlework and embroidered clothing. Although only the high-ranking aristocracy were allowed to wear the inordinately expensive and elaborately embellished costumes, lesser nobility wore ornate though less costly garments. It was still customary for noblewomen, as well as women of the new mercantile class, to participate in the production of this clothing as well as large household embroideries. Lady Montagu's quip makes it clear that needlework skills were essential for a woman's survival:
"It is as scandalous for a woman not to know how to use her needle as for a man not to know how to use his sword."
—*Lady Mary Wortley Montagu*

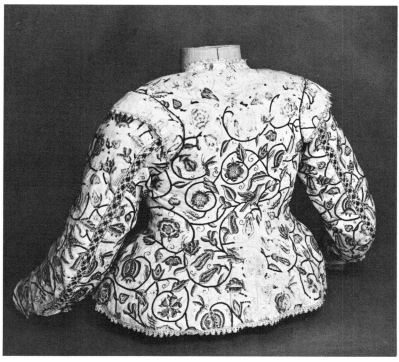

This classic Elizabethan garment demonstrates typical motifs and stitchery done by needlewomen of the sixteenth century.

169

One morning, as the runner was close to completion, I took the dust cover off for yet another day of embroidering black lines – and saw that the runner had been studded with big, luminous pearls! Early that morning Judy had pinned them in place as a surprise. We had long fantasized about putting pearls on Elizabeth's runner, but, knowing how prohibitively expensive an idea it was, we had always laughed it off, saying "When we finish...when we finish." When the runner was nearing completion, Judy had dinner with her lawyer, Susan Grode, and mentioned to her that the Elizabeth runner would be enhanced by the addition of pearls, although we couldn't afford them. Grode didn't say anything, but got up from the table and went into her bedroom; she returned carrying a box of pearls inherited from her mother, which she donated in honor of Elizabeth R.

—*S. H.*

The tiny stem stitches in the runner were made with three strands of Zwicky silk. The tension from the rows and rows of stitching created enormous puckers in the runner. Blocking did not smooth the satin, so the additional stitching for the arabesque forms was done so as to distribute the tension more evenly across the fabric and thereby flatten it.

Detail: back of runner.

Detail: back of runner.

The center of the front of the runner contains a pomegranate image executed by Kacy Treadway in Elizabethan stitchery and blackwork and accentuated by gold couching and pearls.

Artemisia Gentileschi

1590–1652, Italy

Artemisia Gentileschi's runner surrounds and almost engulfs her plate in a mass of draped velvet. The active form of the plate is repeated in the curving, undulating drapery, gathered in folds that twist and turn like the clothed figures in seventeenth-century Italian paintings. The imagery of the runner is derived from the costumes worn by women in these paintings, particularly from those in Gentileschi's own work.

The women in Gentileschi's paintings – primarily heroines of the Bible and mythology – challenged prevailing ideas about the natural inferiority of women. Strong and courageous, these female characters, like Gentileschi herself, attested to women's continual efforts to retain independence and autonomy.

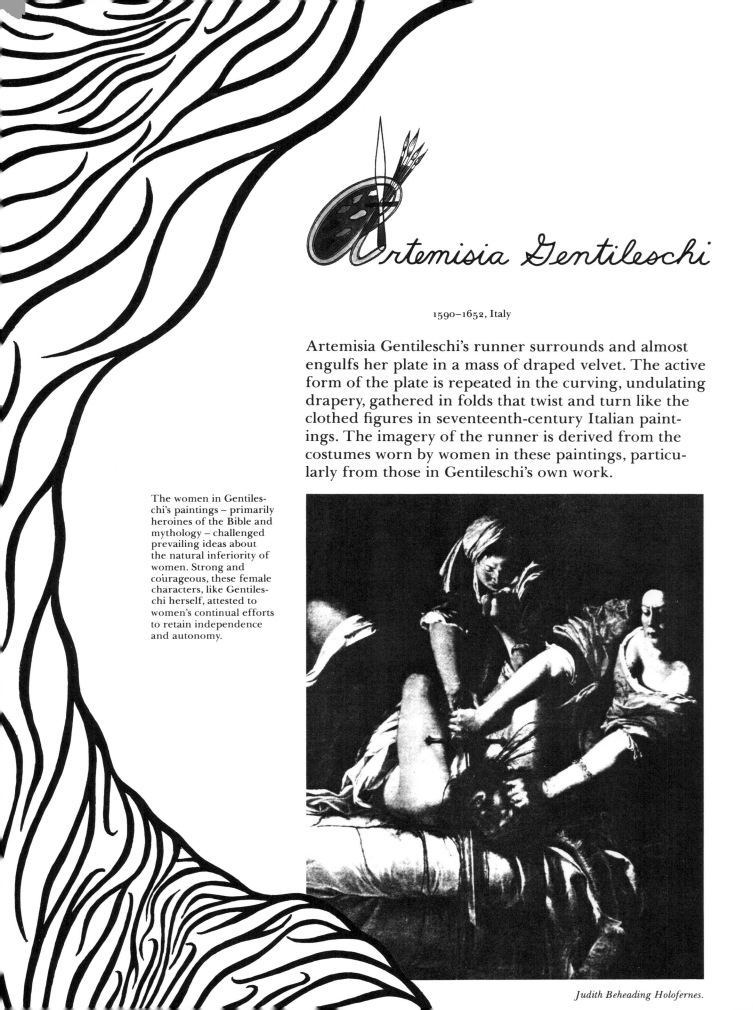

Judith Beheading Holofernes.

The "A" in Artemisia Gentileschi's illuminated capital contains a paint pallette pierced by both the brushes that were the tools of her trade and a sword that refers to the weapon used by Judith in Gentileschi's painting of *Judith Beheading Holofernes.* The sword also refers to the illuminated letter of Judith, whose deed inspired many of Gentileschi's later paintings.

With the decline of monasticism, one of the few ways a woman could acquire artistic training was to be the daughter of an artist who would teach her himself. Apprenticeships – the primary vehicle for training – were available only to men, and the artisan guilds, formerly open to women, were gradually closed. Artemisia Gentileschi's father, a painter, recognized her talent and trained her himself. She went on to become an important artist of the Baroque period and one of the first women to paint from a female point of view.

Artemisia Gentileschi place setting.

When I first saw an example of Bizarre Silk in the Metropolitan's textile department, I thought it was the ugliest fabric I had ever seen. Pattern overlaid pattern until the surface seemed a veritable hodge-podge of lines and forms. But something about this fabric intrigued me. I kept thinking about how I could incorporate some reference to these silks into the runner design for Gentileschi, as it had become popular in Italy less than fifty years after her death.

The rich velvets and brocades of these costumes were further adorned by the development, at the end of the seventeenth century, of a fabric style called "Bizarre Silk." A notable feature of these silks was the way pattern was worked over pattern to create a complex fabric surface, many of which were so fantastic as to be considered bizarre. This style was incorporated into the design for the back of the Gentileschi runner, which was made by painting the subpattern on a red silk fabric ground with white, heat-set textile paint and then embroidering larger patterns over it with two strands of black Zwicky silk in the satin stitch. The subpattern is repeated on the front of the runner in red textile paint on white silk. The painting was done by Susan Brenner and the over-embroidery by Virginia Levie, who worked six weeks to complete the stitching.

The drapery for the runner was made from a high-quality, upholstery-weight silk velvet. We constructed it on a specially built U-shaped frame. The runner design required that we work with the fabric as if it were draped over the table. (If the folds had been made while the runner was flat, they would have been completely ruined when the fabric was bent over the *Dinner Party* table.) We stretched backing linen on the frame, attached the Bizarre Silk pieces in place, and then draped and gathered the velvet. The excess fabric was trimmed away; the folds were tacked to the backing linen; and, before the velvet was secured, the plate, flatware, and chalice were positioned to make sure they were not obscured by the fabric.

Traditional Bizarre Silk.

Bizarre Silk pattern on back of runner.

174

The Gentileschi runner
was constructed by Susan
Brenner, assisted by
Elaine Ireland, on a studio-
fabricated U-shaped
frame. The runner was
shipped on the same kind
of frame, as stretching it
flat would destroy the
forms.

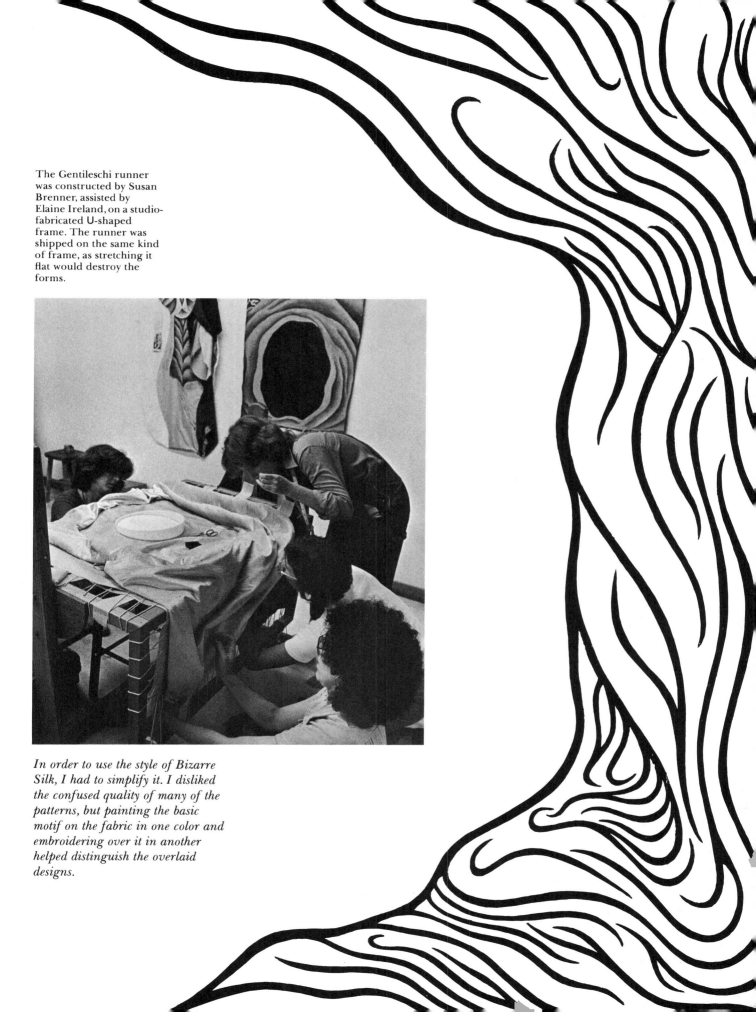

*In order to use the style of Bizarre
Silk, I had to simplify it. I disliked
the confused quality of many of the
patterns, but painting the basic
motif on the fabric in one color and
embroidering over it in another
helped distinguish the overlaid
designs.*

Anna van Schurman

1607–1678, Holland

"Woman has the same wish for self-development as man, the same ideals, yet she is to be imprisoned in an empty soul of which the very windows are shuttered." This phrase, excerpted from Anna van Schurman's writing, is embroidered on the runner in the same cross stitch used by generations of little girls as they painstakingly embroidered samplers with the letters of the alphabet and sometimes with sentimental phrases. By the nineteenth century, in fact, samplers were being done almost entirely by young girls, who made them at school as a first lesson in both needlework and patient, ladylike behavior. Women's educational opportunities were extremely limited by then – a situation Van Schurman had railed against as early as the seventeenth century in her book advocating female education.

Most female education in the eighteenth and nineteenth centuries left girls more able to ply a needle than to use their minds.

Bullion knot and raised buttonhole-stitch flowers.

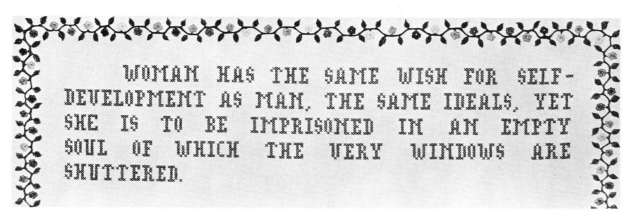

WOMAN HAS THE SAME WISH FOR SELF-DEVELOPMENT AS MAN, THE SAME IDEALS, YET SHE IS TO BE IMPRISONED IN AN EMPTY SOUL OF WHICH THE VERY WINDOWS ARE SHUTTERED.

Embroidered phrase on runner.

Traditional sampler.

Lettering was used on early samplers to identify the embroiderer. As samplers became more decorative, religious sentiments and romantic phrases appeared along with more formalized motifs and alphabets.

Samplers first developed during the late Renaissance and the beginning of the Reformation. The latter period ushered in, along with much-needed Church reforms, the idea that women's work should be entirely confined to the domestic sphere. During the late Renaissance, needlework began to be done by women less for ecclesiastical purposes and more (though not exclusively) for private use.

Anna van Schurman place setting.

Anna van Schurman was a child prodigy who became an outstanding intellectual and theologian as well as an artist. Her interest in religious issues led her to study Greek, Hebrew, and other ancient languages in order to read and interpret the Bible, and although she was allowed to study at the university, she was forced to attend lectures concealed behind curtains. Angered by this and similar injustices, she wrote several important books in which she argued for expanded opportunities for women. These made her famous, but she eventually withdrew from the world, preferring life in a religious community where women had equal rights.

177

The luxury of a Renaissance household was reflected in its embellished fabrics. Women embroidered everything – clothing, linen, bed and furniture coverings, and hangings – using stitches and patterns that had been passed down to them by their female ancestors. Both professional and domestic needleworkers recorded their favorite designs and embroidery techniques on samplers, which in turn became personal encyclopedias that served as sourcebooks for these needleworkers.

Traditional stitch patterns.

Before the advent of pattern books, women passed on their needlework expertise both orally and through treasured pieces on linen. Thus they preserved their patterns and created a personal work encyclopedia.

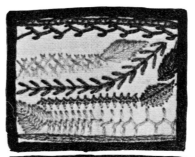

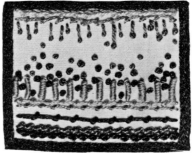

Details of stitches on runner back.

Patterned upon early stitch samplers, these small blocks of embroidery demonstrate many of the stitches used on the Anna van Schurman runner: chain stitch, stem stitch, split stitch, satin stitch, buttonhole stitch, bullion knots and French knots, threaded running stitch, blanket stitch, feather stitch, herringbone stitch, fishbone stitch, filling stitch, couching, and laidwork.

Back of runner.

Detail: back of runner.

The flower basket, one of the most common motifs seen on samplers, is a diminished form of the "tree of life" motif. In Dutch samplers, flowers rising out of a vase or basket signify regeneration.

Detail: Dutch sampler.

The design of this vase of flowers, which was probably taken from a pattern book, was the basis for this image on the runner back.

At first, samplers were stitched without any formal organization and employed a wide range of stitches. Soon, however, conventional arrangements, borders, and motifs developed. With the advent of pattern books, hundreds of designs became readily available, and the purpose of samplers changed; by the eighteenth century, they were primarily decorative. As samplers lost their role as stitch records and became instead a device for teaching, their quality and variety declined.

We modeled the runner for Anna van Schurman on seventeenth-century Dutch samplers using a range of colors that were similar to those in the plate. Both DMC floss and perle cotton were used – one or two strands of the floss for fine stitching and the perle cotton for bolder details. Van Schurman's runner was executed by L. A. Olson, assisted by Mary Helen Krehbiel.

"Of female arts in usefulness
The needle far excells the
    rest
In ornament there's no
    device
Affords adorning's half so
    nice.

While thus we practice every
    art
To adorn and grace our
    moral part
Let us with no less care
    device
To improve the mind that
    never dies."

Two angels with trumpets hover over Anna van Schurman's name. Their figures are embroidered in shaded stem stitch, and their hair is done in bullion knots. Angels such as these symbolize the "trumpeting of the word of God" – an apt image for Van Schurman, who spent the last years of her life as a religious leader.

Detail: front of runner.

The front of the runner contains a series of images commonly found on samplers. These are positioned within the blocks of an interlocking chain that is embroidered in graduated colors using the chain stitch. Many of these images have symbolic significance. For example, the shepherd and shepherdess (whose forms are embroidered in chain stitch) stand on either side of a stylized version of the Tree of Life done in laidwork. Their position flanking the tree indicates that they are married. Just as the Tree-of-Life motif degenerated, so did the image of the rabbit, embroidered in shaded split stitch with a turkey-work tail. Originally a symbol of fertility, by the seventeenth century it had come to signify timidity.

Buttonhole stitch.

The brick facade of the house was done in laidwork. The roof was embroidered in buttonhole stitch to resemble shingles, and the fence was done in chain stitch.

Detail: back of runner.

Embroidering Our Heritage

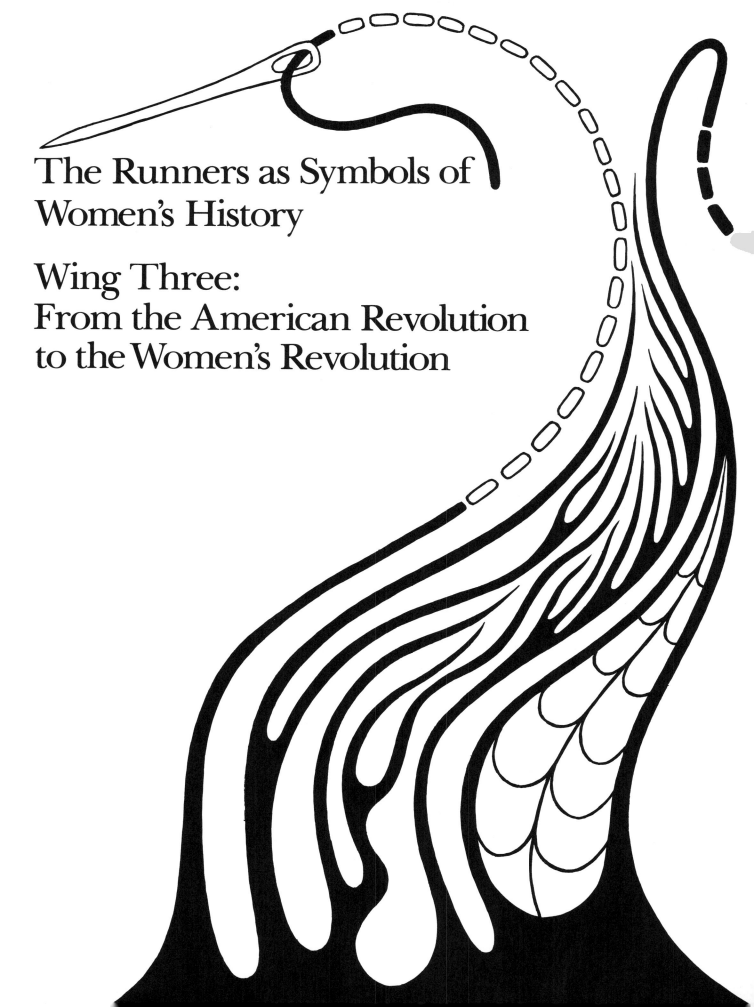

The Runners as Symbols of
Women's History

Wing Three:
From the American Revolution
to the Women's Revolution

"Lucky are you, reader, if you happen not to be of that sex to whom it is forbidden all good things, to whom liberty is denied; to whom almost all virtues are denied; lucky are you if you are one of those who can be wise without its being a crime."

—*Marie le Jars de Gournay* (1565–1645)

These words echo the sadness expressed in the runner for Anne Hutchinson, which begins the third wing of the table. Based on traditional eighteenth-century American needle paintings, the runner mourns the constriction of women's options that started in the Renaissance and was reinforced by the Reformation.

Once again needlework reflects these historical changes. During the Renaissance, embroidery production had been organized into formal workshops in the prospering cities. These continued to turn out church needlework in those European countries that remained Catholic after the Reformation. There was, however, a gradual shift in patronage from the church to the aristocracy as the royal classes appropriated embroidery as a way of emphasizing their growing power, authority, and prestige.

This shift in patronage brought with it a new status for the artist. Painters began to be distinguished from other artisans and viewed as special persons able to infuse their work with their individual identities – something women were considered incapable of doing. It was asserted that women did not have the strength of character to create "forceful designs" on their own.

Pattern books – introduced in the early sixteenth century – reflected this view as well as other prejudiced attitudes toward women. In one book of designs printed on a squared ground, the compiler insisted that he used only counted patterns because women were too lazy to transfer their designs themselves, preferring to count them straight from a book.

This small, early seventeenth century embroidery relates to events of the sixteenth century, when Henry VIII – in a fit of pique against Papal authority – separated England from the Catholic Church, thus ushering in the Reformation.

As the Reformation spread throughout Europe, religious houses were dissolved and their property confiscated. One wonders at the feelings of the homeless nuns and monks as they watched their meticulously worked embroideries being sold for profit or cut up into doublets and saddlecloths.

With these acts, the Reformers completed the process of the destruction of the convents as a viable alternative for women which had begun when the centers of culture shifted from the monasteries to the towns. Needlework then began to be used almost entirely for decorative, rather than spiritual, purposes.

And according to Giovanni Andrea Vavassore, his pattern book, published in 1540, included gridded backgrounds because he had been told that women couldn't draw from free patterns. These attitudes – combined with the end of the convents as a support system for women's art industries and the fact that formal art training was unavailable – had severe repercussions for women.

During the Renaissance, many painters had done embroidery and tapestry designs intended primarily for the professional workshops. With the advent of printing, however, these designs – along with fine engravings and woodcuts – became widely available to needlewomen. Gradually, the major artists stopped creating designs for textiles, and this, along with the general standardization of embroidery that had occurred in the workshops, resulted in a decline in the originality of embroidery patterns. By this time, women were becoming steadily more dependent upon these patterns; the bias against women's ability to create had grown so pervasive it had even begun to penetrate most women's view of themselves.

Pattern books, introduced in Germany and Italy, quickly became popular for both commercial and private use. The most common early motifs and designs were flora, fauna, classical acanthus patterns, and – as is seen in the upper half of this picture – Renaissance grotesques. Designs from the Near East, China, and Mexico were sometimes also included. These books, printed and reprinted, were partly responsible for the development of a standardized embroidery language throughout Europe.

Despite the prejudice that women were incapable of creating their own images, some women continued to design embroideries. The artist depicts herself working at her embroidery frame in this detail of a wall hanging by Luigia Morell. A seventeenth-century hanging measuring 69 inches square and containing twelve medallions representing Morell's family, it is part of the tradition of women's needle painting that developed during the Renaissance. At first these pictorial embroideries were done on cushions, bed hangings and valances, table coverings, and other household furnishings. By the seventeenth century, they were being made as paintings to be hung on walls.

Detail: Morell's embroidery.

During the Renaissance, the nature of the house had begun to change dramatically. The feudal castles, with their large, open, simply furnished halls, had been replaced by palaces situated in or near cities that contained private rooms or chambers. As the family superseded the church as the most important social institution, embellishing one's own living space became a preoccupation of aristocratic women. Furnishings, like clothing, were a visible sign of a family's wealth, and Renaissance women worked with architects, artists, and artisans to "perfect" their environments.

Widening prosperity created an expanding merchant class which tended to imitate upper-class styles. Middle-class women tried to duplicate the expensive wall coverings used by the aristocracy, embroidering cheaper fabrics with motifs from patterned silks and velvets and making needlework pictures that resembled paintings and tapestries. Beds covered with elaborately embroidered hangings, valances, cushions, and linens figured prominently in most households, and other hangings and valances were commonly decorated with pictorial designs, as were the cushions of hard wooden chairs. As a broader segment of society began to enjoy more money and greater leisure, interest in enhancing the home increased. This historical trend coincided with the growing emphasis on the idea that women's sphere should be restricted to marriage and the family.

At first there was a flowering of domestic embroidery – particularly in England after the Reformation ended all ecclesiastical work. Both the scale and the quantity of much of this embroidery were enormous. Highly valued, it was passed down from generation to generation, and women derived considerable social status from their needlework.

This typical seventeenth-century bed hanging by Abigail Pett was embroidered in wool with designs probably derived from pattern books.

Detail of an English needlework screen, inscribed *"Julia Calverley* 1727" and measuring 5′9½″x 20½″.

Smaller needlework pictures, raised embroidery, and samplers became prevalent in the seventeenth century. (Although samplers were in use by the fifteenth century, there are few existing examples of these.) House furnishings such as cabinets, mirrors, sewing boxes, book coverings, and all sorts of personal items, as well as clothing, were ornately embroidered, using silk and woolen thread, on a wide range of materials. Both surface stitching and counted thread were common, as well as many forms of appliqué. As a result of increased trade with the Orient – which produced an abundance of *chinoiserie* designs – there was a renewed interest in quilting. But as women's role steadily contracted, both the size and the quality of their needlework declined.

Engraving.

Needlework upholstery was frequently used on chairs such as this one. Worked in colored wool and silk in the tent stitch, this eighteenth-century piece depicting the rape of Persephone was probably based upon the engraving illustrated here. One wonders if the person who worked this design was conscious of its real meaning. Certainly a rape scene, even one whose roots are in classical mythology, does not seem a sufficiently casual subject to be presented on the back of a chair.

Needleworked chair.

Until the French Revolution, royal women – particularly in France – continued to play a significant role in needlework. Embroidery was extremely popular in the courts, and many queens practiced it and contributed to its development Catherine de Medici, for example, was both an accomplished embroiderer and a patron, and Mme. de Maintenon established a school that emphasized needlework. Because the daughters of nobility from all over Europe were sent there to study, patterns and techniques became rapidly internationalized.

In the seventeenth century it was fashionable throughout Europe, and especially in England, to reproduce paintings in embroidery. Painters, including some women artists, again began to create designs for needlework.

The line between the professional and amateur needlewoman, which had always been unclear, was becoming ever more defined. In 1815, Mary Lamb, author and sister of Charles Lamb, who had worked for 11 years as a paid needleworker, wrote:

"Women should embroider for money, or not at all; only then would they see their work as 'real business'…Moreover, by embroidering for love, women take work away from professional embroiderers."

Early American textiles were economical, practical, and modest. In the absence of any developed industry, linen and wool were produced at home, and the raising of sheep and the harvesting of flax – as well as spinning, dyeing, and weaving – were all part of the responsibilities of colonial women. The need for large quantities of material often led these women to pool their energies, working together at flaxing or spinning parties which were social as well as productive occasions.

By the early seventeenth century, however, professional weavers had begun to set up shops where women could bring their homespun thread to be woven into cloth. As weavers migrated to the colonies, the industry grew, and in 1638 the first textile factory was established by twenty families from England. At that time, restrictions against female weavers were so extensive throughout Europe that it is possible that one reason these families came to America was to escape from the economic persecution of their female members.

Though women in the early colonies had little time for embroidery themselves, they certainly encountered and were influenced by the rich indigenous needlework tradition of Native American women, who were skilled in porcupine quillwork, beadwork, and appliqué. Most Native American embroidery designs had personal or spiritual significance or were symbolic records of important events in a tribe's history. Considered sacred, many of these embroideries were revered, protected, and handed down from generation to generation.

Some important textile traditions of the New World – those of Mexico and of Central and South America – revolved primarily around the decoration of garments, and it is thought that this colorful and elaborate embroidery on clothing has a long history. Because the Spaniards destroyed most of the arts of these conquered cultures, however, there are few surviving examples of early textiles except those from ancient Peru. Archaeological excavations there have unearthed garments and burial shrouds of pre-Inca peoples that were preserved in underground tombs.

These relics indicate a highly developed knowledge of weaving and fabric decoration. In fact, Peruvian weaving has been called "the most perfect in the world." Cotton, vegetable fibers, and wool were woven on backstrap looms, then sewn – with needles made of cactus thorns – into garments containing magical or religious symbols. Spinning, weaving, and embroidery were done by all classes and by both sexes.

This woven image, suggesting a goddess with upraised arms, demonstrates the fine quality of Peruvian weaving.

As the early struggle of the colonists produced a more stable and prosperous society, an embroidery tradition developed among white women that was patterned upon the style and designs of English needlework. At first, blue-and-white embroidery was extremely popular because of the availability of indigo dye and the influence of the blue ceramic Canton ware that was being imported from China. American embroidery gradually became more colorful as trade increased and Native American women taught colonial women to make a variety of dyes from plants, berries, and insects.

This early American work tended to be more naïve than its European counterpart, but, as needlework became an important part of every young girl's education, both its technique and its design improved. However, the quality of women's lives suffered as the simplicity of colonial society was replaced by greater wealth and increasingly rigid ideas about the role of women in the expanding middle and upper classes. By the nineteenth century, these women were being continually admonished that all their energies should be directed toward the domestic sphere. This was precisely at a time when rapidly spreading industrialization was rendering household work – particularly most forms of women's once useful needlework – ever more redundant.

In the early days of the colonies, women worked at a variety of occupations, since there were few restrictions against entering the profession of their choice. But their most important jobs were spinning and weaving, which were done in the home. In fact, work generally was centered in the household, particularly in rural and agrarian regions.

In 1797, Susanna Rowson, an English author and actress, opened a school in America that included needlework as an important part of its curriculum. A specialty of the school was mourning pictures, which played an important role in both the popularity and the high quality of American embroidered pictures. Pictorial needlework continued to be executed in both America and England, especially after Berlin work was introduced by a Madame Wittich. This technique – which has been frequently maligned, perhaps because of its wide appeal – is a tapestry-type embroidery characterized by the use of brightly colored wools.

Berlin work.

Nineteenth-century women's magazines did a great deal to make needlework techniques and patterns accessible to the rapidly expanding market. One of the first of these publications was *Godey's Lady's Book*. Published in Philadelphia in 1830 and edited by Sarah Josepha Hale, this magazine's influence was widespread. In addition to providing information on decorative needlework, Hale kept middle- and upper-class women apprised of technological advances in textiles, as well as emphasizing nutrition, domestic science, and educational rights for women.

189

The Industrial Revolution separated work

The Industrial Revolution – which had a profound effect on women's lives, as well as on the whole of society – was first engineered and experienced in England. Beginning in 1760, an avalanche of inventions rapidly transformed the base of the textile industry from home manufacture to factory production. By 1830, cleaning, carding, roving, and spinning not only had been taken out of the house, but had been removed from women's hands and placed in those of skilled workmen, who used increasingly sophisticated and physically demanding machines that were not designed with women in mind.

In America, when industrialization moved production from the home to the factory, national determination to end all dependency on English goods, combined with the need for men in agricultural work, caused a labor shortage. Therefore, just as upper- and middle-class women were experiencing enforced idleness, women of the lower classes were being encouraged to work in the developing textile mills. Working-class women were supposedly to be "saved" from poverty as well as idleness – which obviously was to be reserved for the upper classes – by factory jobs. Even children were recruited to work in the mills on the basis that "all people should be industrious." These arguments basically disguised the necessity for abundant and cheap labor if American industry was to develop.

In the late nineteenth century, black women slowly moved back into the textile industry. By World War I, more factory positions were opening up, but a study done in 1920 showed that although 12 percent of textile-mill workers were black, their wages were about half that of whites.

The sweatshop system – a total perversion of the home industries of former days – was the turn-of-the-century practice of hiring immigrant women or entire families to labor for subsistence wages in dismal tenements under horrendous working conditions.

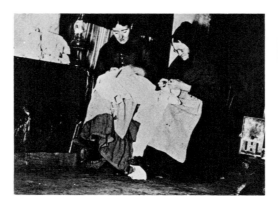

"The golf links are so near
   the mill
That almost every day
The laboring children can
   look out
And see the men at play."
—*Sara N. Ueghorn*

The women who first went to work in the textile factories were usually educated and in search of independence. The opportunity offered by these jobs was especially important because most other fields of employment were closed to women. But instead of finding independence, these women encountered strict regulations, both at the mills and at the boarding houses where they were required to live. Moreover, the working conditions proved to be intolerable: The hours were long and the rooms poorly ventilated. Windows were kept closed to protect the materials – causing unhealthy dust – and at night and during the winter, dark smoke from the oil lamps filled the air.

As more types of work became available to women, the early, educated textile workers were gradually replaced by the waves of immigrants who began to pour into America during the latter half of the nineteenth century. The presence of desperate people who would work for the smallest wages gave the lie to the idealistic slogans which had ushered in the American Industrial Revolution. Instead of leading to a more self-sufficient, decentralized republic, industrialization resulted in the exploitation of human labor on a previously unimaginable scale.

The Industrial Revolution started with the mechanization of spinning and weaving – the earliest creations of women. Women, however, had no part whatsoever in the transformation of their traditional work into a mechanized process over which they had no control. But women's anger at the enforced idleness of their rich and the humiliating labor of their poor led to a women's revolution that – as symbolized in the way in which the last few *Dinner Party* runners break loose from their constraints – helped all women in their efforts to rise up and become free.

"The shuttle drops from the fingers of the weaver, and falls into iron fingers that ply it faster. For all earthly, and some unearthly purposes, we have machines and mechanical utterances...Not the eternal and physical alone is now managed by machinery, but the internal and spiritual also."

These words, written by Thomas Carlyle in 1829, exemplify the way in which writers, very shortly after the Industrial Revolution began, started to protest its dehumanizing effects. Visual artists also became involved in trying to counteract the debasement of crafts and the disregard for the quality of design which accompanied the industrial emphasis on faster work for greater profits. Looking back to pre-industrial society, when craft production was centered in the family as an integrated part of everyday life, artists like William Morris attempted to revive or promote traditional crafts, particularly embroidery.

"I do not want art for a few, any more than education for a few, or freedom for a few."
—*William Morris*, 1877

Industrialization, which basically involved the separation of work from the home, resulted in the loss of an economically productive role for middle- and upper-class women. By the mid-nineteenth century, household work had ceased to be seen as possessing any economic value. Moreover, "privileged" women were supposed to demonstrate, through their leisure, the economic and social status of their husbands. The rapid increase in wealth and upward social mobility during Victorian times quickly expanded the ranks of women forced into false idleness. The idea of a vast number of members of one sex being supported by members of the other was an entirely new phenomenon in history and totally without precedent. Upper- and middle-class women were expected to be merely the "helpmates" of men, and they were required to be submissive and demure. Women's needlework reflected this profound restriction of women's role; it became more obsessive, more trivial, and more grotesque – until every possible article of clothing and household item was engulfed by the same artificiality that threatened to smother a large segment of the female population.

In America, as in most countries, women were excluded from higher education until the nineteenth-century women's movement forced open the doors of the colleges. Until then, girls were allowed only minimum schooling, mostly through academies where middle- and upper-class young women received a "genteel education" that featured embroidery as its main focal point. For a long time these schools were the chief avenue for obtaining both needlework designs and techniques, as pattern books were quite scarce. Later, during the second half of the century, ladies' magazines began to publish embroidery instructions and designs.

1853—"Reticule : to be worked on rich, deep blue velvet with network gold braid laid flat; the fleur-de-lis must be worked in white silk, the rose in red silk, the five dots in the center in gold beads."

1866—"Quilted Bed Pocket": with a place to contain a watch; to be quilted in blue with added ribbon work. "Appliqué and Embroidery for What-not:." (*Peterson's Magazine*, February.)

Victorian painting, *Family Circle*.

Along with suggestions for embroideries, Victorian needlework books usually included illustrations such as these, which attest to the endless forms of "busy work" women were urged to do.

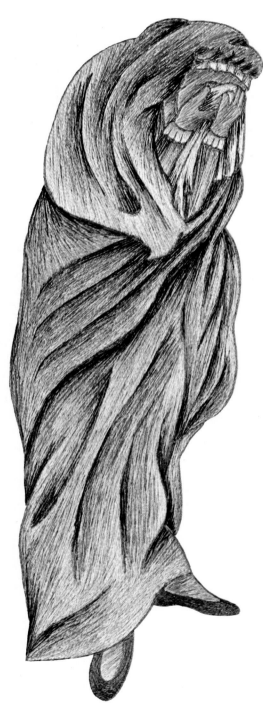

Figure on runner front.

Grieving for women, grieving for the

Full runner.

Anne Hutchinson plate.

Detail of tree.

loss of our power.

Section of runner back.

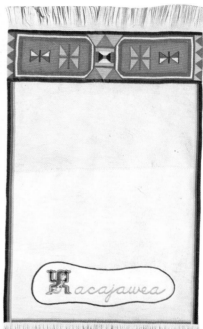

Full runner.

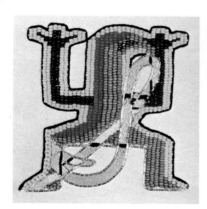

Illuminated capital.

Detail: cradle board.

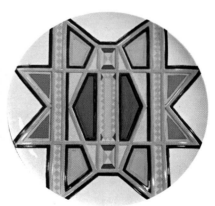

Sacajawea plate

Trying to expand our universe.

Illuminated capital.

Caroline Herschel plate.

Full runner.

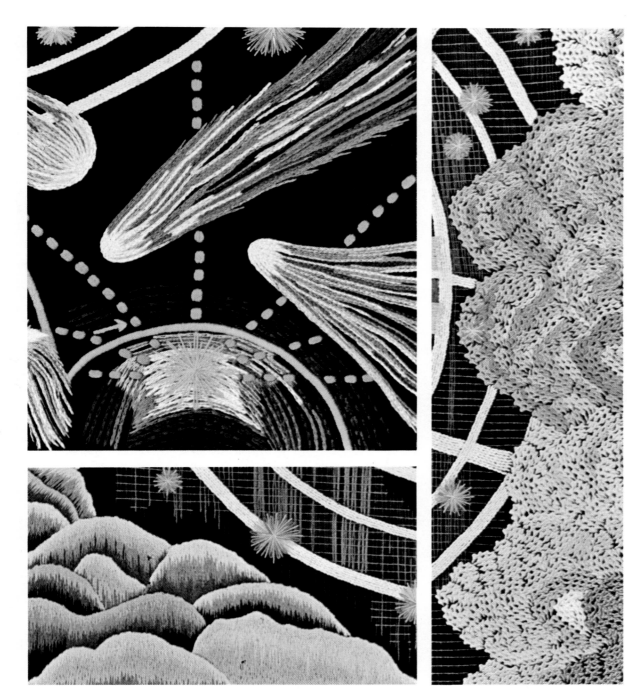

Runner details.

Education is a right, not a privilege.

Full runner.

Mary Wollstonecraft plate.

Runner detail: top.

Runner details: front.

Runner details: back.

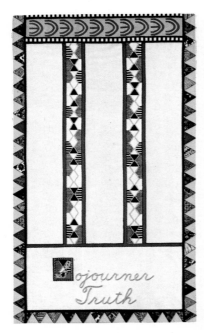

Full runner.

Sojourner Truth plate.

Illuminated capital.

Section of runner back.

Full runner.

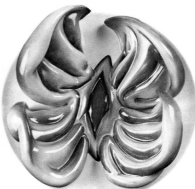

Susan B. Anthony plate.

Section of quilted back.

Illuminated capital.

Elizabeth Blackwell plate.

Full runner.

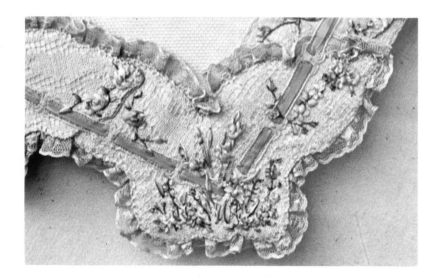

Full runner.

Runner details: ribbon work.

Emily Dickinson plate.

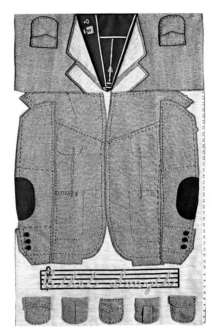

Full runner.

Detail: back of runner.

Ethel Smyth plate.

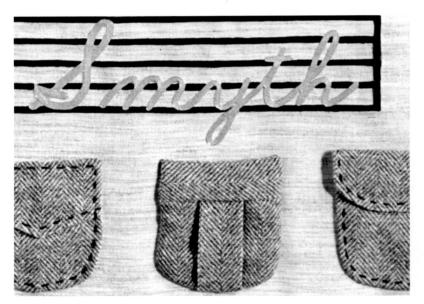

Detail: front of runner.

Center of runner back.

Full runner.

Margaret Sanger plate.

The butterfly as a symbol of liberation.

Detail: beading.

Natalie Barney plate.

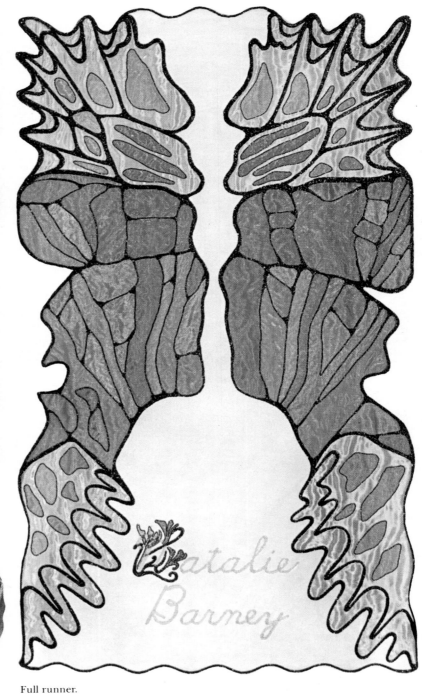

Full runner.

Illuminated capital.

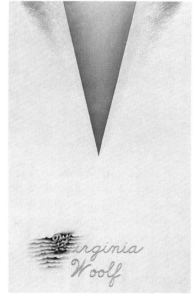

Full runner.

Virginia Woolf plate.

Regaining our creative power.

Full runner.

Detail of stitching.

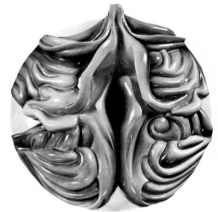

Georgia O'Keeffe plate.

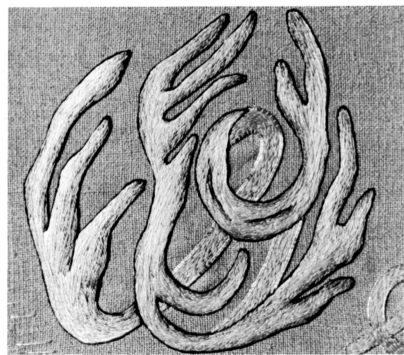

Illuminated capital.

The compressed energy in the
third Millennium triangle –
located between flat, confining
runners for Anna von Schurman and Anne Hutchinson
– symbolizes the nadir of
women's history. At this point
in the table, women's lives were
becoming as confined as their
needlework: small in scale,
obsessive, and indistinct.

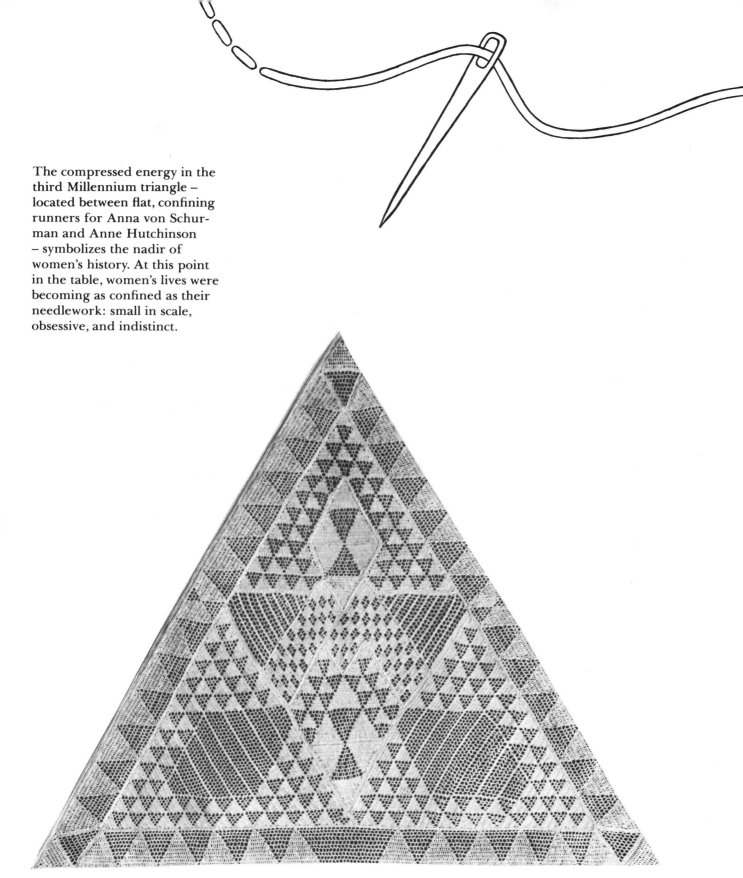

The illuminated capital for Anne Hutchinson, embroidered by Terry Blecher, repeats the center forms of the plate.

Anne Hutchinson

1591–1643, United States

The runner for Anne Hutchinson is based on an original American art form: the mourning picture. This type of needle-painting first appeared in the eighteenth century and became especially popular after the death of George Washington in 1799. Throughout the next fifty years, many of these pictures were created – some in mourning for Washington, others as a way of expressing grief at the death of a family member or sympathy for a neighbor's loss. Mourning pictures were generally done on silk, frequently combining watercolors and silk thread to create images that had consistent motifs: lamenting female figures dressed in the neoclassical style; a weeping-willow tree; and a Grecian urn set on a tombstone with an embroidered memorial phrase.

Chicago's drawing for plate and runner.

One evening in the summer of 1976, I took a long walk on the beach in Santa Monica because I was upset. Having been educated – like most people – to believe in the idea of progress, I had thought that women's position had improved through the centuries. But historic research was leading me to other inevitable conclusions: Women had actually been better off before the Renaissance than after it; the Reformation had confined women to their homes for the first time; and finally, as a result of the Industrial Revolution, the work women had always done in the home became completely devalued. I hated what I was finding out, preferring not to know the reality of my historic circumstances – it was too painful. But I had to confront this information – information that was not only verified, but expanded by the research team for the Heritage Floor.

The seventeenth century was a low point in women's history, clearly demonstrated by Anne Hutchinson's experience. I decided that her runner should express my grief about the tragedy of women's loss of power, loss of legal and educational rights, and, worst of all, loss of esteem in the eyes of society. I mourned our degradation through the form of the "mourning picture," a traditional mode for the manifestation of women's sorrow.

Anne Hutchinson place setting.

Anne Hutchinson – a midwife and healer, preacher, theologian, and teacher – held religious discussions in her home, since women were not allowed to participate in the after-church debates. Her belief that the Holy Spirit dwelt in everyone led her to encourage her followers to pursue their own inner powers. This resulted in women beginning to challenge church doctrine that required blind submission not only to ministers, but to husbands as well. Persecuted, excommunicated, and banished from Massachusetts and Rhode Island, she and her family died tragically during an Indian raid.

One of the leading exponents of the neoclassical school of painting, Angelica Kauffman created images of women that helped shape the iconography of mourning pictures.

Traditional mourning picture.

grieving for women,

One thing that impressed me about mourning pictures was the way emotion was conveyed through the stitching itself. The motion of the thread is generally downward, accentuating the sadness of the scene. In preparation for embroidering the images I had drawn, the needleworkers and I examined blown-up sections of historic mourning pictures to determine how the stitching had been done. The fact that the scale of the originals was generally much smaller than our runner presented a problem. The scale change required that we recreate the effect of the stitching rather than try to duplicate it. The work Terry Blecher and Connie von Briesen had done in translating my images on previous runners provided a method of stitching that could convey the anguish I wanted to express.

Detail: tree surrounding plate.

During the early nineteenth century, due to the neoclassical revival, lamenting female figures suddenly became prominent on everything from ceramic ware to paintings. Modeled upon images from Greek friezes and urns, grieving women were represented wearing short-waisted white dresses of the Empire style, but their true origins were decidely pre-Greek. Similar figurines have been excavated at sites of early civilizations, where they were customarily placed in graves or attached to sarcophagi. Later, goddesses were depicted as lamenting or wailing, and it was from these representations that the Greek mourning figures evolved.

grieving for the loss of our power.

Goddesses were traditionally associated with the willow tree, a form of the Tree of Life. The willow tree was sacred to pre-Greek goddesses as well as to Hecate, Circe, Hera, and Persephone and later to witches. In fact, the words "witch" and "wicked" are derived from the same ancient word as willow. Because it has the regenerative power to grow again after being cut, the willow tree was also associated with the Resurrection in Christian theology. And the willow has always been connected with burial sites because it drains the ground of water, keeping the site dry for the digging of the grave and protection of the corpse.

This image demonstrates the historic identification of the urn with the Goddess or female spirit.

The mourning figure Chicago had drawn for the front of the runner was both strong and sad, and I wanted to express this through the stitching. One of the major differences, however, between drawing and stitching is that stitches are straight, and I had to use them to create the illusion of a drawn, rounded body form. I wanted the stitching to accentuate the long, sad gesture of the hunched body and to create the feeling of the folds gathering and knotting near the center of the figure.

—*Terry Blecher*

Images of lamenting or wailing women date back to the earliest days of human history. This Egyptian fresco contains a particularly good example of pre-Greek mourning figures.

Greek vase painting.

The eighteenth-century revival of interest in classical art inspired images of women in Grecian attire which appeared on Wedgewood ceramics as well as in popular design and painting. Few people realized that the origin of these images was in the ancient practice of placing mourning female figurines in graves and summoning the female musicians to sing mourning songs whenever a member of the community died.

Mortuary urns, like mourning figurines, date from ancient times. Not only were they receptacles for the ashes, bones, or vital organs of the deceased, but they were also symbols for the death aspect of the Goddess. (In early societies, the Goddess represented both life and death, which were seen as inseparable.) Urns had another identity as containers or vessels of the female spirit. Interestingly, witches, like many Goddess-worshiping peoples, practiced their rites around an urn or cauldron.

The historical origins of these images suggest that the popularity of mourning pictures – which were a singularly female creative form – may have been an expression, not only of nineteenth-century women's grief, but also of their attraction to symbols that had unconscious significance to them as women.

Chicago wanted very subdued coloring for the Hutchinson runner and chose over thirty colors, ranging from dark, dull grey-greens and grey-blues through various middle-value neutral transitions to pinks, beiges, and finally off-whites. These were used to create a color and value shift across the tree – a somber shadow on the right and a soft roseate light on the left.

Blecher and I worked out the color transitions and value changes on the tree, as well as the technique of embroidering the branches to create the illusion of motion.

—*Connie von Briesen*

Hill stitching on back of runner.

I embroidered the memorial stone and urn on the back of the runner, using very fine stitches for the difficult shading. I loved the uninterrupted stretches of focused work, especially after many months of the daily pressure of administration. It was a pure joy to stitch.

—*S. H.*

Front of runner.

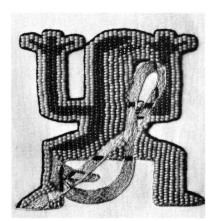

The beaded bird form in the capital letter for Sacajawea, done by Cherie Frainé, refers to the Indian meaning of Sacajawea's name, "Bird-Woman."

Sacajawea place setting.

The only woman on the Lewis and Clark expedition, Sacajawea was their interpreter and guide, although it was her husband who had been formally hired. Sacajawea was responsible for foraging and preparing the food, gathering herbs to make healing potions, nursing the sick, and, in several instances, saving the entire expedition. Unfortunately, she had no way of knowing that her help in opening up the Northwest Territory would eventually lead to the wholesale slaughter of Native American tribes.

One of the sources for the runner design was the beautiful beaded and fringed dresses made and worn by Native American women. The first imported beads to be used by the Indians were called "pony beads" because they were brought here by European traders and explorers on pony packtrains. Pony beads were large, opaque, irregular china beads made in Venice. This beadwork, mentioned in the journals from the Lewis and Clark expedition, gradually replaced the traditional and extraordinary quillwork unique to Native American art. We explored the possibility of doing quillwork for the Sacajawea runner, but realized that the technique was too difficult and time-consuming. Instead of pony beadwork, we based our beading techniques on later work done with seed beads, which were introduced about 1830.

Indians had used beads made from bone before the arrival of the Europeans. These bone beads required such great expenditures of time and labor, however, that European-manufactured beads quickly became popular. By 1860, beads were easily available and Native American women began to bead large areas instead of their earlier narrow beaded or quilled bands. Traditionally, beadwork was only for personal or family use, for ceremonial purposes, or sometimes for barter. Skill with beads and quills was handed down from generation to generation among the American Indians.

Beadwork designs were similar to those painted on the *parfleches* (rawhide paintings), which influenced not only the runner, but the plate as well. The flat, chalky quality of the painted parfleche contributed to our choice of matte, rather than gloss, china-paints on the plate and also suggested covering the runner with deerskin, which has a similar surface. Only straight lines were used in the runner design – containing authentic Indian motifs – because the women of the Shoshone tribe, to which Sacajawea originally belonged, used no curved forms in their art.

Beaded dress.

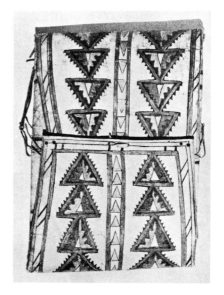

The Sioux parfleche paintings were done by both women and men. Women painted only geometric forms – like squares, bands, and triangles – while men painted realistic images – such as birds, animals, and humans. This stylistic distinction, which exists in many parts of the world, has not yet been adequately explained.

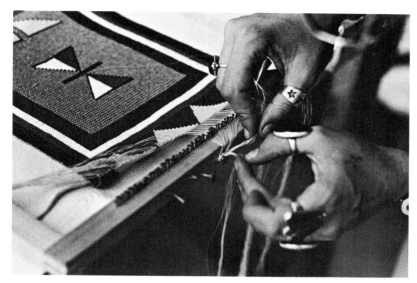

Preparing beadwork for back of runner.

For me, the quality of the surface, the color, and the rhythmic texture of quillwork is more beautiful, though more subtle, than beadwork. I really wanted to use this technique on the Sacajawea runner, but even I – who tended to totally disregard the time the needlework designs would take – had to admit that quillwork required more technical skill and time than we could spend.

I tried to create the feeling of an authentic Native American design, incorporating both the butterfly and the triangle, which appear in Native American iconography and are used repeatedly in The Dinner Party. *Using triangular motifs caused considerable difficulty for Kathleen Schneider, however, when she translated the design into beadwork, which is customarily done only in horizontal and vertical lines.*

The fringe on the front and back is, of course, adapted from fringed clothing. It was cut after the runner was completed. We had to let the runner hang over a bar for several months to allow the leather to stretch and settle.

Back of runner, beaded by Kathleen Schneider.

Traditionally, beads were worked in two ways: sewn to the deerskin (and later to fabric) or woven on looms – either simple wooden frames or a weaving bow, the original ancient method. Both the sewn and woven systems were combined in the beadwork for the runner.

Traditional quill work.

The same visual elements were carried into the design of the cradle board (which is attached to the plate), a reference to Sacajawea leading the Lewis and Clark expedition with a baby on her back. Cherie Frainé, a Native American woman versed in authentic Indian techniques, came to the studio in the summer of 1978 to construct the cradle board and help assemble the runner. In addition to making the cradle board, Frainé saw to it that the hides were stitched together and the beading attached in a historically accurate method.

To construct the cradle board, Frainé cut the leather headboard shape from the thinnest and most supple section of the hide. The leather was backed with white felt, and both fabrics were stretched on an embroidery hoop. The beading was done by hand in the overlay stitch – the same technique used for the illuminated capital. When the surface beading was complete, the leather and felt were trimmed and backed with another piece of leather. Leaving the bottom of the form open, Frainé bound the edges with cotton thread and beaded them. The cradle-board form was slipped over a specially constructed plexiglass support which had been bonded to the plate stand. The hood was then carefully constructed, sewn to the base of the cradle board, wrapped around the plate, and tied in the front.

This traditional Native American cradle board, which is lavishly embellished with beadwork, provided the inspiration for the cradle board in Sacajawea's place setting.

206

The association between
female deities and the textile
arts remained prominent in
Native American myths and
legends. In many tribes, Spider
Woman was associated with
female creation deities or seen
as the representative of the
feminine principle. In Navaho
mythology, she was described as
the greatest weaver of all time
and attributed with having introduced women to weaving.

To the Hopi, Spider Woman
was the guardian of Mother
Earth. She was one of the most
important supernatural beings,
described as "the little gray one
who always lives in corners of
houses." (For this reason, no
Hopi woman ever destroyed
the spider or the web.) According to legend, the Grandmother
Spider was the supreme "master" of the art of embroidery
and transmitted designs for
quill and beadwork through
dreams.

Cradle board and hood attached to plate.

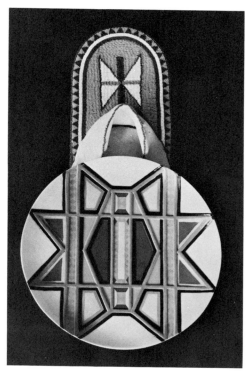

Chicago's study for imag-
ery for Sacajawea's plate
and runner, from authen-
tic Shoshone design.

"O our Mother the Earth
    O our Father the Sky,
Your children are we, and
    with tired backs
We bring you gifts that
    you love,
Then weave for us a gar-
    ment of brightness.
May the warp be the white
    light of morning,
May the weft be the red
    light of evening,
May the fringes be the
    falling rain,
May the border be the
    standing rainbow.
Thus weave for us a gar-
    ment of brightness,
That we may walk fittingly
    where birds sing,
That we may walk fittingly
    where the grass is green,
O our Mother the Earth,
    O our Father the Sky."
                    —Tewa song

Bird=Woman

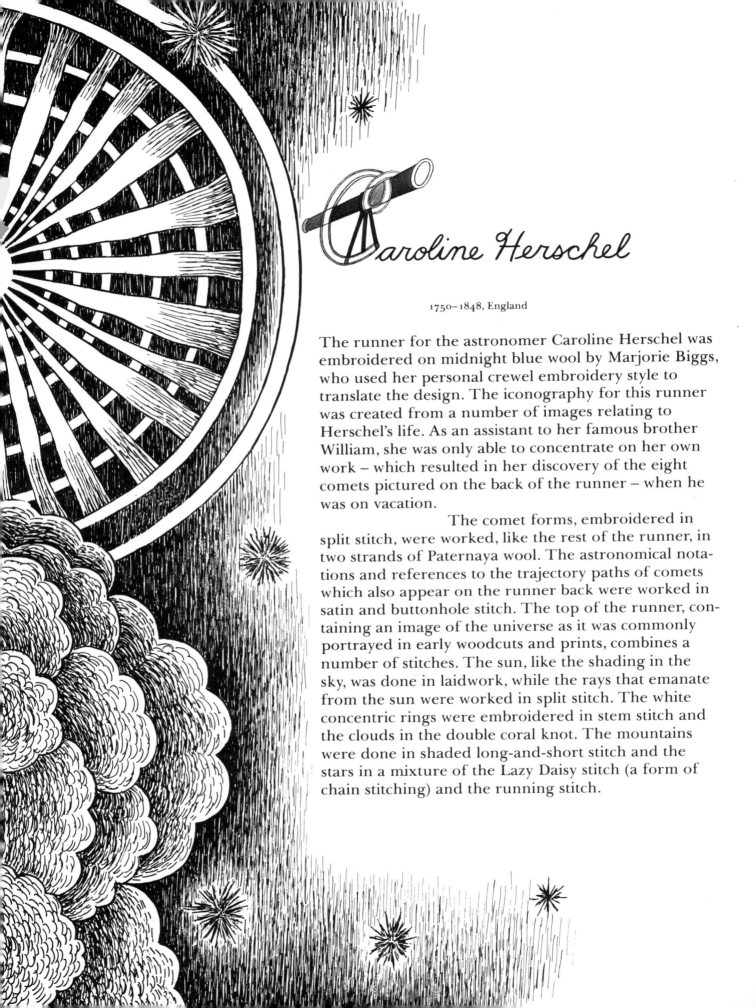

Caroline Herschel

1750–1848, England

The runner for the astronomer Caroline Herschel was embroidered on midnight blue wool by Marjorie Biggs, who used her personal crewel embroidery style to translate the design. The iconography for this runner was created from a number of images relating to Herschel's life. As an assistant to her famous brother William, she was only able to concentrate on her own work – which resulted in her discovery of the eight comets pictured on the back of the runner – when he was on vacation.

The comet forms, embroidered in split stitch, were worked, like the rest of the runner, in two strands of Paternaya wool. The astronomical notations and references to the trajectory paths of comets which also appear on the runner back were worked in satin and buttonhole stitch. The top of the runner, containing an image of the universe as it was commonly portrayed in early woodcuts and prints, combines a number of stitches. The sun, like the shading in the sky, was done in laidwork, while the rays that emanate from the sun were worked in split stitch. The white concentric rings were embroidered in stem stitch and the clouds in the double coral knot. The mountains were done in shaded long-and-short stitch and the stars in a mixture of the Lazy Daisy stitch (a form of chain stitching) and the running stitch.

After the mockup was painted, Marjorie Biggs and I discussed how to translate the image into embroidery. I knew by then that her needlework was extraordinary, and I trusted her to interpret the design. In order to aid her in establishing the length and density of the stitches, I did a carefully hatched line drawing, which she took home along with the mockup.

After two months of eighteen-hour workdays, Biggs brought the completed runner to the studio and I nervously brought out the Herschel plate. I was concerned about the plate relating to a runner as elaborately embroidered as this one. When I placed it on the runner, it didn't work. But fortunately, another plate for Herschel — I had several successfully completed versions — matched Biggs' embroidery perfectly. We all felt that some mysterious process had determined both Biggs' color choices and mine.

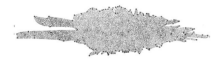

When we found Caroline Herschel's drawing of the Milky Way, we became very excited. It was attributed to William Herschel, but our research suggested that the calculations and technical drawings were all done by Caroline. We had the study blown up photographically, and then I altered it to fit the front of the runner.

Detail showing comets on back and top of runner.

Caroline Herschel place setting.

Caroline Herschel was an astronomer and one of the leading women in science in the eighteenth and early nineteenth centuries. As an assistant to her famous brother – one of the few ways women could participate in the professions – she was the first woman to discover a comet. Because women weren't allowed membership in the Royal Astronomical Society, she was made an "honorary" member for her achievements in science. Herschel was further honored by being named the first woman to receive a salary as an astronomer to the king; however, that salary was only one-fourth of her brother's.

209

A section of traditional
seventeenth-century
crewel-work embroidery
made by Abigail Pett.

During the nineteenth
century, crewel work al-
most became a lost art as a
result of the Industrial
Revolution and the avail-
ability of printed fabrics.
Crewel embroidery has
recently been revived, but
it is used in a less literal
way than the traditional
definition implies. This
ecclesiastical hanging by
Marjorie Biggs demon-
strates the kind of crewel
embroidery being done
today and is also representative of Biggs' work.

Section of Marjorie Biggs'
crewel-work hanging, *The
Peaceable Kingdom.*

Detail of runner showing clouds.

A linen panel containing Herschel's name was inserted between the wool front of the runner and its linen backing, and a section of the dark fabric was then cut away to reveal the name. The edges of this cutaway form – derived from an outline of Herschel's diagram of the Milky Way – were bound to the linen with rows of stem stitching. The illuminated capital, embroidered in the split stitch with silk thread, describes a telescope, the instrument through which Herschel gazed at the stars.

Front of runner.

This twenty-foot-long telescope was built by William and Caroline Herschel and used by both of them in their astronomical studies.

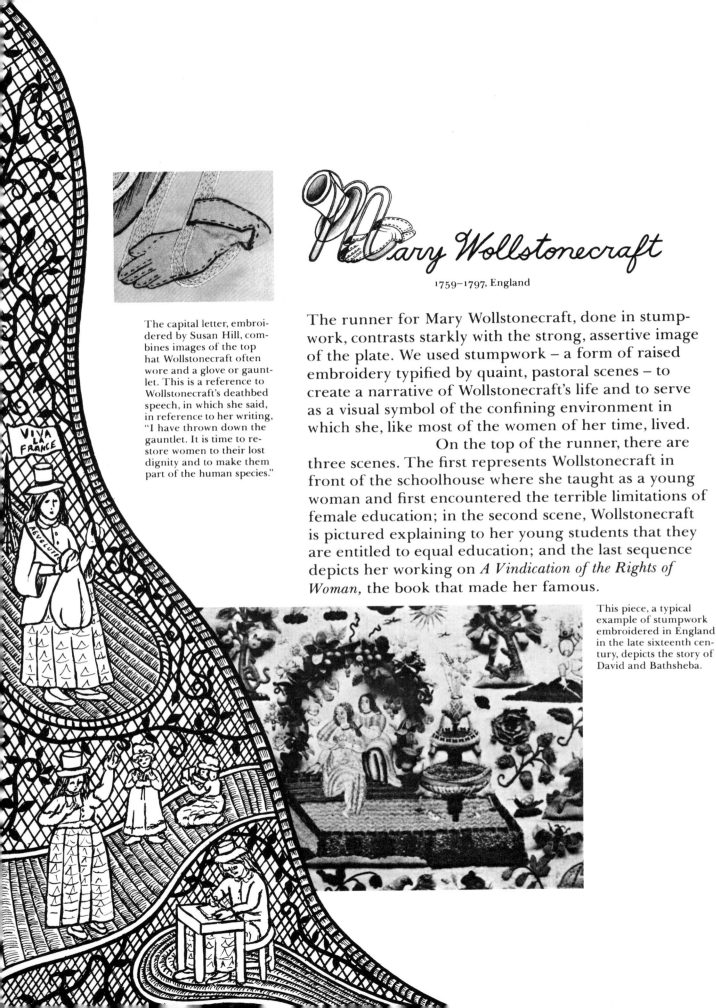

Mary Wollstonecraft

1759–1797, England

The capital letter, embroidered by Susan Hill, combines images of the top hat Wollstonecraft often wore and a glove or gauntlet. This is a reference to Wollstonecraft's deathbed speech, in which she said, in reference to her writing, "I have thrown down the gauntlet. It is time to restore women to their lost dignity and to make them part of the human species."

The runner for Mary Wollstonecraft, done in stumpwork, contrasts starkly with the strong, assertive image of the plate. We used stumpwork – a form of raised embroidery typified by quaint, pastoral scenes – to create a narrative of Wollstonecraft's life and to serve as a visual symbol of the confining environment in which she, like most of the women of her time, lived.

On the top of the runner, there are three scenes. The first represents Wollstonecraft in front of the schoolhouse where she taught as a young woman and first encountered the terrible limitations of female education; in the second scene, Wollstonecraft is pictured explaining to her young students that they are entitled to equal education; and the last sequence depicts her working on *A Vindication of the Rights of Woman,* the book that made her famous.

This piece, a typical example of stumpwork embroidered in England in the late sixteenth century, depicts the story of David and Bathsheba.

Stumpwork was a style of needlework that became popular in England in the seventeenth century. Used primarily for needle pictures and to decorate cabinets, boxes, and frames, it was characterized by the padding and stuffing of various parts of the design. Biblical, allegorical, or idyllic scenes were crowded with figures, animals, insects, fruits, vegetables and flowers, landscape elements, and architectural motifs without regard to distinctions in scale or spatial relations. Designs were directly drawn, traced, or stamped on fabric and the flat details embroidered. The raised elements were constructed separately, padded, and then sewn to the surface. Much of this work was done by young girls as part of their embroidery training, which accounts in part for the rather naïve quality of this form of raised embroidery.

The origin of the term "stumpwork" comes from several sources. Small wooden molds from France called "stumps" were used to raise the body parts of the figures in this "embroidery on the stump." Patterns printed or stamped on fabric became available for the first time, and these led to the term "embroidery on the stamp." The French word for "work" was "estompe." A combination of these phrases resulted in the designation "stumpwork."

Written shortly after her return from France, *A Vindication* expressed Wollstonecraft's disillusionment at the revolutionaries' apparent disregard of women. It argued that the principles of democracy that were the underpinnings of revolutionary activity in France as well as America must be extended to the female sex. The serious tone of this book, the title of which appears on a satin banner over Wollstonecraft's name, is belied by the array of miniscule objects that surround the words – crocheted apples, pears, and bananas; Pekinese-stitched vines and herringbone leaves; intricately embroidered fish and seaweed; and turkey-work birds and appliquéd butterflies. These cover the front of the runner and trivialize the meaning of her work, a metaphor for the repeated trivializations of women's accomplishments. The contrast between the meaning of the images and the way they have been stitched sets up a tension which we tried to emphasize by making the embroidered surface and figures incredibly obsessive. This also increased the inherent contradiction between the imagery of the runner and that of the plate.

Mary Wollstonecraft place setting.

Mary Wollstonecraft, a novelist, pivotal feminist writer, and theoretician, applied the principles of the French Revolution to the situation of women. In her major work, *A Vindication of the Rights of Woman*, she insisted that the tyranny of men must be broken both politically and socially if women were to become free.

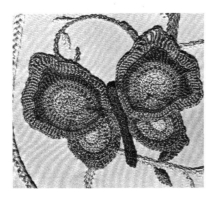

Butterfly crocheted by Stevie Martin.

"Flowers, plants, and fishes
    beasts, birds, flies and bees,
Hills, dales, plains, pastures,
    skies, seas, rivers, trees,
There's nothing near at hand
    or farthest sought
But with the needle may be
    shaped and wrought."
                    —*John Taylor*

The irregular shape on the top of the runner – meant to create a sense of compression in the scenes – was made in an adapted trellis stitch over a gridded foundation of Ver au Soie thread (which was used throughout the runner), outlined with handmade braid. The figures on the top of the runner, as well as on the back, were formed of white cotton over layers of felt and individually dressed in elaborate clothing. The faces were embroidered, bullion knots were added for hair, and the heads were appliquéd to the figures before being secured in place.

The three figures representing Wollstonecraft are dressed in post-revolutionary garb. A top hat she wore in a painting by one of her colleagues inspired the use of the gray satin hat that identifies her. Like the shoes of all the figures, hers were constructed from well-worn kid gloves, carefully cut so that the finger seams form the outline of the feet.

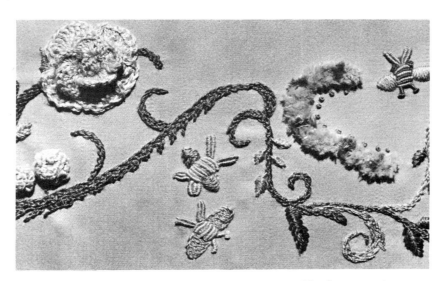

The flowers on the top and front of the runner were done in either the raised cup stitch or crochet. The vines – embroidered in Pekinese stitch – and the leaves – worked in the closed herringbone – were done by Dorothy Polin.

Adrienne Weiss, who supervised the production of the Wollstonecraft runner, organized a stumpwork team of seventeen people – the largest needlework group in the Project. Through the sheer force of Weiss' enthusiasm, even short-term workers got caught up in the spirit of stumpwork. Some needleworkers came to the studio for a few days and left with assignments that occupied them for weeks. Tiny crocheted garments, lovely small butterflies, and miniature fruits arrived in the mail. Weiss put them all into a box, and months later, as if from nowhere, produced the most amazing array of miniscule objects we had ever seen.

In this scene Wollstone-craft is standing in front of a schoolhouse done in needlepoint, and the path to the door, worked in a variation of the trellis stitch, is edged with a fine silk braid. An embroidered collar and silver beads for buttons embellish her satin cloak. Her skirt is embroidered with one strand of silk in the cloud stitch, and her petticoat is bordered with lace. The young women are both wearing crocheted "mob" caps. The jacket of the woman in the back right was done in the trellis stitch and her skirt embroidered in the Ceylon stitch; the other is wearing a crocheted skirt and a satin cloak finished with the feather stitch.

Detail: Chicago's drawing.

Detail: top of runner.

Weiss provided preparatory sketches from which I made the drawings for the runner. Her style was closer to the quality of stumpwork than mine, which sometimes tends to be too refined.

The back of this runner was a difficult image for me to create. I wanted to depict Wollstonecraft dying in childbirth – a common experience for women of her time, and one I felt compelled to represent in The Dinner Party. *There are, however, very few images of women's childbed sufferings, and thus there is an absence of esthetic tradition upon which I could draw. Working with such clear subject matter, I was afraid the image would be gross, but I discovered that by making each part of the scene – the petit-point rug, the crocheted doily, the embroidered window, and, most of all, the bed and the figure of Mary – as beautiful as possible, the harsh content could be transformed into sophisticated art.*

The back of the runner depicts Wollstonecraft dying after giving birth to her second daughter, Mary Shelley, author of *Frankenstein.* Her grieving husband is William Godwin, a publisher and staunch advocate of women's rights. The figures and furnishings, which accentuate the contrast between the needlework technique and the grisly scene, were made separately and applied. The bed was built over a dimensional cardboard and wooden frame, creating a kind of shadowbox into which the body was placed. The drapery was made over felt cylinders and the bed linens carefully sewn; the blood was embroidered, and the lace-edged pillows, like the blankets and the sheets, were made to seem dirty and slightly disarrayed. The face and hair were worked over in order to convey the anguish of this great woman's tragic death.

None of the traditional yarns used in needlepoint produced the effect we wanted for the mirror. I tried out different kinds of yarns and threads, making little samples of each. Chicago chose the one I had almost ripped out because it was so difficult to do. But my conscience wouldn't let me, as I had somehow felt it was the one she would like.
—*Thelma Brenner*

Detail: back of runner.

When I had the body for Wollstonecraft finished, I pinned it to the bed and then carefully ironed and neatly arranged the sheet and blanket around the figure, placing the pillows under the head. Before stitching the pieces in place, I called Chicago over for her okay. She looked for a while, then said that Mary looked too relaxed and at peace; she should seem ill and weak, her hair wild, oily and sweaty, her gesture exaggerated to express her exhaustion. Chicago manipulated the fabric, crushing the blanket and making it look as if it were about to fall off the bed, crumpling the pillows and pushing them askew. At her urging, I restitched the face with light and dark gray thread to give it a haggard expression, using Chicago's technical drawing as a guide. Instead of a woman in restful sleep, the finished bed scene was a graphic portrayal of the horror and tragedy of Mary Wollstonecraft's death.

—*Julie Brown*

Detail: back of runner.

I practiced for a long time before I had the courage to start on the Wollstonecraft runner. Working with so many people was difficult, and there was some dissension at first. Then we had a team meeting where we all expressed our feelings about certain problems and aired our grievances. I had never done anything like that, but the results were fantastic. I spoke in a group for the first time. Working on the runner became an emotional experience for me. I was moved by the charm and beauty of the front of the runner and deeply saddened as the death scene on the back began to take shape.

—*Dorothy Polin*

Detail: Chicago's drawing.

Detail: back of runner.

The window, through which a London street scene is visible, was stitched by Adrienne Weiss. A gifted artist, she was determined not to leave the project until she had proven that she was as skilled with a needle as with a brush.

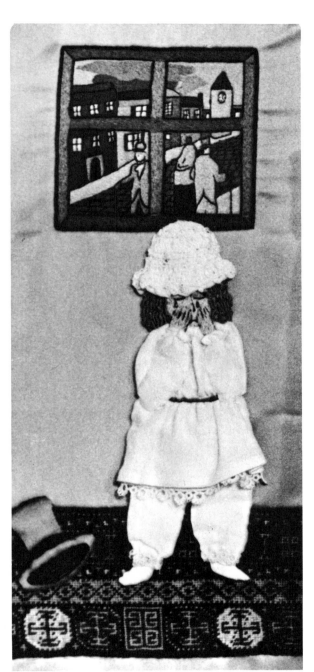

Detail: back of runner.

The tearful child repre-
sented on the back of the
runner is Wollstonecraft's
first daughter, Fanny,
whose father was the
painter Gilbert Imlay. She
stands on a petit-point
Persian carpet upon which
her mother's hat has fallen
– a signal of her death.
The carpet, which is
worked with 484 stitches
to the square inch, was
made by Marny Elliott
and Thelma Brenner,
based on the design of Elliott's living-room rug.

The illuminated letter, which repeats the patterns used in the runner, was embroidered in DMC cotton floss by L. A. Olson.

ojourner Truth

1797–1883, United States

The bold black, brown, and yellow runner for Sojourner Truth repeats the colors of the plate and extends its design. The runner is a pieced quilt with sections that included bands woven in a technique patterned on African strip-weaving. We chose a pieced quilt for the Sojourner Truth runner as a way of acknowledging the Afro-American influence on quilts. When African women came to America, they brought their own rich textile traditions with them, and both appliqué and pieced quilts reflect this. Some black women created appliqué quilts which were similar to African hangings; others constructed pieced quilts which included scraps of African strip-woven fabric carefully worked into the overall design. Pieced quilts were introduced to America by European women, and we combined their traditional technique with that of African strip-weaving as a way of representing the merging of these two traditions in the development of American quilts.

In constructing this runner, we first embroidered the name, then cut the linen into sections and joined these sections with the separately made woven strips. We stretched a piece of muslin on the embroidery frame, applied the quilt to it with running stitches, and padded the fabric parts of the quilt with flannel to even out the differences in thickness between the linen and the weaving. The linen and the side and bottom pieced triangular borders were difficult to attach, and it required repeated efforts to establish the proper balance between the woven strips and the thinner fabric and pieced sections. We then corrected the

irregularities and made the edges of the forms more exact by first adding black bias tape at the joins between the linen and the pieced borders, then edging the tape with two rows of couched brown cotton thread and couching a black outline around the triangular shapes on the borders.

　　　　Two black-and-white bands, the ladder-like forms of which were entirely pieced, were sewn to the top and bottom edges of the woven back strip. The brown color from the woven strip on the back was repeated on the top and along the front edge of the runner. We worked these narrow bands in the raised stem stitch and rows of black couching to help unite this stitching visually with the side strips of black cotton tape.

Chicago's study from African motif.

My study was inspired by the phrase "Look at this arm... Ain't I a Woman?" from Truth's famous speech.

Sojourner Truth place setting.

A former slave who became an abolitionist and a feminist, Sojourner Truth was one of the first people to identify the similarity between the problems of Blacks and those of women. She lectured throughout the country, published her autobiography, and helped the newly freed slaves find jobs and establish themselves after the Civil War. Truth, who chose her own name when she was freed, was a proud symbol of black women's struggle to transcend the opression of both their sex and their race.

African women learned quilting as part of their oppressive plantation experience, and this quote makes the drudgery of their work quite clear. Nonetheless, many of their quilts helped to preserve the cultural and personal memories of their heritage.

"My mammy she work in the field all day and piece and quilt all night. Then she has to spin enough thread to make four cuts for the white folks every night. Why sometime I never go to bed. Have to hold the light for her to see by. She have to piece quilts for the white folks too."
—*Fanny Moore,* ex-slave from North Carolina

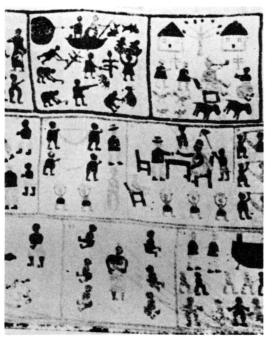

Detail: Fon hanging.

Appliquéd quilting – another form of patchwork – allowed greater design freedom than piecing, but it did not really flower until cloth became more easily available. The appliquéd Bible quilt by Harriet Powers has a great resemblance to this Fon wall hanging. Born in Georgia, Powers would have received her knowledge of African textiles verbally, for slaves passed on their knowledge of cultural traditions and techniques as a way of preserving them. Though Powers' ancestry is unknown, slaves were being kidnaped primarily from the Congo-Angola region at that time. This was the only area in Africa where appliqué work (though not quilting) was done.

Although Harriet Powers' quilts use biblical subject matter, their style can be traced to African appliquéd textiles and their content to the slave experience. Interestingly, although biblical characters are traditionally depicted as Caucasians by white artists, in Powers' quilts they range from black to white. Perhaps she used a biblical story to express her feelings about the relations between races.

Powers' quilt.

"It took me more than twenty years, nearly twenty-five, I reckon, in the evenings after supper when the children were all put to bed. My whole life is in that quilt. It scares me sometimes when I look at it. All my joys and all my sorrows are stitched into those little pieces. When I was proud of the boys and when I was downright provoked and angry with them. When the girls annoyed me or when they gave me a warm feeling around my heart. And John too. He was stitched into that quilt and all the thirty years we were married. Sometimes I loved him and sometimes I sat there hating him as I pieced the patches together. So they are all in that quilt, my hopes and fears, my joys and sorrows, my loves and hates. I tremble sometimes when I remember what that quilt knows about me."

—anonymous woman in Ohio
referring to a pieced
quilt she had made

This section of the runner shows the way piecing and weaving were combined. The front and side borders – made by Judy Mathieson, who did all the pieced sections – were fashioned from fabrics similar to those used in nineteenth-century quilts. The construction was done by Judy Mulford and Peter Fieweger, who did the embroidery as well.

Pieced quilt.

This pieced quilt was done by the artist Sophonisba Anguissola Peale (named after a famous Renaissance painter), who was a member of the influential Peale family of artists. Quilts were brought here by early European immigrants when they came to America. As these quilts wore out, they were "patched" with scraps of fabric; thus the patchwork quilt was born.

African strip weaving is done by women and men, but there is a difference both between their techniques and between their finished work. Women's cloth is usually woven on a vertical loom, and the fabric is quite wide; men tend to work on horizontal looms and produce thin strips of cloth. We crossed over these historic distinctions in sex roles – as we often did in the Project – and, basing the pattern for the top bands on "women's weave," made narrow strips on vertical looms.

Detail: women's weave.

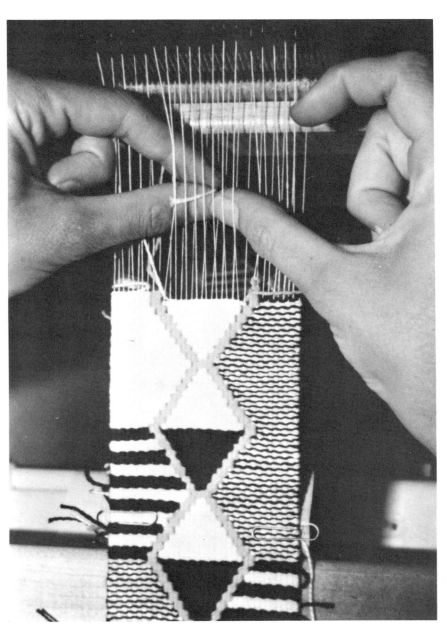

Karen Schmidt strip-weaving bands for top of runner.

The bands for Truth's runner were woven by Julie Brown and Karen Schmidt with a fine cotton warp and a heavy cotton weft. This same heavy cotton thread was used for the stitching and the couching.

Judy Mathieson and Judy Mulford piecing quilt.

All three of the capital letters in Susan B. Anthony's name are embellished – she is the only woman so honored – because I consider her the "queen of the table." The illuminations relate to her achievements and also chronicle her life, which is a continuing inspiration to me. The first letter depicts her as a young woman with symbols of the WCTU, where Anthony began her political career as an advocate for temperance reform. She became involved with the feminist movement and with Elizabeth Cady Stanton, who is portrayed with Anthony in the letter "B." The theories these two developed together sparked decades of agitation for women's rights. In the last illumination, Anthony is seen with white hair, marking the five decades of her struggle for equality. Her loyalty to women is represented by the Amazon's double axe and her importance as a patriot by the American flag. The three illuminated letters were embroidered in single strands of Zwicky silk by L. A. Olson and Susan Hill.

As I embroidered the words "We demand equal rights" in tiny satin stitches, I thought about my father. I wished that he could see this phrase and understand that feminism was not a joke and was not threatening.
—L. A. Olson

usan B. Anthony

1820–1906, United States

On their visit to England in 1883, Susan B. Anthony and Elizabeth Cady Stanton proposed to the suffragists there that an international women's movement be formed which would bring together representatives of women's organizations all over the world. By 1889 this International Council of Women had, through its affiliated groups, a membership of six million women. Though it changed in both organizational structure and leadership, the international movement made enormous strides in the late nineteenth and early twentieth centuries toward improving the status of women. The leaders of this movement are commemorated by the memory bands on the top of the Anthony runner, which are patterned after the embroidered memorials to family members or friends that women sometimes stitched into their quilts.

Illuminated capital "S" for Susan.

We Demand Equal Rights

"B" for Brownell.

"We hold these truths to be self-evident: that all men and women are created equal; that they are endowed by their Creator with certain inalienable rights; that among these are life, liberty, and the pursuit of happiness; that to secure these rights governments are instituted, deriving their just powers from the consent of the governed. Whenever any form of government becomes destructive of these ends, it is the right of those who suffer from it to refuse allegiance to it, and to insist upon the institution of a new government, laying its foundation on such principles, and organizing its powers in such form, as to them shall seem most likely to effect their safety and happiness. Prudence indeed, will dictate that governments long established should not be changed for light and transient causes; and accordingly all experience hath shown that mankind are more disposed to suffer, while evils are sufferable, than to right themselves by abolishing the forms to which they were accustomed. But when a long train of abuses and usurpations, pursuing invariably the same object evinces a design to reduce them under absolute despotism, it is their duty to throw off such government, and to provide new guards for their future security. Such has been the patient sufferance of the women under this government, and such is now the necessity which constrains them to demand the equal station to which they are entitled."

– From the Preamble to the Declaration of Sentiments issued at the first Women's Rights Convention in Seneca Falls, N.Y., 1848 – at which women openly demanded equal rights.

"A" for Anthony.

Susan B. Anthony place setting.

The "queen" of the *Dinner Party* table, Susan B. Anthony worked unfalteringly for fifty years to improve women's lives. In the face of enormous resistance, she – with her colleague, Elizabeth Cady Stanton – introduced reforms that transformed the position of women in America. Additionally, Anthony helped organize an international feminist movement that sought to extend these reforms to women all over the world.

Each of the white satin memory bands was worked separately on a small embroidery frame by Elfie Schwitkis, who was primarily responsible for this runner. Rather than embroidering the names with double-strand thread, Schwitkis, using black Ver au Soie, did two rows of single-strand stem stitching because it made a cleaner line of writing. After the names had been completed, the edges of each band were folded over and pieced with the black velvet strips. The triangular points of the memory bands – derived from the sashes worn by suffragists – were faced with satin and gently pressed into shape.

This top section of the runner was secured to stretched muslin and butted against an appliquéd triangular piece of felt – the lining for the red silk fringed triangle based on the famous shawl worn by Susan B. Anthony. Because the silk crepe was so difficult to work with, Schwitkis first made a prototype and then, when she was satisfied that she had solved the technical problems, fabricated the real shawl. The triangle was cut and the edges trimmed by hand, the fringe carefully attached, and the whole form appliquéd.

When Susan and I saw the exhibit of Susan B. Anthony's study and her silk shawl, we both had the same feelings of respect and awe. The shawl was something Anthony treasured and one of her few possessions; she had always given her money, like her life, to the suffrage cause. On her sixty-fifth birthday, she received a present of $100 and a note urging her to buy herself a gift. The red shawl she then purchased was worn by her for twenty years.

Top of runner.

The women commemorated on the memory bands are Amita Augsburg (1857–1943), a German suffragist; Frances Balfour (nineteenth century), a Scottish advocate of women's rights; Harriet Stanton Blatch (1856–1940), an American feminist, lecturer, and daughter of Elizabeth Cady Stanton; Amelia Bloomer (1818–1894), an American temperance worker, journalist, and advocate of dress reform; Lydia Maria Child (1802–1880), an American abolitionist, reformer, and author; Emily Davidson (d. 1913), an English suffrage worker and martyr; Pauline Kellogg Davis (mid-nineteenth century), an American educator, orator, and suffragist; Julia Ward Howe (1810–1901), an American writer, reformer, women's rights advocate, and author of *The Battle Hymn of the Republic;* Alice Duer Miller (1874–1942), an American feminist author; Ernestine Rose (1810–1892), a Polish reformer, orator, and radical writer who emigrated to America and became active in the suffrage movement; Mary Wright Sewall (fl. 1900's), an American suffragist who was active in the international feminist movement and served as President of the International Council of Women in 1902; Anna Howard Shaw (1847–1919), an American doctor of medicine and theology, an ordained Protestant minister, a social reformer, and a leader of the National Women's Suffrage Association for twenty years; and Emma Willard (1787–1870), an American educator, author, and advocate of women's education.

Independence Is Achieved by Unity

Back of runner.

Crazy quilt with buttons carrying Anthony's famous phrase, "Failure Is Impossible."

In the late nineteenth century, many women turned their needlework skills to the production of sashes, banners, and flags, which they bravely wore or displayed in the demonstrations for womens' rights. The suffrage movement was part of the larger reform movements of the nineteenth century in which women played a major role: abolition, temperance, social welfare, peace, missionary work, revolutionary activity, and utopian experiments. These movements, many of them international in scale, brought about significant economic and social changes.

Suffrage march.

The crazy quilt on the back of the runner was also done in appliqué and embroidered with three variations of the traditional feather stitch. The handpainted satin band carrying the phrase *Independence Is Achieved by Unity* was sewn over the quilt as another reference to suffrage dress. The red buttons that repeat the color of the Anthony shawl were specifically made for the runner; they assert Anthony's belief that in the struggle for equal rights, "Failure Is Impossible." The triangles in the front quilted border were pieced rather than appliquéd, and the border was visually broken by the addition of white satin triangular forms. When the runner was finished, a velvet ribbon was used – as it was in historic crazy quilts – to wrap the entire edge.

Traditional crazy quilt.

The "crazy quilt," made of scraps of leftover fabrics and intended primarily for practical use, was one of the earliest forms of American pieced quilting and provided the basis for the design of the Anthony runner. As quilting techniques developed, the popularity of these quilts declined. The late nineteenth century brought about a revival. But, rather than being utilitarian, crazy quilts came to be used for display. Quilters used only the finest materials – satin, velvet, silk – and embroidered the joins with variations of the feather stitch.

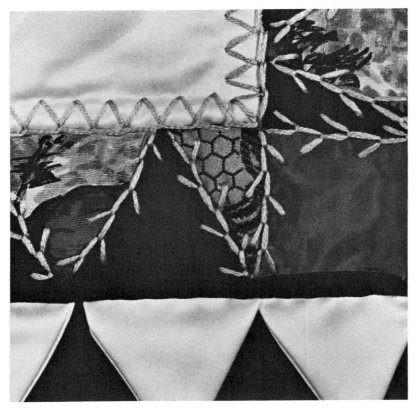

Detail: front corner of runner.

Early American painting of quilting bee.

The quilting bee, usually an all-day affair, had great social importance as well as being a popular event in the nineteenth century. Quilting bees were the place where women exchanged news, discussed social and political issues, revealed personal problems, swapped fabric scraps and new designs, and initiated their daughters into both quilting and female community life.

The popular impression of quilting bees has been that quilts were made collaboratively by the attending group. In actuality, the women worked on an already finished top which had been designed and made by an individual woman. She usually chose the quilting stitches, as well as the quilters, and supervised the work. Those who were not expert with a needle had to retire to the kitchen and prepare food. Bad stitches were ripped out by the quilters, or, at night, by the woman who had created the quilt.

"The Original Cubist"

This cartoon, published in a New York newspaper after the Armory Show (which introduced Americans to modern art), demonstrates early-twentieth-century attitudes toward both quilting and avant-garde art. Although this satiric drawing indirectly acknowledged that quilting prefigured nonobjective art, abstract painting became widely accepted while quilts remained "woman's work." Women generally considered quilts – especially the later, more elaborate ones – an art form, yet quilting has only recently been looked upon as anything more than a "craft."

Elizabeth Blackwell

1821–1910, United States

The Blackwell runner, which was executed in a reverse appliqué technique, extends both the forms and the colors of the plate and continues the gradual alteration of the contour of the runner that began with Wollstonecraft. The free scalloped shapes on the side of the runner contrast with the firmly secured forms on the front and back – a symbol of the tension that still existed between women's aspirations and social and legal restraints during Blackwell's lifetime.

The various colors of the undulating forms were cut from patterns, basted to the runner, trimmed, and then covered with two large pieces of black cotton which overlapped down the center of the runner. After these had been sewn in place, we cut through the black fabric to reveal the rainbow colors. All the edges were rolled back and six strands of black DMC cotton floss couched along each interior edge to achieve a smooth outline.

The Blackwell runner was completed in eight weeks – record time. The needlework team was elated. However, when the plate was placed on the runner, it was clear that – despite our careful matching of the colors – they did not work together. The runner tones, though in the same color families, were brighter than those in the plate. At first we toyed with the idea of allowing that difference, but the implications were not consistent with Blackwell's historical circumstances.

The color relationship between the plate and the runner had to have a certain congruence to express the fact that Blackwell's struggle to become a doctor took place during a period when women's options, though still limited, were sufficiently enlarged to allow her to achieve her goals.

We decided to subdue the runner's color by covering it with a layer of gray chiffon. The many days' work of couching had to be taken out. The chiffon was basted to the runner with a network of stitches to prevent it from rippling, and the edges were sealed with Stevie's Paste. The colored shapes were couched again, the scalloped sides of the runner faced with black cotton and a layer of silk chiffon, and the seams covered with three strands of black perle cotton. The overall effect of this, like the plate, finally reflected both the sadness and the triumph of Blackwell's unending struggle to break free.

Choosing fabric colors at Beverly Hills Silks and Woolens.

Example of traditional mola work.

I wanted to incorporate mola into one of the runners, but it never seemed right for any of the earlier runner designs. Cutting away the fabric, however, seemed like an apt metaphor for Blackwell's efforts to remove the obstacles against women in medicine.

Elizabeth Blackwell place setting.

Elizabeth Blackwell was the first woman in America to graduate from a medical school and become a licensed physician. She struggled throughout her lifetime to open the medical profession to women, and, with her sister Emily, began the New York Infirmary for Women and Children – the first hospital where female doctors could get both training and clinical experience.

One day, early in my association with the Project, I brought to the studio a picture of my mother as a bride. Framed in a satin mat embroidered with silk ribbon flowers, this type of "ribbon work" was a popular technique during the late nineteenth and early twentieth centuries. I also brought an old box filled with halved calling cards wrapped with myriads of the ombré ribbon my mother had used to create the flowers. The cards were engraved with the name of my mother and of my grandmother, who had taught her the nearly lost art.

Because ribbon work was done by women in Dickinson's milieu, combining it with lace seemed a perfect way to symbolize the quality of life for a woman in her time. Initially, this technique was to be used only for the capital letter, but when Chicago saw the embroidered "E" she decided to carry the ribbon work through the overall runner design. Then Frances Budden – a young woman from Australia – and Karen Schmidt asked to learn the technique. As we made the tiny flowers, it was a source of joy to me that the efforts of generations of women, including my grandmother and mother, should be preserved in a work of art and, through the younger women, be revived.

—*Connie von Briesen*

Emily Dickinson

1830–1886, United States

Lace was always our choice for the Dickinson runner – a logical extension of the image on the plate. The mockup was made using commercial lace to establish the basic design, but we knew that the quality of the runner would emerge only with the use of fine lace. We had been developing a lace collection, to which Connie von Briesen – who supervised this runner – added some rare pieces. Because they were of various shades of white, Von Briesen tinted them by bathing them in her tub in a solution of tea and coffee with a few mysterious household ingredients thrown in. When she brought them back to the studio, all an even shade of beige, we worked with these pieces directly on the runner surface, uniting their dissimilar patterns by placing them on a background of cotton net.

We used ribbon work – a nineteenth-century flower-making technique that was nearly lost – on the band of lace that borders the ruffles on the back. The flowers continue down the sides, along the butterfly border, and around the "E" in Dickinson's first name. Pink ribbon was inserted through the lace at intervals to create visual continuity between the back, the front, and the sides.

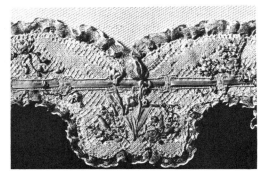

The front border of the runner was made with antique, handmade filet lace butterflies. These were attached, then overlapped and edged with fine, ruffled lace.

I took my power in my hand

The capital letter for Emily Dickinson was executed in ribbon work by Connie von Briesen.

My concept for the Dickinson runner, as well as the plate — the two are closely related both visually and symbolically — was influenced by the poet Adrienne Rich. In an essay on Dickinson, whose work she greatly admires, she wrote: "Probably no poet ever lived so much and so purposefully in one house; even in one room...I have come to imagine her as somehow too strong for her environment, a figure of powerful will..."

By making her room a sanctuary where she could pursue her work, Dickinson locked out the demands of a world that would never understand her. I wanted to express this contrast between the poet's sense of herself and the Victorian concept of womanhood that would have strangled her autonomy. Despite the layers of porcelain lace and the lacy, beribboned runner that surrounds the center of the plate, this core, though painted in pale colors, remains strong and untouched.

Emily Dickinson place setting.

Emily Dickinson, one of America's greatest poets, led an outwardly uneventful – but intensely focused and productive – life. Using her room as a refuge from the repressive Victorian society, she wrote "letters to the world" in the form of 1,775 poems, which she bound into booklets with a darning needle and carefully placed in trunks to be found, read, and published after her death.

235

and went out against the world.

Each ribbon was threaded into a needle as if it were thread. The basic stitch with the ribbon was a loop one-eighth to one-quarter inch long. The different flowers were made by varying the combinations of this loop to form the type of flower desired. In addition to making daisies and roses – the flowers on my mother's picture frame – we invented ways of using the ribbons to make irises, violets, and lady slippers. The overall technique is best described by explaining how we made a rose.

To fashion the center of the flower, we made French knots with different shades of ribbon, all darker than those used for the petal forms. These were made around the cluster of knots by bringing the needle up and down through the fabric, each stroke overlapping the one before (a bud required two or three petals, while a fullblown rose took six or eight). The flowers were done in one or two colors with shaded ombré ribbon to create the color fades. The leaves were made like the petals except that the ribbons were not overlapped; the stems and branches were worked with tones of green floss in the stem stitch.

—*Connie von Briesen*

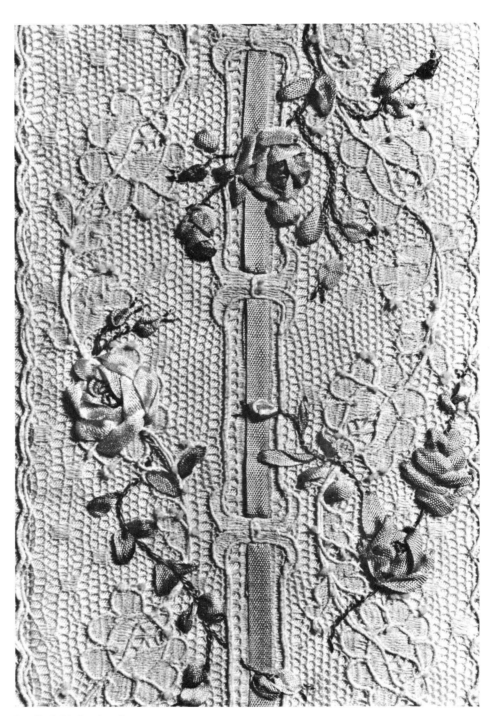

Detail of side border showing ribbon work.

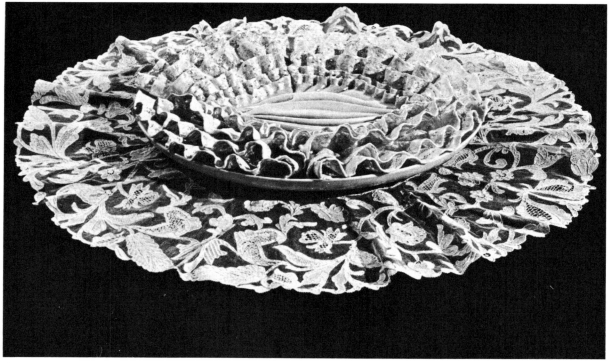

Plate on lace collar.

"I hide myself within my flower,
That wearing on your breast,
You, unsuspecting, wear me
    too –
And angels know the rest.

I hide myself within my flower,
That fading from your vase,
You, unsuspecting, feel for me
Almost a loneliness.

A sepal, petal and a thorn
Upon a common summer's
    morn,
A flash of dew, a bee or two,
A breeze
A caper in the trees –
And I'm a rose!"

—*Emily Dickinson*

One day a woman named Alice Chew, a college professor who had been impressed with the Project when she came to an open house, appeared at the studio with several pieces of lace and offered us our choice. Unwrapping the carefully folded tissue paper, she revealed an extraordinary collar, passed down to her through generations by an ancestor who had collected lace. We were ecstatic, as we had been unable to resolve the top of the runner, and the collar was just what we needed underneath the plate.

This lace collar is a fine example of needle-made lace, one of the two methods used to produce handmade lace (the other being the use of bobbins). Made in France in the mid-nineteenth century, the collar has a *point de gauze* pattern of stylized pomegranate blossoms, a popular lace motif at the time.

237

The runner was constructed by basting one layer of pink china silk to the linen, which repeated the color in the plate, and then applying the net. A slightly deeper shade of pink silk was added to the back of the collar, the side lace bands, and the *filet* lace butterflies that form the front border; these were then stitched in place. We had originally planned to ruffle the collar around the plate edge, hoping to make a transition between the porcelain and the fabric lace, but there was no way to form the gathers so that they either butted against the edge or emerged from beneath the plate. The ruffled tiers on the back of the runner, however, do echo the layers of lace on the plate.

While attending the ecclesiastical embroidery class, a woman who knew of the Project brought in a cardboard box that had been donated to the church thrift shop, which, as the minister's wife, she ran. I took the box to the studio, and Judy and I tried to decide if we should buy the odds and ends of lace inside. Neither of us knew whether the pieces were valuable, but we offered twenty dollars and put the lace away. Some time later, I spent six months' worth of Sundays washing the different pieces of lace. Eventually, we used the best ones for the ruffles on the back of the Dickinson runner.
—*S.H.*

Section of back runner.

The origins of lace are unknown, although records show that lacemaking was practiced by the Egyptians, Jews, Greeks, and Romans. No examples of their work remain, however. In the early days of Christianity, lace was made in convents from designs based on scriptural subjects or church emblems and used exclusively for ecclesiastical purposes. During the Renaissance, lace became part of royal dress, and it was common for noblewomen to make it themselves. Pattern books became available specifically for this purpose. While this practice continued among the aristocracy and the nuns, it gradually became a commercial activity as well. Cottage industries developed throughout Europe and later in America; male jobbers brought thread and designs to lower-class women who were trained from childhood and consistently underpaid.

The seventeenth and eighteenth centuries were the high point for the production of lace, which was used not only on every article of a nobleperson's undergarments, but also on collars, ruffles, knee and boot trimmings, and bed and bath linens. When the French Revolution overthrew the aristocracy, the lace industry was greatly altered. In addition, the invention of the lacemaking machine further diminished the production of handmade lace.

Lacemaking has continued to the present, but neither the scale nor the quality is the same. Lacemakers, however, are still exploited.

Noblewoman making lace.

This wedding veil for a princess indicates how excessive the use of lace became. This extravagance was particularly scandalous when one considers how long lace took to make and the horrendous conditions under which lacemakers worked; they certainly never benefited from the enormous sums of money that high-quality lace generated.

In order to fully appreciate Dickinson's struggle, one must see her life against the background of the late nineteenth century. The contrast between the Victorian Ideal and the reality of women's lives resulted in intense suffering among women in every economic class. A middle-class woman was as imprisoned in the all-pervasive concept of the "perfect lady" as she was in the corsets that wasted her body and caused her organs to decay. Expected to be chaste and virtuous, morally superior, idle, and entirely dependent on her husband for both her economic welfare and her social status, the Victorian woman had few ways of supporting herself if she did not marry. She could be a governess, and be paid a pittance to live in someone's house in a lonely and degraded position, or a seamstress who worked twenty hours a day.

Working-class women were oppressed in different ways, especially as industrialization took work out of the home. A lower-class woman was expected to contribute to the family income; after the textile factories opened, she – and usually her children – worked from eight in the morning till late at night for intolerably low pay and under working conditions that presented a constant threat to life and health. Despite the fact that she could never live up to it, the image of the "perfect lady" haunted the working-class woman too.

This nineteenth-century painting and poem clearly demonstrate the expectation that "Women's mission was the easing of the burdens of men."

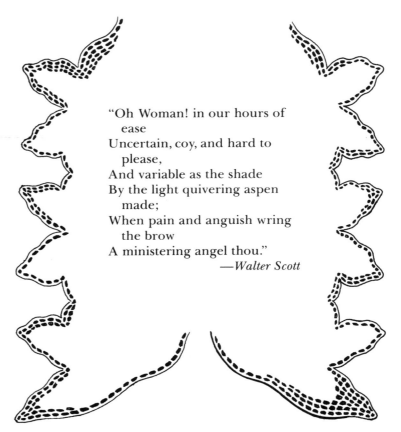

"Oh Woman! in our hours of
    ease
Uncertain, coy, and hard to
    please,
And variable as the shade
By the light quivering aspen
    made;
When pain and anguish wring
    the brow
A ministering angel thou."
                    —*Walter Scott*

240

"In poverty, hunger and
   dirt
Sewing at once, with a
   double thread,
A shroud as well as a shirt.

              —*Thomas Hood*

When sewing machines
were invented, factory
owners, in an effort to get
more work produced,
crowded the workers to-
gether in dark, badly lit
rooms, most of them fire
traps. "Sometimes in my
haste," one woman said, "I
get my fingers caught.
The needle goes right
through it. It goes so fast,
though, that it doesn't
hurt much. I bind the
finger up with a piece of
cotton and go on working.
We all have accidents like
that."

Some painters and writers
attempted to deal sympa-
thetically with the hard
life of a working woman.

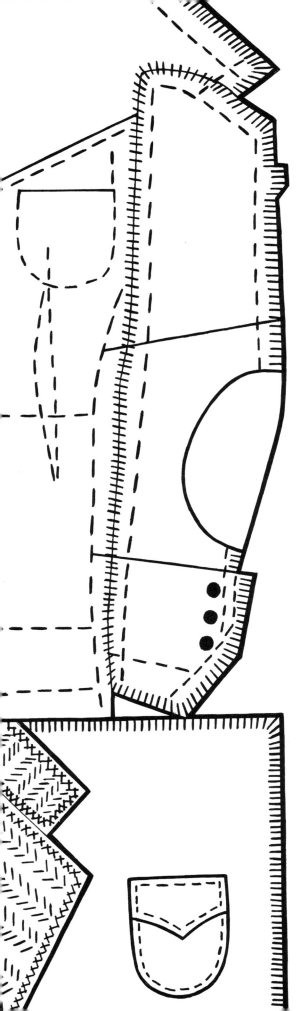

Ethel Smyth

1858–1944, England

The runner for Ethel Smyth combines several iconographic references: a musical staff and metronome to symbolize her profession; a tailored suit to represent her mode of dress, a series of pockets that allude to men's clothing and also to the historic pockets worn by women of the past, and a linen tape measure on one side of the tweed jacket – intended as a pun on the word "measure," which is used in both music and tailoring.

The Pendleton wool jacket pieces, made from a suit pattern, have been "taken in" with darts above the breast pockets to emphasize the way Smyth's talents were constricted by a musical establishment that wanted to "cut her down to size." The sleeves overlap the fronts of the jacket and are finished – like a professor's coat – with buttons and patches, ironically implying a position in a university music department, something Smyth never enjoyed. We overcast the raw edges of the fabric with the whip stitch and embroidered the bold tailoring marks in the running stitch with double strands of black cotton carpet thread. To increase the feeling of compression, we outlined the runner in black soutache braid.

Ethel Smyth, who usually dressed in masculine attire, was part of a long tradition of women who "cross-dressed." In many ancient civilizations, it was common for women and men to dress alike. For example, in Egypt both sexes wore tunics – a custom adopted by the Jews. Later, Jewish law forbade cross-dressing, calling it "an abomination unto the Lord," an attitude that continued and eventually made cross-dressing illegal. The insistence that men and women dress differently correlates with the diminishing status of women and the development of more distinct sex roles.

However, almost as soon as dress codes were established, women began to resist them. By Greek times there were women who disguised themselves as men in order to attain professional training, particularly in medicine. During the Middle Ages, there was supposedly a Pope who was revealed to be a woman. John Angela – whose real name was Joan – has been recorded as reigning for two years, five months, and four days during the 850's A.D. Centuries later, Joan of Arc was burned at the stake for refusing to recant either her visions or men's garb. There are records of many other women who participated in military activities dressed as men. Deborah Sampson fought in the American Revolution and later traveled throughout New England telling her life story. It is known that at least four hundred other women participated as soldiers in the Civil War.

The back of the runner continues the image of the suit, this time combining beautifully lined pockets with unfinished lapels. Inside the open jacket there is a brown wool metronome, which was appliquéd to the runner, embroidered with stem stitching, and couched in Japanese gold. After the runner was finished, we accidentally discovered a piece of fabric that had been slipped under the wool. It turned out that one of our needleworkers, an anarchist, wanted to make known her objections to what she perceived as a rigidly hierarchical studio structure. Rather than openly expressing her feelings – which was encouraged in the Project – she had embroidered the slogan "Anarchists arise, overthrow authority" on a doily, which she had enclosed in the runner in the hope that someone in the future would discover it.

Ethel Smyth place setting.

A British composer who tried to move into the major ranks of the music world, Ethel Smyth wrote symphonies, operas, and large choral works. She encountered overwhelming prejudice because of her sex and became active in the struggle for women's rights, composing the famous "March of Women" which was sung by the suffragists to bolster their spirits when they marched and when they were imprisoned.

As women's clothing became more confining, the frequency of cross-dressing increased. The impulse to wear men's clothing, however, did not necessarily express the desire to be a man; rather, it was an attempt to transcend the limits of female role. In the eighteenth century, George Sand, like other women writers who wanted to be taken seriously, adopted a male name and, in order to gain greater social mobility, wore male attire. Rosa Bonheur, the nineteenth-century painter, dressed as a young man and – carrying a permit from the government to protect herself from arrest – went to the slaughterhouses and horse fairs to learn about anatomy. Dr. James Barry, the inspector-general of British hospitals, lived virtually her entire life as a man and was discovered to be a woman only after her death.

The nineteenth-century women's movement was determined to free women from all that restrained them, including the corsets, crinolines, and bustles that ensured physical immobility. The dress-reform movement in America was led by Amelia Bloomer, after whom the trousers she wore were named. For a while, many women adopted them – not only feminists, but housewives as well. These "bloomers" were ridiculed so severely, however, that eventually most women gave them up.

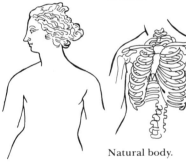

Ethel Smyth and her dog.

"I dressed as a boy...It must have been successful, because no one looked at me at all suspiciously – never once, out of the many times I did it...It was marvelous fun...I never felt so free in my life."
—Vita Sackville-West, quoted in *Portrait of a Marriage*

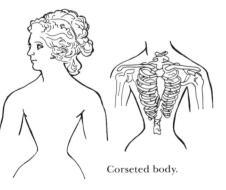

Picture showing compression of female organs resulting from wearing a corset.

Natural body.

Corseted body.

In addition to making it difficult for women to move around and causing an occasional cracked rib, corsets also created perforated organs and prolapsed uteri.

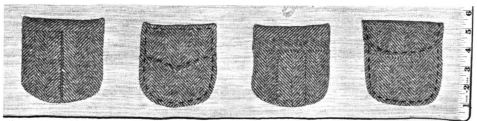

Traditional women's pockets.

Eighteenth- and nineteenth-century women tied large unattached pockets around their waists and under their skirts, which were slit to provide easy access to the pockets. Generally made of linen and embroidered in wool or quilted, they were used to carry needlework supplies, money, and household keys.

The lapels were made by Mary Ann Glantz, a Los Angeles artist who generously contributed advice, students, and moral support to the Project. Using the methods of fine tailoring, she constructed the lapels, deciding with Chicago that their unfinished quality provided an interesting visual contrast with the rest of the runner and also alluded to Smyth's "unfinished" career.

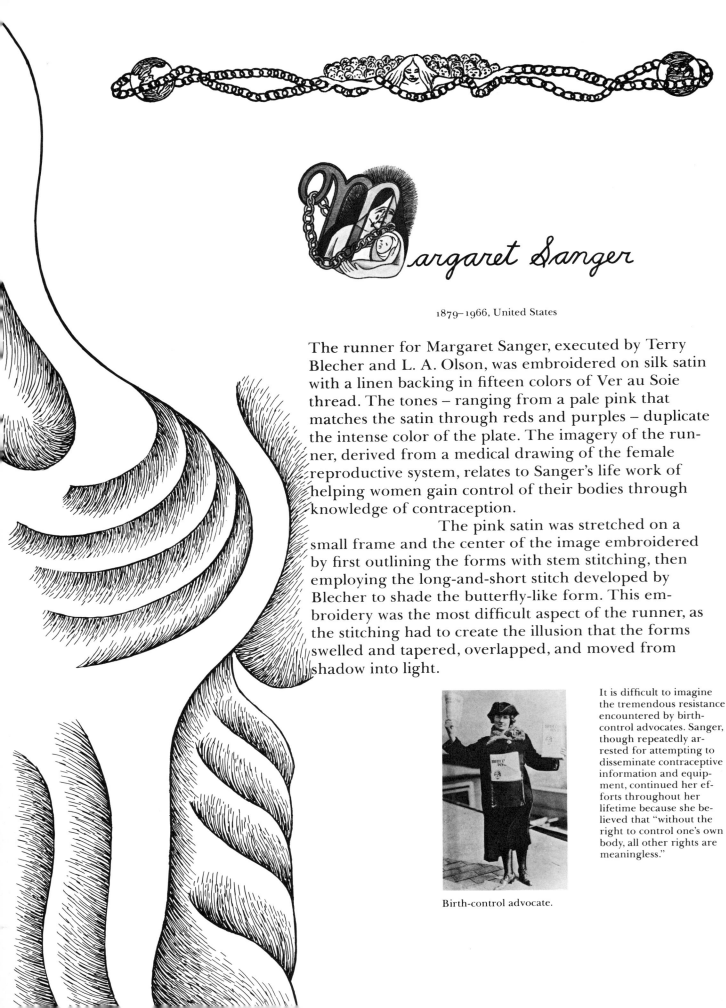

Margaret Sanger

1879–1966, United States

The runner for Margaret Sanger, executed by Terry Blecher and L. A. Olson, was embroidered on silk satin with a linen backing in fifteen colors of Ver au Soie thread. The tones – ranging from a pale pink that matches the satin through reds and purples – duplicate the intense color of the plate. The imagery of the runner, derived from a medical drawing of the female reproductive system, relates to Sanger's life work of helping women gain control of their bodies through knowledge of contraception.

The pink satin was stretched on a small frame and the center of the image embroidered by first outlining the forms with stem stitching, then employing the long-and-short stitch developed by Blecher to shade the butterfly-like form. This embroidery was the most difficult aspect of the runner, as the stitching had to create the illusion that the forms swelled and tapered, overlapped, and moved from shadow into light.

It is difficult to imagine the tremendous resistance encountered by birth-control advocates. Sanger, though repeatedly arrested for attempting to disseminate contraceptive information and equipment, continued her efforts throughout her lifetime because she believed that "without the right to control one's own body, all other rights are meaningless."

Birth-control advocate.

Free motherhood/free world.

"For this is the miracle of free womanhood, that in its freedom it becomes the race mother and opens its heart in fruitful affection for humanity. How narrow, how pitifully puny has become motherhood in chains." The capital letter was inspired by this quote from Sanger, which expresses her idea that once women acquired reproductive freedom, they would contribute to the creation of a better world. The letter was embroidered with Japanese gold, Ver au Soie, and Zwicky silk, combining couching and the split and stem stitches.

The great German artist Käthe Kollwitz also believed in the power of motherhood, as can be seen in her sculpture of Woman as the protector of the human race.

Margaret Sanger place setting.

A visionary and feminist theoretician, Margaret Sanger believed that if women were freed of involuntary child-bearing they could change the world. As an early advocate of birth control, she opened her first clinic in 1918 and battled her whole life to break through the curtain of silence that surrounded all matters of sex and reproduction.

247

I had originally planned to make the runners on the last wing of the table become, like the plates, increasingly dimensional. In Sanger's mockup, we attempted to repeat the plate's fleshy folds by building up layers of fabric, but this didn't look good. We then decided to try to develop the dimensional form by extending the embroidered sections with padding to create areas of high relief. In an effort to repeat the plate gesture – the image reaching around the edges and trying to lift itself off – we made a prototype for the runner that was flat in the center and dimensional on the sides. This looked so contrived, however, and like soft sculpture (which Susan and I both hate) that I went back to relying on the visual illusion that embroidery can create.

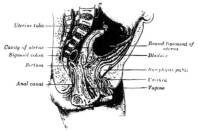

Chicago made a hatched and shaded technical drawing to help Terry Blecher and L. A. Olson with their stitching. They pinned the mockup and the drawing side-by-side on the wall next to their embroidery frame so they could refer to the colors and the line work as they stitched.

This anatomical drawing was transformed into a sensual image to emphasize the importance of women gaining control of not only their reproductive functions, but also their sexuality. In designing the runners, we often made use of historic or scientific images as well as art, enlarging them photographically – in a graphic process introduced by Helene Simich – and then cutting, altering, or combining them as we pleased.

Working on Sanger runner.

Embroidering the colors so they were shaded properly was a challenge. Each stitch had to be the exactly right color, length, and position to create the illusion of consistent shading despite the varying shapes of the sections. This took an enormous amount of time and concentration and often a lot of ripping out and restitching.

—*Terry Blecher*

Another problem Blecher and Olson encountered was that one side of the form was harder to do because of the relationship between the stitcher and the runner frame. In order to share this burden, the two frequently exchanged sides, and – because embroidery is like handwriting in that each person's is different – this helped to merge their personal stitching styles.

The shaded long-and-short stitch was used throughout the runner, which was completed on our regular embroidery frame. The outline of the runner shape was drawn directly on the fabric after most of the embroidery had been done. The stitching was then extended so that the rounded outside forms moved smoothly into the edges, which were cut, rolled, and then hemmed.

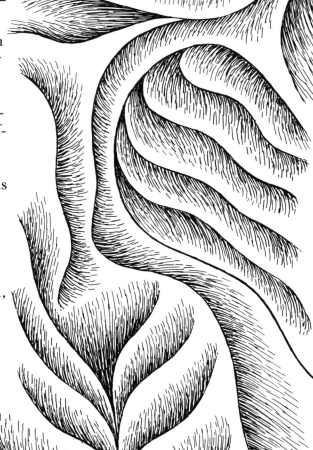

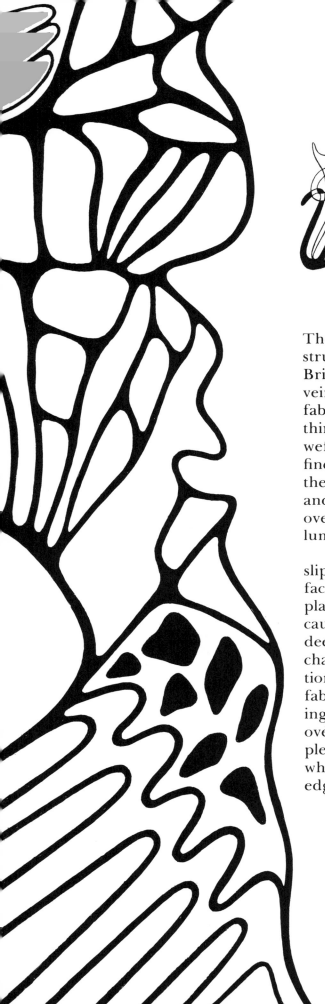

Natalie Barney

1876–1972, United States

The Natalie Barney runner, a butterfly image, was constructed with successive layers of fabric by Connie von Briesen. An outline of the butterfly form and internal veining was transferred to the linen, and the ground fabric – iridescent art-deco silk from the twenties or thirties with a colored silk warp and an anodized metal weft – was basted in place with silk sewing thread in a fine double running stitch. The gold and black silk of the center section and tips of the wings and the silver and white in the front and back were trimmed, then overlaid with as many as five varying shades of luminaire – a sheer, opalescent French fabric.

This procedure, made difficult by the slippery quality of luminaire, was not helped by the fact that the colors had to be coordinated with the plate, which was being painted at the same time. Because of the repeated firings required to build up the deep iridescent tones, the lusters would unexpectedly change colors in the kiln. We kept having to take sections of the runner out; this meant not only cutting fabric without slitting the silk ground, but also spending hours matching colors and appliquéing the new overlays. When the color segments were finally completed, the runner was covered with fine black net, which both unified the hues and protected the raw edges of the silk.

The capital letter, beaded by Connie von Briesen, is derived from the stylized lily form popular in Art Nouveau. It was chosen for both the plate image and the illumination because of its association with Barney, who was sometimes called "The Lily."

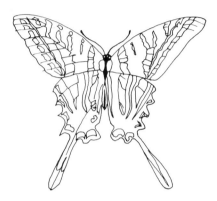

Enlarging and combining these two butterflies provided the pattern for the wing forms and internal striations in the runner.

Natalie Barney, a writer and aphorist, was one of the first women to live openly as a lesbian. Committed to an independent lifestyle, she organized a salon in Paris where women writers and artists could explore their own attitudes and sexuality to create works that reflected a lesbian point of view.

Natalie Barney place setting.

Chicago's drawing.

The portrait of Barney included in this drawing is by Romaine Brooks, her lifetime companion. Barney is depicted with a statue of a horse, referring – in both the title and the image – to Barney's daily horseback rides, in which she appeared dressed as an Amazon, and to the books about her by Rémy de Gourmant addressed to "L' Amazone." Barney's own words, however, seem a particularly appropriate description of this gallant woman: "The courageous being is not one who has done a courageous act, but whose entire life has been an act of courage."

L'Amazone, by Romaine Brooks.

In this drawing, I tried to create the feeling of la belle époque, *that extravagant period in Paris when artists, writers, and intellectuals mingled in café society and salons, creating an explosion of ideas and avant-garde art. When someone donated an outrageous black beaded dress – which suggested the clothing of this period and Barney's fabulous style – I incorporated it into the drawing, then added beading to the edge of the drawn plate to convey the close relationship I wanted between the plate and the runner.*

The way the lily form in the center of this Tiffany bowl relates to and repeats the undulating pattern around it provided the basis for the relationship between the plate and the runner. The visual context for the plate was extremely critical because it had to suggest that Barney's salon provided an environment where she and other women could be free. To imply this freedom, the contours of the runner – the outside edges of the butterfly form – are completely broken from the rectilinear format. I wanted to emphasize the importance of context or environment: If women do not have a supportive atmosphere, they cannot freely express themselves. I painted the plate after the runner was in progress, insisting that Barney's identity, symbolized by the plate, was inseparable from her milieu.

Tiffany bowl.

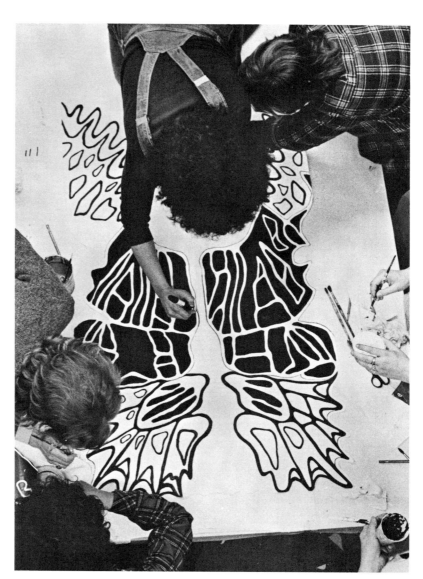

Painting Barney mockup.

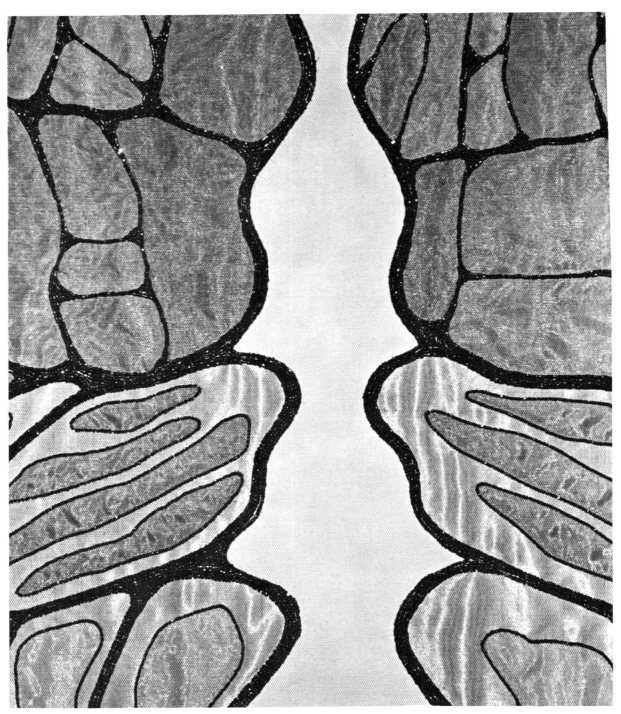

Detail: top of runner.

The beading of the runner, supervised by Von Briesen and Audrey Wallace, took a team of seven people and several months to complete. They first tried stringing the small, greenish-black glass beads on silk thread and couching the whole string at once, but the long strings were awkward to handle and didn't make an even line. Instead, a double strand of sewing silk was threaded into a beading needle – an exceptionally long, fine tool made to pass through the tiny holes in seed beads. This needle was used to pick up a few beads at a time, and the beads were positioned, then couched in place. The intersecting veins between the forms and the undulating outlines of the wings required such careful manipulation of the beads that only the most skillful beaders were able to handle those areas.

Both needleworkers and non-needleworkers were attracted to the Barney runner, which was considered the most "glamorous" of the thirty-nine. A practice runner was set up for those interested in beading, and when their proficiency had been demonstrated they became part of the beading team. This tedious work was done during a summer of record heat, with as many as five perspiring women seated around the embroidery frame with only one fan.

Beadwork in process.

As a member of the design team and eventually the runner mistress for Barney, I kept worrying about the overall concept of the runner. Thoughts about Tiffany lamps and their segmented, colored glass shapes, the flowing organic lines of Art Nouveau, the Impressionists' concern for light, the beautiful fabrics of Paris haute couture, kept whirling in my head – until one day I had this idea: huge butterfly wings with the sections done in various soft colors and outlined with the beading Chicago wanted to use.
                    —Connie von Briesen

Detail: front of runner.

Virginia Woolf

1882–1941, England

The waves on the front of the runner refer to Woolf's book of that name and also to her suicide by drowning.

The runner for Virginia Woolf, like those for the other highly reliefed plates on the end of the last wing of the table, presented many visual problems. Our tendency in designing runners was to make them very elaborate, and we kept conceiving of sculptural runners which would repeat both the forms and the dimension of the plates. The enormous physical presence of these plates, however, required simpler runner designs which would visually and symbolically reinforce the implications of the plates: that these women had begun to transcend the confines of female role.

Emanating from the top of the plate is a representation of a light beam – a reference to Woolf's book *To the Lighthouse* and to the quality of her writing, which seems to penetrate to the core of reality. This beam was sprayed on the linen with acrylic paint in an airbrush and outlined in stem stitch through the chiffon. A field of graduated color was embroidered on either side of the beam, creating a glow around it and repeating the colors of the plate.

Stitching the waves presented many technical and esthetic problems. I had Chicago's prismacolor drawing and a selection of Zwicky silk embroidery floss she had chosen. The thread colors were very much like the colors of the ocean, but not at all like the colors in the drawing. I had to translate the forms from a pencil technique to an embroidery technique as well as translating from one set of colors to another. Most importantly, I had to make it look and feel like waves.
—*Susan Brenner*

Illuminated capital.

and feminine values.

Chicago's drawing for plate and runner.

The image of the lighthouse in Woolf's book To the Lighthouse *captivated me. I had intended to include a carved light beam in her plate, but I wasn't able to work it out technically. I was therefore determined to incorporate it into the runner. The lighthouse seemed a perfect metaphor for the integration of masculine and feminine traits which I, like Woolf, was trying to achieve in my work. Its hard, phallic form enclosed a hidden interior space from which emanated a light beam that circled the horizon, illuminating everything in its path. The latter aspect reminded me of something Anaïs Nin had said about singularly feminine perception. In her opinion this trait was characterized by an ability to pass through and reveal all the layers of the human psyche.*

Virginia Woolf place setting.

A brilliant and prolific novelist, Virginia Woolf was a pioneer in the development of a female form language in literature. According to her philosophy, the subjugation of women was the key to most of the social and psychological disorders of Western civilization. She believed that only by integrating masculine and feminine traits on the personal, social, and esthetic levels could the world become sane, and she attempted to express this through the form and content of her work.

eorgia O'Keeffe

b. 1887, United States

Detail: capital letter.

The capital letter for O'Keeffe – embroidered by Terry Blecher, who executed this runner – is derived from the reaching antler forms that are typical of O'Keeffe's skull paintings. Anaïs Nin spoke for many female creators when she said: "The woman artist has to fuse creation and life in her own way, or in her own womb... Woman has to create within the mystery, storms, terrors,...do battle against the abstractions of art. She has to sever herself from the myth man creates, from being created by him... Woman wants to...recover the original paradise."

The runner design for Georgia O'Keeffe – like those for Sanger and Woolf – went through several phases, becoming progressively simpler at each stage. Though the rough canvas mockup was probably our most successful attempt at a three-dimensional design, we decided not to use it, as it seemed redundant in relationship to the plate. Instead we made a runner that incorporated painting and needlework to symbolize the transformation of women's experience into a form through which it could be more clearly expressed. While women have made many images that reflect their lives, these have generally not affected or altered the culture – particularly if created with traditional feminine techniques. O'Keeffe built a visual language that reflected that way she, a woman, saw the world. Because her painting entered and influenced the mainstream of art, it represents a significant breaking of the historical silence about women's point of view. This "breaking out" is suggested by the way the runner edges were cut free from the frame and left raw, a symbol of O'Keeffe's independence and of the risks she had to take to succeed as an artist when opportunities for women were few.

In 1868, the Pennsylvania Academy took the radical step of allowing women students to take a "life class." Obtaining adequate training, however, was only the first step in the long struggle women have waged to gain their place in the world of art.

Nineteenth century life drawing class.

The O'Keeffe runner is made of the fine Belgian linen that painters use and is stretched over specially made cherrywood stretcher bars. The runner was embroidered by Terry Blecher with Ver au Soie thread in her shaded-stitch technique. This embroidery was done over sprayed paint in colors that reiterate the tones of the plate, graduating both the density and the length of the stitches until they merged imperceptibly with the painted fade.

When I began china-painting in 1972, I intended to put my spray guns away forever in favor of the more "painterly" quality of a brush. But because the highly reliefed plates were so fragile, and would break with repeated firings, I reinstated my airbrushes, using them to apply heavy coats of china-paint. Somehow it seemed natural to extend my sprayed color fades to the runner surface, which created a fusion of painting and embroidery that stretched the boundaries between the so-called "fine" and "decorative" arts.

Chicago's study for capital letter.

Georgia O'Keeffe was the first contemporary woman artist to create a visual language that anthropomorphized the world in female terms. Her work provided a foundation for the development of a female form language in art. Part of the group of American painters who exhibited at "291," the influential gallery run by the photographer Alfred Steiglitz (O'Keeffe's husband), O'Keeffe is a major figure in twentieth-century art.

Chicago spray-painting colors on runner.

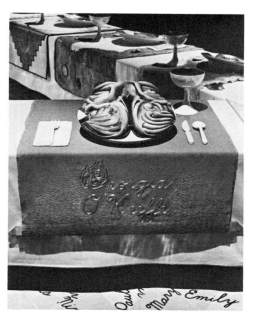

Georgia O'Keeffe place setting.

The Dinner Party
as Sacrament

Our Table Linens and Altar Cloths

The sacramental nature of *The Dinner Party* is a deliberate part of its imagery. It may seem strange for me – Jewish and basically irreligious – to create a work of art that aspires, as *The Dinner Party* does, to spiritual significance. But part of what comprises my attitude about the meaning of life was probably passed down to me through the twenty-three generations of rabbis whose mission my father was expected to carry on. Rebelling against the strictures of institutionalized religion, however, he chose to be a labor organizer and social reformer rather than a rabbi. By example and through discussions, he taught me to respect the dignity of all human beings and the historical importance of their struggles for independence.

Although we rarely attended temple as a family, I used to go to services alone from time to time. Even though I didn't understand the Hebrew words, I remember the chills that went through me at the rhythmic sound of the cantor's voice. It was awesome to watch the Torah being carried from the tabernacle and reverently placed on the lectern. The Torah cover – which was, like other temple furnishings, embellished with embroidery – was slowly lifted off and the scroll unrolled. I was so involved with the ceremony that I never really noticed that it was only men whose shoulders were draped with the *tallis* or sacred shawl and who chanted while the rabbi read.

When I was sixteen, something occurred at the temple that kept me from ever going back. It was Yom Kippur, the highest holiday of the year, and the traditional *yiskar* or memorial services were being held. I wanted to commemorate the death of my father, who had passed away three years before. During the service, which was quite emotional, envelopes were passed around with printed requests for donations so that our "loved ones [could] rest in peace." The idealistic young woman I was then was horrified; I fled the temple crying at what seemed a perverted practice. I never again attended religious services, but some aspects of their meaning stayed with me and became connected in my mind with the best parts of being related to a large, second-generation Russian Jewish family.

My own family was small, but my father had many siblings, most of whom lived in Chicago, where I was raised. There was, along with continual bickering, a profound warmth among them. Their deep sense of caring about each other and the world somehow became associated, for me, with the meaning of the ritual and spirituality embodied in the temple services. Perhaps the cadence of my grandmother's speech or the lilt of my aunts' voices when they all talked at once reminded me of the rhythm of the Hebrew incantations; perhaps the level of feeling expressed in my father's voice when he spoke to me about human suffering made me think of the emotion in the rabbi's voice when he read from the Torah; perhaps the sense of belonging which enveloped me at our noisy family gatherings was similar to the feeling which filled the synagogue at the ancient sound of the *shofar* being blown on Yom Kippur.

At any rate, those experiences stayed with me for years. In the early 1970's, when I began to work on the problem of creating an art language which could express my faith in the potential power of women and the importance of those feelings and values that have been relegated to the "feminine sphere" – from somewhere deep inside me – those early memories began to come into play. They helped shape my sense of ritual, my connection with history, and my belief that the force of the human spirit could best be expressed through art.

In 1976, Susan took me to an exhibition of work done by the ecclesiastical embroidery class in which she was enrolled. My knowledge of Christian rituals and the vestments associated with them was quite limited. I had studied medieval and Renaissance art, but my only direct experience with the practice of Christianity was when I was six years old. Because I had a crush on a Catholic boy in my building, I began to listen to the Sunday radio broadcast of the Mass. After a few weeks of dutifully kneeling on the floor of my room throughout the service, I abruptly lost interest. When my mother asked me about it, I told her that I had decided not to be a Catholic because the floor was too cold and I got cramps in my legs.

Perhaps it was precisely my lack of knowledge about the meaning of the needlework Susan and I saw exhibited which precipitated the response I had. The room was full of chasubles and altar cloths, all beautifully embroidered by women who were proudly standing close by or demonstrating their needle techniques at embroidery frames in the corner. They seemed totally oblivious of the fact that they were using their incredible needlework skills to aggrandize the trappings of a church which – like most organized religions – had systematically deprived women of equal status for centuries. Moreover, the needlewomen received absolutely no credit for their work. There was no documentation, and they were not encouraged to embroider their signatures on the vestments they had done. As soon as the work left their hands, the women became as anonymous as those who had embroidered the Torah covers I had scarcely noticed when I was a child.

I was outraged and saddened. It was as if I were seeing our whole condition as women embodied in that room. Instead of devoting their energies and skills to honor each other and their own heritage, women were submerging their time and efforts in support of male institutions and male-dominated belief systems. Why couldn't these women direct their abilities toward bettering the conditions of their own sex? After we left the exhibition, I began thinking about extending the religious metaphor of *The Dinner Party* by incorporating into it more of the objects traditionally associated with Christian worship. I wanted to turn these around so they would honor the female principle instead of a male deity. The opportunity to explore this possibility soon presented itself.

A few weeks later, we constructed a mockup of one section of the table. Until that time, we had planned just to butt the tables – with their tablecloths – up against each other. But it became obvious as soon as we had tried this that the corners where the two wings met needed to be covered. I began to pin white materials together – silks, satins, and brocades – to form a corner covering that hung almost to the floor. I embellished it with gold cords and a heavy white braid, trying to make some kind of altar cloth. Susan and I both liked the idea, although we knew it wasn't quite right yet. Then Susan brought in a pile of crocheted doilies, and, intrigued, I began to play with them. Although they are not considered art, I had always loved doilies, and they provided a perfect example of the way women's needlework has been ignored or dismissed in spite of its beauty. As I worked with the doilies, they seemed to form themselves into the triangular sign of the Goddess, thereby changing the whole character of the corner and somehow making the table "feel" like an altar or shrine. The problem of the table corners was thus solved, and, additionally, traditional male symbols were transmuted into a female form.

Our altar cloths – which adorn all three corners of the *Dinner Party* table – combine ecclesiastical whitework techniques with other forms of whitework, most of which have been used for domestic purposes. Combining these techniques emphasizes the central position of the table in both religious and secular needlework traditions. During early Christian times, the household table was transformed into an altar simply by covering it with a clean, white cloth. Some of the finest needlework, particularly whitework, has been done on tablecloths and altar cloths. In conventional needlework history, however, an unjustified distinction has been made between ecclesiastical and domestic embroidery, the former being viewed seriously and the latter dismissed as "amateur." (But in neither case have the needlewomen been sufficiently acknowledged.)

The other reason for combining religious and secular needlework in the altar cloths has to do with the way the values associated with the altar have been transposed to the *Dinner Party* table. One form of the Eucharist has been traditionally conducted at the church altar; another has been enacted at the dinner table. For centuries, women have given of themselves so that their family and guests could be sustained and renewed. But this repeated act, which requires considerable sacrifice, has never been considered particularly important – merely an expected part of the female role. The work women have done to embellish and enrich their home environments and to support and nourish their families has been ignored or trivialized and has remained undocumented for thousands of years. The association of women's domestic acts with Jesus' martyrdom may seem ridiculous or even blasphemous to some, but it is an association I consider to be rooted in truth.

The *Dinner Party* altar cloths are called "Millennium runners," M being the thirteenth letter of the alphabet and thirteen being the number of women represented on each wing of the table as well as the number of guests at the Last Supper. The Millennium is a symbolic reference to that moment in the future when the double standard – which defines men's rituals as not only significant but sacred, while rendering women's invisible – will end, and all human effort will be honored for its part in the richness of human experience.

The Dinner Party is, on one level, a reinterpretation of the Last Supper from the point of view of those who have done the cooking and serving throughout history. It is also a work which uses women's traditional needle skills to record and celebrate women's lives and achievements. These two works – Leonardo da Vinci's famous *Last Supper* and this detail from Queen Matilda's Bayeux Tapestry – help to illuminate these intentions. The images show the close connection between the "holy" table and the secular banquet feast. In both cases, no women are present, even though events like those depicted here were usually made possible by the work of women. Additionally, the embroidery was done by women who plied their needles to honor men.

It is women's historical invisibility, both as participants and as creators, that *The Dinner Party* tries to rectify – to give credit to the preparers of the feasts, the setters of the tables, the makers of the tablecloths, the advisors and recorders of men's activities. *The Dinner Party* acknowledges these contributions and simultaneously challenges the way women have inadvertently participated in their own oppression by not using their energies and skills to nurture and acknowledge themselves and their own accomplishments.

Women at their domestic tasks have been popular subjects for art for centuries. These two paintings – one from the Middle Ages, the other contemporary – are good examples of this tradition. In each picture, the woman, whether mistress of the house (as in the medieval version) or servant (as in the Matisse painting), is involved with the preparation of the table or the serving of food.

Interestingly, the body gestures, as well as the actions, of both women are the same, despite the span of centuries and the historic changes that separate them. Both have a compliant attitude and a total lack of facial expression. Both seem resigned to their roles. Both are images of women as men have seen us. What is not seen is the rage and despair that women have often felt and expressed as they labored for hours over yet another meal to be quickly consumed and forgotten.

The Dinner Party employs a Eucharistic metaphor in the use of not only altar cloths, but also plates or *patens* (the surface that holds the wafer during Communion); chalices (which hold the wine); and fair linens (rectangular cloths placed over the altar during the service), which are the basis for our runners. In *The Dinner Party* the "Communion" is performed as the audience moves around the table, viewing this assembled community of women – Apostles, if you will – all of whom have served women through their lives and work. The viewers participate in the joy of women's heritage, but also experience the sadness that comes with the realization that this heritage has been obscured, fragmented, and denied for so long.

This act of participation in the meaning of a work of art hearkens back to the early Christian Masses, when the community was involved very directly in the religious act. The laity brought bread, wine, and sometimes animals to be ritually consecrated and then consumed. As the ceremony of the Eucharist – the word derives from the Greek and Roman words for thanksgiving – became more elaborate, it also became more symbolic and esoteric. Gradually the involvement of the congregation was limited, and the sharing of a meal became a ritual act.

I like to think of the potluck suppers we often had in the Project as a kind of return to the original celebration of the Mass: a coming together to share our feelings, a time when we became renewed through the assembling of our community. Moreover, I hope that the piece itself suggests the importance of the role art can have in communicating human values, and the way it can provide a spiritual, even religious, meaning to life.

The Dinner Party plates and chalices extend the Eucharistic reference. In addition to relating to the traditional objects at a dinner table, they suggest ecclesiastical patens as well as chalices or Communion cups. The paten, like the ritual goblet, can be traced back to ancient times. Plates resembling patens have been found in Minoan and Mycenaen archaeological excavations. These are thought to have been used either to prepare sacred bread or to contain food offerings for the snake – a household animal identified with the Goddess and worshiped as the embodiment of the spirit of the dead. The chalice has its antecedents in Minoan and Mycenaen effigy vessels used in the Goddess cults, as well as in the later Greek *calyx,* or wine cup.

Chalice.

Paten.

In this image representing Christ on a paten with a chalice beside it, the ritual objects rest on an altar covered with a sacred cloth. In the photograph of the luncheon setting, the plate, glass, silverware, and accoutrements sit on a crocheted cloth – a beautiful example of whitework, which has been used almost interchangeably in ecclesiastical and secular work. The juxtaposition of the two realities exemplified in these place settings – the "holy" and the "everyday" – provides the basis for the iconography of *The Dinner Party.*

Sharing food at a meal is a very ancient way of celebrating community or expressing the joy or solemnity of a particular occasion. Moreover, certain ritualized household meals demonstrate the close connection between domestic and religious traditions. This is particularly clear in the Passover seder, which was, of course, the scene of the Last Supper.

For a sacred feast such as this it is customary for Jewish women to do needlework, as is illustrated by this embroidered matzo cloth. The very nature of this work, used only on special occasions, helps identify the meal as a significant event. During the Passover ceremony, in fact, the household table becomes an altar as well as the setting for an important meal. The ritual foods are offered on a ceremonial plate; the wine glass is transformed into a holy cup; and even the napkin takes on spiritual significance.

Extensive samples were made before we arrived at a design and an edge quality that we liked.

Napkins also have both a domestic and a religious connotation. They have been used in all classes of households. Originally quite large, they were first worn over the shoulders rather than being placed in the lap. The "maniple," from the Latin word meaning napkin, was a square of linen worn over the left arm of the priest and used to cover his hand during the administration of the sacraments. Initially appearing during the ninth or tenth century, the maniple gradually evolved into a long, elaborately embroidered strip worn over the priest's shoulder.

The Dinner Party napkins – which refer to both the domestic linen and the maniple – have carefully embroidered edges, worked in split stitch and couched with Japanese gold. Positioned on every runner, the napkins – like the form of the place settings themselves – symbolize the way all women have been treated alike, irrespective of their differences.

Fifty napkins were made for *The Dinner Party*. They are large, measuring 10 by 5¼ inches, their proportions consistent with the scale of formal dinner napkins and the oversized porcelain flatware. They were hand-embroidered with silk and gold and constructed to appear flat, smooth, and elegantly folded.

269

In preparation for designing the Millennium triangles, I studied a number of examples of whitework techniques. Projecting slides of lace, crochet, drawn thread and cutwork, embroidery on net, shadow work, and other forms of whitework was particularly helpful, as it allowed me to see some of the minute patterns that are otherwise difficult to appreciate. It seemed to me that the most important visual issue in almost all whitework is the manipulation of the light and dark areas. This is achieved primarily by cutting away or withdrawing parts of the design, using shadowed effects of raised work or – as in crochet or lace – actually working the thread to create a network of negative spaces. The sophisticated use of positive and negative space in some of this work, which requires a high level of visual sensitivity, is truly impressive.

I decided to create a pattern that had a rhythmic field of shapes, primarily triangles, which would be broken by open areas, changes in configuration, and scale variations. Although I did not design specifically for any particular method, I tried to make an image which would translate well into almost any whitework technique.

The entryway to The Dinner Party marks the merging of past and present.

In many churches, the altar is the central focus of the building. To the pious Catholic, it is literally a "holy and dreadful place ..." (*Genesis* XXVIII. 17), positioned on an elevated surface in order to preclude the possibility of defilement.

Chicago's design for Millennium triangle.

This drawing of mine was the basis for the whitework triangles which embellish each of the three corner cloths on the *Dinner Party* table.

270

Millennium triangle 1:
cutwork and petit point.

The first Millennium triangle is the clearest of the three translations of the original design. Worked by a team of seven people, including L. A. Olson, Julie Brown, Karen Schmidt, Peter Fieweger, Pat Akers, Thelma Brenner, and Marny Elliott, the piece combines five techniques. Of these, trailing, cutwork, and shadow work are traditional whitework methods generally used for tablecloths and napkins. Petit point and satin stitching were added to provide contrast with the delicacy of the whitework.

Our altar cloths are composed entirely of silk, as we wanted to distinguish them from the linen tablecloths in both surface and texture. All three cloths are identical in construction and materials, but each of the triangular center pieces is done in a different whitework technique. The fabrics used in the Millennium runners included heavy slipper satin for the triangular wings; silk linen (which relates the altar cloths to the tablecloths through color and weave) for the top diamond shapes; and *peau de soie* for the skirts or frontals.

Millennium triangle 2: white silkwork.

Millennium triangle 3: crochet.

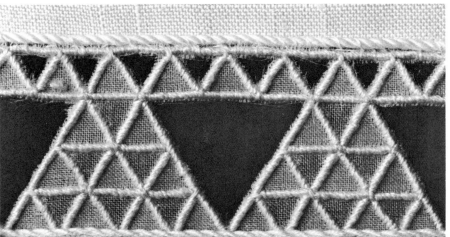

Border detail of the first Millennium runner.

The border of this cloth clearly demonstrates the dramatic effect of cutwork and shadow work. The triangles are outlined in trailing, which was stitched along the foundation at a 60-degree angle so that the intersections would be sharp and clean. Some of these triangles are completely cut away, while others have had one layer of organza removed.

Of the various techniques used on the altar cloths, crochet is most directly linked to the most devalued part of the domestic needlework tradition. It is difficult even to look at a crocheted piece without thinking of afghans, dresser scarves, table mats, or ruffled dolls' dresses. Even within the context of the home, however, where women's needlework is at least appreciated by her family, crocheted objects are overlooked and easily lost. Why, then, would we choose to include this technique in a serious work of art?

First, crochet had a visual and expressive potential which Susan and I thought could be used to embody the entire tradition of obsessive needlework. Second, by placing a dishonored needlework technique in a prominent position in a museum-scale work, we intended to implicitly challenge the whole value framework of what constitutes art.

Piecing crocheted section of third Millennium triangle.

During my first few months on the Project, Chicago asked me about translating her complicated design for the Millennium runner into crochet. Having had some experience in hook and yarn, I accepted. I had no idea, however, of the difficult technical problems I would encounter. It took three months just to find a crochet stitch that could be used for the alternating open and closed triangles. Finally I decided to use a simple, staggered filet pattern, as it was one of the few stitches that would produce legible triangles. Because of the minute scale of the design, only a size 50 cotton thread and a size 12 metal hook could be used.

The complexity of the pattern was so demanding and required so much concentration that I could sustain work for only a limited amount of time. I broke the overall pattern into four sections, worked them separately, joined them with a simple whip stitch, and appliquéd them to a black China silk ground. The Millennium runner took me twenty-one months to complete.
—*Stephanie Martin*

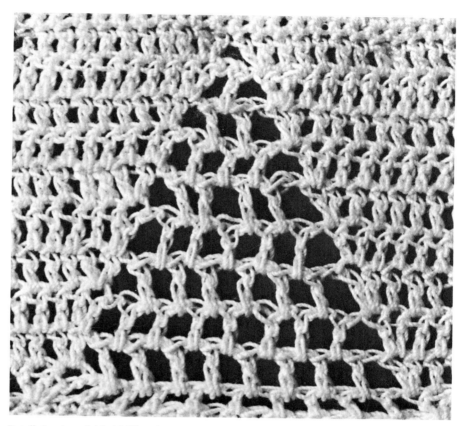

Detail: border of third Millennium runner.

Martin crocheting Millennium runner.

The border pattern of each Millennium triangle was repeated in the ninety-inch strips which edge the skirts of the altar cloths. These borders also repeat some of the techniques incorporated into the embroidered triangles.

The "M" in the centers of the Millennium triangles, like the overall pattern, changes in appearance with shifts in technique. The first "M" – worked in petit point – dominates the delicate areas surrounding it. The assertion of this central form is a symbol for the strength of the female principle as it existed in pre-history and as it is emerging today.

The first wing of the table, chronicling the gradual decline of women's social position, ends with the second triangle, which is softer in appearance. Although the "M" is still differentiated from the other stitched areas, it is more difficult to perceive.

By the end of the second wing, women's status had reached its lowest point. The thousands of tiny stitches in the third Millennium triangle reflect the suppression of women's autonomy at this time. The bold technique of the petit-point "M" has been replaced by a crochet pattern that renders the apocalyptic symbol an indistinguishable part of the whole design.

The wide range of whitework techniques available allowed us to express the historical changes in women's condition within the framework of one image. This emphasizes the richness of this needlework tradition – one that has been largely ignored.

Petit-point "M" against a background of silk organza worked with satin stitch, trailing, cutwork, and shadow work.

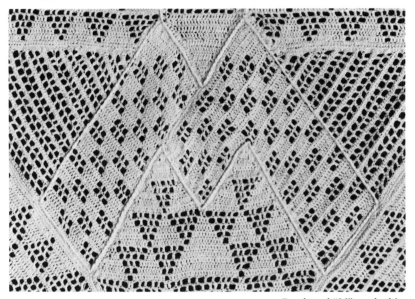

Crocheted "M" worked in chain stitch and double-crochet in a filet pattern against a surface worked in the same techniques, varying the pattern.

Detail of "M" on ground, showing the complexity of the stitched surface and the way the light enhances the richly embroidered surface.

Whitework "M" worked in silk using the long- and -short stitch against a ground of varied types of stitching.

In this Millennium runner, Marjorie Biggs included every stitch and technique traditionally employed in ecclesiastical embroidery. Because she executed her version of the triangular design on a solid white background in white silk floss, she could not depend on the visual contrast provided by the open and closed areas that occur in the usual forms of whitework. Instead, the black-and-white design had to be rendered in such a way that the light play across the surface would emphasize the direction and texture of the carefully delineated and differentiated stitched areas.

When I first learned of *The Dinner Party* through Susan Hill, I was impressed by the enormity of its scope, by its purpose, and by the dedicated and precise way it was being researched and carried out. I wanted to be part of such a project, and I am proud to have contributed to the needlework of this tremendous undertaking. I hope it will serve as an inspiration to dedicated needleworkers for many years to come.
—*Marjorie Biggs*

The Needleworkers' Dictionary

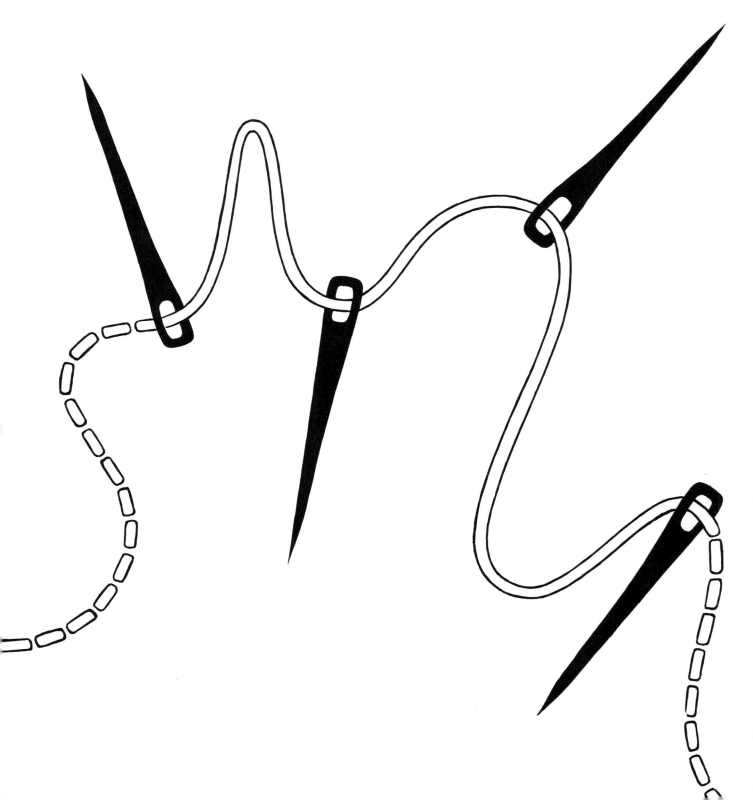

Recognizing Our Community

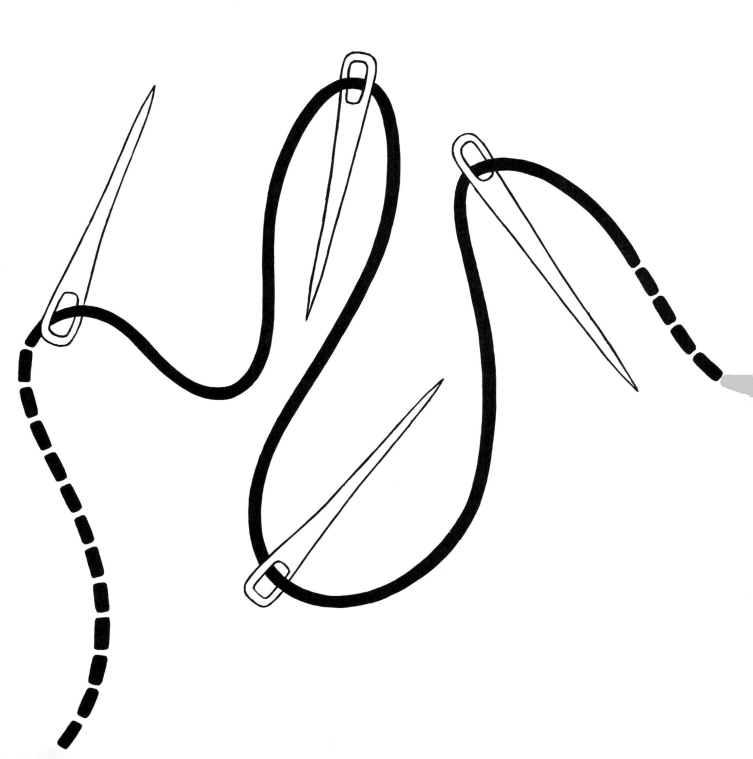

Because the development and execution of the runners involved so many people, it seems important to clarify our work process. From the time we began working on the runners, I invited people in the studio to participate in the formative stages of each design, while always retaining the right to determine its final form myself. At first – because the imagery came so directly from the plates – people basically helped me paint the designs I drew on the fabric we used for the mockups. But gradually this changed, particularly after the early images had been successfully translated into embroidery.

Susan and I decided to encourage the needleworkers who had been involved in all the stages of these first runners – from concept to completion – to participate more fully in the next series of runner designs. By then, I had expanded the parameters of the runner concept to include more specific historical styles and iconography. This allowed those needleworkers who were interested in the design process to do research for a runner that appealed to them, bringing examples of patterns, stitches, or relevant material to the design sessions. Not all needleworkers wanted to be involved in this activity, however; some preferred to simply stitch.

In the design sessions for runners whose format was already established, needleworkers would have some input into the specific form the runner would take, and they always contributed substantially to solving the technical problems presented by the type of embroidery we chose. Occasionally a design session would begin without a preconceived plan – only the plate or plate drawing, historical information about the woman represented and the techniques of her time, and our imaginations.

Chicago on Needlework Loft.

This photograph shows me trying to decide whether to apply white satin triangles to the bottom of the Susan B. Anthony runner in order to break the linearity of the front edge. Watching me solve visual problems, particularly in the Needlework Loft, was one way people learned from me as an artist.

Faith holds the Distaff;

The reason I insisted on esthetic control of all aspects of the Project was that first, it was my concept; second, I was the most developed artist; and last, my control ensured visual consistency in a work of art that contained an enormous range of images, styles, and techniques. However, establishing a balance between my ultimate authority and an open esthetic process was one of my goals in the studio. This was sometimes difficult to achieve, particularly in the Needlework Loft. There was a distinct difference in levels of development, both artistically and intellectually, not only between me and the needleworkers, but also among themselves; moreover, the fact that many of the needleworkers were not professional artists produced a gap between their approach and mine. The greatest difficulty, however, resulted from the fact that Susan and I were generally the only ones on the continually changing design teams who had an overall view of the piece. This meant that we could anticipate how runner would relate to runner in a way that other people simply couldn't do. Inevitably, someone on a design team would suggest a wonderful idea which, unfortunately, simply would not work with the runners around it.

Although I am convinced that without the framework of my overall vision this pluralistic approach would never have succeeded, having so many varied points of view greatly enriched the runners. Learning how to extend this idea of incorporating different points of view into the actual conceptual structure of my work is one of my future goals.

I want to take this opportunity to thank the many people who participated in the making of the runners and cloths, especially those who took responsibility for executing individual runners, supervising work, and assuming leadership. Most of all, I wish to acknowledge Susan Hill, without whom the needlework could never have been accomplished.

Chicago choosing thread colors for edging of woven strips on Hypatia runner, with Olson (l.) and Hill (r.).

Hill and Chicago discussing development of runner imagery on third wing of table.

Hope winds

I came to the project with no background in needlework – or even any thought of doing needlework. I came with only a heritage of embroidery skills in my family. My great-grandmothers had provided for their families by sewing, and my sister and I grew up within a large clan of women who took pride in their domestic skills. Even as a child, however, I felt that this work was not really valued, and I was driven by a strong but unfocused urge to do something important in the world. I studied sociology, then began a career as a freelance photographer, working first in New York and eventually moving to Los Angeles. My pictures expressed concern for the social issues I felt strongly about, but I was frustrated by my own critical attitude.

In the fall of 1976, I drove 150 miles to hear Judy give a lecture. I was already familiar with her work and had great respect for her ideas. I had read *Through the Flower,* and I remember thinking that I'd be interested in working on one of her projects. During the lecture, someone asked "Do you make collective art?" "No, I don't," Judy replied, "but I am working on a large piece, and I need assistants." I volunteered. We agreed that I would produce the embroidered tablecloth, and we expected the work to take six months. It seemed worthwhile to put

photography aside for a short time in order to gain new skills and explore new ideas. Within a few weeks, however, we knew that our initial concept of six months' work had been ridiculous; yet I gave little thought to leaving the Project. By then we had developed the idea of the runners, and, despite my inexperience, I felt fully responsible for their production. Also, Judy and the studio members were providing a kind of support I had never encountered before; I was challenged, encouraged to succeed, and given room to flounder. Most of all, I believed in the work; I felt that the information and the vision of *The Dinner Party* superseded the work I could produce as an individual.

I was directly involved in the needlework research and the runner designs; here I was very much the apprentice, and I learned a great deal from Judy. I saw myself primarily as a facilitator, directing the process of translating Judy's designs into needlework and integrating people into the Needlework Loft. Often this meant convincing experienced stitchers otherwise when they insisted that techniques couldn't be used the way Judy had conceived them. I, like Judy, worked on the principle that just about anything could be done, and I set about to make it happen.

Most of the four hundred people who worked on the project were involved in the needlework, but few arrived with embroidery skills; most had to be taught. I supervised work and took care of the materials, gradually building a team of people who shared these tasks with me. We coordinated the jobs and the people in the loft – matching people's stitching styles, time schedules, and needlework abilities with the different chunks of work – and consoled innumerable people innumerable times when hours' worth of stitching had to be taken out.

For me, the beauty of the work and the gratitude I have received from *The Dinner Party*'s audience totally compensate for my three years of personal and technical struggle. In turn, I feel enormously grateful to the people who worked with me for making our needlework a reality.

—S.H.

Pictured here are those who made a significant contribution to the execution of *The Dinner Party* needlework. In addition, the many people who helped bring the needlework to completion are listed on page 283.

the shining thread on Fairy Spools;

Marilyn Akers, *art student*
Hatshepsut, Hildegarde

Pat Akers, *community worker*
Millennium Runner #1; Sappho, Eleanor of Aquitaine, Hildegarde, Artemisia Gentileschi, Sojourner Truth, Ethel Smyth, Virginia Woolf, Georgia O'Keeffe

Marjorie Biggs, *director, L.A. Episcopal Diocesan embroidery class*
Millennium Runner #2, Theodora, Caroline Herschel

Terry Blecher, *artist*
Judith, Boadaceia, Marcella, Anne Hutchinson, Margaret Sanger, Georgia O'Keeffe; Ishtar, Kali, Sappho

Susan Brenner, *artist*
Artemisia Gentileschi, Virginia Woolf, Tablecloth; Saint Bridget, Hildegarde, Susan B. Anthony

Thelma Brenner, *needle-woman, fundraiser*
Millennium Runner #1; Christine de Pisan, Anna van Schurman, Mary Wollstonecraft

Julie Brown, *art student*
Millennium Runner #1, Mary Wollstonecraft; Hildegarde, Sojourner Truth, Virginia Woolf

Audrey Cowan, *homemaker, weaver*
Eleanor of Aquitaine; Fertile Goddess

Ellen Dinerman, *artist*
Elizabeth Blackwell; Elizabeth R, Tablecloth

Jan Marie Du Bois, *bookkeeper, weaver*
Hypatia; Snake Goddess, Marcella

Marny Ennis Elliott, *mother, church needlework designer*
Hrosvitha; Millennium Runner #1, Mary Wollstonecraft

Peter Fieweger, *archeology student*
Millennium runner #1; Primordial Goddess, Hatshepsut, Hypatia, Trotula, Sacajawea, Mary Wollstonecraft, Sojourner Truth, Margaret Sanger, Georgia O'Keeffe

Cherié Frainé, *artist*
Sacajawea

Dorothy Goodwill *home-maker, needlewoman*
Hildegarde; Snake Goddess

Elaine Ireland, *artist*
Ishtar, Petronilla de Meath; Fertile Goddess, Aspasia, Marcella, Saint Bridget, Eleanor of Aquitaine, Artemisia Gentileschi, Mary Wollstonecraft, Ethel Smyth

Sharon Kagan, *artist*
Saint Bridget; Snake Goddess, Hatshepsut

Love turns the wheel of time.

Mary Helen Krehbiel,
homemaker, needlewoman
Ishtar, Hatshepsut, Judith,
Aspasia, Anna van Schurman

Judy Mulford, *homemaker,*
graduate student – textiles
Amazon; Primordial Goddess,
Aspasia, Isabella d'Este, Hildegarde, Mary Wollstonecraft,
Sojourner Truth

Karen Schmidt, *editor*
Millennium Runner #1;
Sojourner Truth, Emily Dickinson, Natalie Barney

Kacy Treadway, *fashion*
design student
Elizabeth R

Ruth Leverton *business-*
woman, artist
Hatshepsut, Sappho, Aspasia,
Boadaceia

L.A. Olson, *educator*
Millennium Runner #1, Hildegarde, Anna van Schurman,
Margaret Sanger; Isabella d'Este,
Christine de Pisan, Sojourner
Truth, Susan B. Anthony

Kathleen Schneider, *artist*
Sacajawea; Fertile Goddess,
Snake Goddess, Sappho

Karen Valentine, *artist*
Sophia, Conservation System;
Fertile Goddess, Aspasia

Stephanie Martin, *artist,*
mother
Millennium Runner #3, Sophia,
Aspasia; Mary Wollstonecraft

Dorothy Polin, *homemaker*
Napkins, Runner Backs; Snake
Goddess, Aspasia, Trotula, Anna
van Schurman, Mary Wollstonecraft, Elizabeth Blackwell

Elfie Schwitkis, *homemaker,*
student
Isabella d'Este, Susan B. Anthony;
Amazon, Sappho, Eleanor of
Aquitaine, Natalie Barney

Constance von Briesen
needlewoman, artist
Kali, Christine de Pisan, Anne
Hutchinson, Emily Dickinson,
Natalie Barney; Hatshepsut,
Saint Bridget

Kathy Miller, *student*
Trotula; Petronilla de Meath,
Isabella d'Este

Linda Preuss, *businesswoman*
Fastening System; Saint Bridget,
Eleanor of Aquitaine, Mary
Wollstonecraft

Catherine Stifter,
art student
Elizabeth Blackwell, Runner
Backing

Adrienne Weiss, *artist*
Fertile Goddess, Petronilla de
Meath, Mary Wollstonecraft;
Primordial Goddess, Aspasia

We wish to thank:

Joyce Aiken
Marilyn Anderson
Susan Anderson
Mariona Barkus
Shirley Bierman
Frances Budden
Susan Chaires
Pamela R. Checkie
Alice E. Chew
Aldeth S. Christy
Marguerite Clair
Joyce Cowan
Ruth Crane
Lynn Dale
Sandi Dawson
Elizabeth Eakins
Faye Evans
Marianne Fowler
Libby Frost
Jan Gandelman
JoAnn Garcia
Winifred Grant
Estelle Greenblatt
Judy Hartle
Margaret Herscher
Arla Hesterman
Robin Hill
Anita Johnson
Nancy Jones
Sherrie Lederman
Julie Leigh
Susan Leverton
Virginia Levie
Margaret Litchfield
C. Alec MacLean
Shelley Mark
Beth Martin
Judy Mathieson
Marie McMahon
Juliet Myers
Natalie Neith
Laura Nelson
Charlotte Ranke
Pauline Schwartz
Sue Severin
Manya Shapiro
Dee Skolnick
Raveli Soltes
Millie Stein
U.C. Santa Barbara
  Women's Center
Betty Van Atta
Audrey Wallace
Judith Wilson

Freya Alexander
June Alexis
Barbara Amelia
Eva Anda
Jane Anderson
Mandy Arrington
Marian Banks
Lisa Beavis
Valerie Bechtol
Grace Beresford
Virginia Berkenseer
Shirley Bess
Leah Blackburn
Belle Blecher
Elizabeth Bloser
Hilda Bolotin-Hardy
Bonita Boulio
Amelia Breit
Harriet Brown
Jo Ann Brown
Edith Bubar
Judy Buffaloe
Molly Burns
Connie Cesario
Jane Chapman
Walter G. Chapman
Diane Chorier
Gloria Clark
Molly Cleator
Kate Connell
Elaine Cole
Carrie Colburn
Mary Crawford
Sallee Crookston
Roz Cross
Laura Dahlkamp
Mary Damiano
Holly Davis
Laura De Lacy
Donna den Boer
Suzanne Doells
Roberta Dreis
Lisa Druckman
Barbara Du Bois
Mary Dudek
Cindy Dunham
Ann Dunn
Elisabeth Eldred
Laura Elkins
Janet Ewing
Gloria Falick
Nan Ferrin
Kelly Finnerty
Starr Fiore
Mary Frances Flynn
Louise Fox
Brenda French
Stephanie Galli
Diane Gelon
Judy Gernsbacher
Cynthia Gersch
Sally Gilbert
Roberta Gilman
Pat Goldstene
Shirley Goodman
Karen Gray
Gretchen Greene
Conte Guzman-Hoffman
Vivian Hallbauer
Holly Hampton
Nancy Handley
Jan Hansen
Cheryl Haynes
Donna Heider
Lynn Hickey
R. Romh Hinsley
Sally Holstrom
Linda Hood
Helen Hotchkins
Robin Hurst

Linda Jacaway
Victoria Johnson
Joan Hill Jordan
Michele Kamen-Posner
Kay Kaminski
Lisa Kaplan
Linda Kaun
Julie Keller
Anne-Marie Kennedy
David Kessenich
Judye Keyes
Debra Knoppow
Marva Kopels
Anne Kugler
Linda Lanker
Anne Laudecker
Estelle Lauter
Aurelia Licari
Lynn Lindahl
Leah Linsky
Tiffnie Lothrop
Nancy Lundy
Sherry MacGregor
Mary Lou Maniff
Pat Mauceri
Linda McGlasson
Jean McGregor
Terri McMains
Carole McMilan
Gloria McPearson
Kathleen Menzies
Mary Michaels
Phyllis Mottola
Rayle Mozur
Maureen Murphy
Kathleen Mussachia
Victoria Olivetti
Aletha Olson
Neil Olson
Elisa Ann Orozco
Victoria Ortiz
Florence Paul
Annie Pavlicek
Ellen Perlmutter
Michael Perlmutter
Wendy Piuck
Janis Ratliff
Jenny Raven
Nancy Raven
Karen Reed
Michelene Reed
Alexandra Robinson
Carol Robinson
Margaret Rompf
Roberta Rothman
Kathleen Rowley
Esther Rubin
Ruth Shorr Saltzberg
Deirdre Sartorius
Nancy Schulman
Elizabeth Schwartz
Howard Schwitkis
Kent Schwitkis
Miriam Shapiro
Linda Shelp
Tawny Sherrill
Stephen Shotland
Penelope Simison
Odine Sinneville
Betty Sirkin

Helen Slater
Elizabeth Smith
Diane Sophia
Judi Sowell
Jill Spurgin
Beverly Stefanski
Liesbeth Steffens
Jenny Stern
Hannah Stone
Leslie Stone
Dixie Swift
Carolyn Taylor-Olson
Julie Trachtenberg
Mitzie Trachtenberg
Sally Turner
Eileen Walsh
Linda Young
Will Vroom
Adele Watson
Peg Wood
Sharon Wood
Nelleke Woortman
Angela Zoe Zerdavis
Rita Zerull

We are indebted to
the Runner Graphics team

Helen Simich
Martie Rotchford
Shannon Hogan
Sandra Marvel
Louise Simpson

The entry banners were
woven by the San
Francisco Tapestry
Workshop

Jean Pierre Larochette
Cynthia Betty
Terry Blecher
Jan Marie Du Bois
Amanda Haas
Catherine Heach-Meese
Elaine Ireland
Cathryn Keller
Linda Preuss
Rudi Richardson
Mary Schoenbrun
Sally Torrance

I would like to thank all those whose efforts helped make this book possible – first and foremost, Kate Amend, without whose support and substantial intellectual contribution I would have been lost. In addition, I would like to thank Loretta Barrett for her belief in and commitment to the *Dinner Party* Project; Angela Cox, whose careful scrutiny of the manuscript ensured its clarity; and Peggy Kimball, who inherited the difficult task of making sure my words retained their meaning while correcting my often awkward phrasing.

Invaluable research was provided by Barbara Baldwin in particular, as well as Julie Brown, L. A. Olson, Mary Markovski, and Karen Schmidt. Thanks also to Sherrill Kushner for her endless patience in obtaining photographs and permissions from often obscure sources; to Terry Blecher and Dorothy Polin for their help in assembling the Needleworkers' Dictionary; to Mary Ann Glantz and Rachel Maines for their advice, information, and aid; to Aline Lapierre for her acute visual design skills; and, as always, special thanks to my colleague Diane Gelon, whose staunch support continues to sustain me.

Most of the work of printing the enormous number of black-and-white photographs fell to Juliet Myers, who accomplished this monumental task in record time. Additional thanks go to Don Miller, who gave generously of his expertise to the photographers – including Mary McNally and Beth Thielen, who photographed the overall runners and supplied many of the other pictures, with the help of A. Springer Hunt, Lyn Jones, Thea Litsios, Amy Meadow, and Linda Shelp.

Twinkle, twinkle, pretty spindle;

Glossary/Index of Terms

Appleton wool. Brand name of fine wool yarn used in embroidery.

Applique. Ancient technique of sewing a shaped piece of fabric onto larger fabric to form a design. (Pp. 45, 52, 60, 64, 70, 80, 84–85, 111, 114, 117, 119, 122, 127, 134, 154, 187–88, 192, 213-14, 220, 222, 228, 230, 250, 273)

Assisi work. (Pp. 162–63)

Back stitch. Small stitch taken while working a row of running stitches. (P. 126)

Backstrap loom. Loom that places tension on the warp by means of a belt tied to the warp threads and worn around the weaver's waist. (P. 188)

Bargello. American term for a needlepoint technique; also called Hungarian point, flame stitch, or Florentine stitch. Specific counted-thread pattern is worked to produce shaded wavy or flame-like design. (Pp. 158–59)

Basket-weave stitch. Term used in embroidery, needlepoint, and weaving to describe pattern created by two or more threads alternately crossing over and under each other. (Pp. 81, 120)

Basting. Use of running stitches to mark or sew fabrics together temporarily. (Pp. 45, 80, 233, 238)

Beadwork; Beading. Use of beads to create an outline, texture, or solid surface. (Pp. 64, 188, 202-3, 250-52, 254-55)

Berlin work. Form of needlepoint originating in Germany which became popular in 19th-century England and America. (P. 189)

Blackwork. (Pp. 166, 168, 171)

Blanket stitch. Variation of the buttonhole stitch. (P. 178)

Bobbin lace. One of two major categories of lace (the other is needlemade lace). A design is drawn on parchment, then secured to a hard pillow. Linen threads, held by bobbins, are braided and twisted to follow the pattern. (P. 237)

Brick stitch. Filling stitch consisting of even and parallel rows of satin stitches arranged in brick formation. (Pp. 44-45, 93)

Bullion knot. Fancy embroidery stitch producing a delicate coil. (Pp. 177–78, 180, 214)

Buttonhole stitch. Basic stitch of embroidery and plain sewing. (Pp. 177–78, 181)

Byzantine silk. (P. 122)

Cable knitting. Raised interlace design, worked on knitting needles. (Pp. 114–15)

Canvas. Mesh-like ground for needlepoint.

Cartoon. Artist's painted design used directly behind the warp threads of a loom as the pattern of a tapestry. (Pp. 88–89, 141–42)

Cavandoli work. (Pp. 164–65)

Ceylon stitch. Filling stitch of closely looped threads. (P. 215)

Chain stitch. Basic, looped embroidery and crochet stitch with many variations. (Pp. 30, 70, 178, 180–81, 208, 214)

Chinoiserie. Style of design based on objects imported from China. (P. 187)

Cloud stitch. A filling stitch. (P. 215)

Cloth of gold. Luxurious fabric made by weaving strands of gold thread through colored silk threads. (P. 168)

Coptic. Designs and tapestry techniques associated with Egyptian Christians called Copts. (Pp. 84, 88)

Cord. Thick, plied length of thread used for decorative edges and surfaces or to create relief. (Pp. 65, 67, 80, 120)

Cording. Use of cord – sewn to the surface or inserted in a casing – to create relief. (Pp. 64, 80)

Couching. Method of visibly securing one strand of thread with another, usually finer, thread. (Pp. 48–49, 52, 68, 70, 80, 95, 98–99, 119–20, 122, 144, 146–47, 154, 166, 171, 178, 232-33, 255)

Counted-thread work. Embroidery worked by making stitches over threads counted in the fabric ground (Pp. 92, 95, 124–30, 158–59, 162, 168-69, 187)

Crazy quilt. Pieced quilt made of varying, random shapes, popular in 19th-century America. (Pp. 229, 231)

Crewel work. Embroidery done with fine, two-ply wool, usually on a linen ground. (Pp. 132, 210)

Crochet. Technique of looping single strands of thread with a hook. (Pp. 214, 268, 270, 272-74)

Cross stitch. Two stitches crossing diagonally. (P. 176)

Cutwork. Areas of the ground are cut away, and the resulting space is patterned with bars of thread worked in a buttonhole stitch. (Pp. 93, 270–72, 274)

DMC. Brand name for cotton embroidery threads.

Distaff. Rod or staff with one forked end; used to hold fleece or flax prepared for spinning. (Pp. 26–27, 101, 104)

Domestic embroidery. Embroidery done in the home for furnishings or clothing. (Pp. 102, 169, 178, 186, 264)

Double coral knot. Complex embroidery stitch, worked in a single line or as a filling stitch. (P. 208)

Double crochet. Basic stitch in which the hook takes the thread through two loops. (P. 274)

Double running stitch. (Also, Holbein stitch.) Straight, regularly spaced stitches worked to form a solid line. (Pp. 162, 246)

Double-weft weaving. Indian technique for weaving with beads. (P. 202)

Drawn loom. Early, complex loom in which the harnesses are controlled by cords manipulated by weavers. (P. 100)

Drawn threadwork. (Also, pulled threadwork.) Embroidery technique creating an openwork design by withdrawing threads from the fabric, then strengthening the remaining strands. (Pp. 30, 92, 126–28, 270–71, 274)

Drop spindle. Spinning tool with one end weighted – usually by a disk or whorl – to promote continuous rotary motion. (Pp. 4, 41–42, 92)

Ecclesiastical embroidery. Needlework done on religious garments and furnishings. (Pp. 95–96, 105, 184, 264, 275)

Feather stitch. Decorative stitch with many variations. (Pp. 178, 215, 230)

Filet lace. Net or lace made with a simple pattern worked on a square mesh background. (Pp. 238, 271, 273–74)

Filling stitch. Category of stitches used to fill areas of design with color or texture. (P. 178)

Fishbone stitch. A filling stitch of interlaced straight lines. (P. 178)

Flame stitch. See also Bargello. (P. 158)

Florentine stitch. See also Bargello. (P. 158)

Floss. Fine, non-plied embroidery thread.

Frame loom. Simple loom made by fashioning a wooden frame and securing the warp across it. (P. 202)

French knot. Complex, single knot formed on the surface of fabric. (Pp. 52, 166, 168, 178, 236)

French seam. Narrow seam sewn on both sides to hide raw edges of cloth. (P. 50)

Goldwork. Embroidery done with metallic gold threads. (Pp. 103, 120–21, 144, 146–47)

Ground. Fabric upon which embroidery is worked.

Herringbone stitch. Interlaced stitch with many variations. (Pp. 49, 178, 213–14)

High-warp loom. French tapestry loom. Warp threads are stretched vertically between rollers and held under tension. Opening and closing of the warp are controlled by hand-held loops, or heddles. (P. 100)

Horizontal loom. Any loom in which the warp threads are held in tension horizontally. (P. 101)

Hungarian point embroidery. See Bargello.

Hymo. Stiff fabric made of wool, linen, and horsehair; used as interfacing. (P. 17)

Inkle-loom weaving. Using a narrow, simple loom to make a tape called "inkle." (Pp. 48–49)

Italian shading. (Also, Or Nué.) Gold or silver threads couched in a pattern with colored silk thread. (Pp. 44, 122)

Japanese gold. Trade name for thread made by wrapping gold leaf around a silk core.

Join. Seam attaching one fabric to another. (P. 230)

Knitting. Technique of interlocked, looped stitches worked in yarn with two needles. (Pp. 114–15)

Lacis. Early form of lace: net or mesh containing patterns worked in darning stitches. (P. 94)

Laidwork. Embroidery technique in which long, straight threads are laid flat on the surface of the material, then secured by a pattern of stitches. (Pp. 98, 144, 146–48, 178, 180–81, 208)

Lazy Daisy stitch. Variation of the chain stitch. (P. 208)

Long-and-short stitch. Variation of the satin stitch; straight stitches are worked alternately in long and short lengths, in even, parallel rows, for filling. (Pp. 46, 52, 57, 119, 246, 249, 252)

Long-armed cross stitch. Variation of the cross stitch, worked so that the stitches interlock. (Pp. 93, 162)

Low-warp loom. Flemish tapestry loom. Warp threads, stretched horizontally between rollers, are raised in groups by foot-controlled pedals. (P. 140)

Maltese silk. Trade name for silk couching thread.

Modified long-and-short stitch. *Dinner Party* term; technique of shading with varied-length threads, developed to translate Chicago's drawings into embroidery. (Pp. 47, 52, 67, 69)

Mola. Panels worked in reverse appliqué by women of San Blas Islands, Central America. (P. 233)

Mourning picture. (Pp. 189, 194, 197)

Needlemade lace. One of the two major categories of lace (the other is bobbin lace); made with a needle. Involves covering threads attached to a paper pattern with buttonhole stitches, then cutting the lace free from the paper. (P. 237)

Needlepoint. Embroidery worked on a canvas ground. (Pp. 158–59)

Ombré ribbon. Silk ribbon containing one or more colors shaded across its width. (P. 236)

Opus anglicanum. Medieval style of embroidery. (Pp. 94–96, 144, 146, 148–49)

Opus teutonicum. Style of embroidery which developed during the Middle Ages in German convents. (Pp. 92–93, 124–26, 144)

Or nué. See Italian shading.

Outline stitch. Category of stitches used to work the fine lines in a design. (Pp. 30, 98)

Overcast stitch. See also Whip stitch. (Pp. 74, 202)

Padded satin stitch. Satin-stitch embroidery worked over a foundation to create a raised surface. (Pp. 52, 122, 151)

Palampore. Printed cotton fabric woven in India. (P. 133)

Patchwork. Small pieces of fabric sewn together to form a pattern. (Pp. 222–23)

Paternaya wool. Brand name for a wool used in embroidery and weaving.

Pekinese stitch. Decorative embroidery stitch created by looping a thread through a foundation of back stitches. (P. 213)

Perle cotton. Plied embroidery thread.

Petit point. Needlepoint embroidery done in tent stitch on extremely fine mesh canvas. (Pp. 219, 270–71, 274)

Piecing. Sewing two or more fabric shapes together with a seam. (Pp. 220, 223, 228, 230)

Plain sewing. Term to differentiate functional stitching from embroidery.

Plaiting. (Also, braiding.) Diagonal interlacing of strands. (Pp. 24–26)

Plied wool. Twisted length of two or more single strands. (Pp. 43, 154)

Plunge. To pull the ends of couched threads or cords through fabric with a heavy needle.

Point de Gauze. Type of needlemade lace. (P. 237)

Pulled threadwork. See Drawn threadwork.

Quillwork. Technique worked by Native American women, in which dyed animal quills are secured to a leather or bark surface to create a design. (Pp. 188, 204–5)

Quilt. Bedcovering made by the process of quilting. The top layer has a patterned surface which is traditionally made by the quilting stitches themselves or by piecing, appliqué, cording, or patchwork. (Pp. 132, 134)

Quilting. Process of sewing several layers of fabric together with running stitches. (Pp. 133–35, 187)

Raised stem stitch. Stem-stitch embroidery worked over a ladder-like foundation of thread. (Pp. 84, 106, 221)

Raised work. Embroidery done over padding to create a reliefed surface. (Pp. 144–45, 151, 187)

Reverse appliqué. Shapes cut in surface layer of fabric to reveal one or more different fabrics beneath. (P. 232).

Ribbon work. A 19th-century embroidery technique of making flowers, using narrow silk ribbons. (Pp. 213, 234, 236)

Roving. Clean fleece loosely twisted into thick strands. (P. 24)

Running stitch. Series of straight, even stitches made at regular intervals. A basic technique of embroidery and plain sewing. (Pp. 70, 80, 134, 166, 178, 208, 220)

Sampler. Piece of fabric worked in a variety of stitches and/or designs. Originally used as a reference for techniques or patterns. (Pp. 132, 176–79, 187)

Satin stitch. Straight stitch worked in dense, parallel rows. (Pp. 19, 64, 72, 86, 93, 119, 124, 126, 151, 174, 178, 271, 274)

Shaded long-and-short stitch, Shaded split stitch, Shaded stem stitch. *Dinner Party* terms for basic filling stitches used in a range of blended colors (Pp. 166, 180, 208, 249, 259)

Shadow work. Embroidery technique in which herringbone stitches or pieces of fabric are applied to the underside of a sheer fabric to create a muted effect. (Pp. 270–72, 274)

Shot. In weaving, one pass of the shuttle across a section of warp threads. (P. 142)

Shuttle. Tool used to hold thread in weaving and tatting. (Pp. 63, 130)

Silkwork. Embroidery done entirely in silk thread. (Pp. 271, 274-75)

Soutache. Commercially woven flat, silky braid. (Pp. 44, 242)

Spindle. Tool resembling a shaft with tapered ends; used in the hand to spin prepared fleece or flax into thread. (Pp. 26-27, 29-30, 101, 104)

Split stitch. Very old, basic embroidery stitch used for outline or filling. (Pp. 60, 68, 72, 119, 124, 145, 147, 151, 166, 178, 208, 211, 253, 259, 269)

Stem stitch. Fundamental, linear embroidery stitch; used for outlines and filling. (Pp. 46, 72, 76, 80, 93, 111, 127, 134, 151, 166, 178, 181, 208, 211, 228, 236, 243, 246, 252-53, 256)

Stevie's Paste. *Dinner Party* term for textile glue made from a rice-flour base. (Pp. 74, 168)

Strip weaving. Basic structural technique in many West African textiles. (P. 224)

Stumpwork. Style of raised embroidery popular in the 17th century. (Pp. 212-13)

Surface stitching. Embroidery worked across a fabric ground.

Tabby weaving. (Also, plain weave.) Simplest form of weaving, in which warp and weft alternate evenly at right angles. (P. 108)

Tapestry. Weaving technique used to create pictorial patterns. (Pp. 84, 87–88, 92, 98, 100, 138, 140, 144)

Tent stitch. A very even, flat, firm, basic counted-thread and needlepoint stitch. (Pp. 56, 60, 187)

Trailing. Technique of cutwork; stitching used to strengthen and bind the edge of the design. (Pp. 271–72, 274)

Trapunto. Technique of selectively stuffing areas of a quilted design from the back of the fabric. (Pp. 38–39, 133–34)

Trellis stitch. Interlaced series of stitches detached from the fabric except for the beginning row. (Pp. 214–15)

Turkey work. Tufted embroidery stitch. (P. 180)

Twining stitch. Ancient, universal weaving technique employing multiple weft threads which twist on the warp. (Pp. 30–31)

Upright loom. See also Vertical loom. (P. 142)

Ver au Soie silk. Trade name for silk embroidery floss.

Vertical loom. (Also, upright loom.) Any loom in which the warp threads are held in tension vertically. (Pp. 84, 88, 142)

Warp. Long threads on the loom which are held under tension.

Weft. Weaving threads which cross and interlock with the warp; carried in a shuttle and worked horizontally.

Wheat-ear stitch. Open, looped embroidery stitch. (Pp. 115, 117)

Whip stitch. (Also, overcast stitch.) Simple, straight stitch worked over the edge of a fabric. (Pp. 272–74)

Whitework. Embroidery of any method worked in white thread on a white ground. (Pp. 92–93, 105, 264–65, 268, 270–71, 274–75)

Whorl. Disk attached to one end of a spindle for weight. (Pp. 26–27)

Zwicky silk. Brand name for silk embroidery floss.

Let the white wool drift and dwindle.

Attributions and Endnotes

P. 25, **Cave painting:** From copy by M. Almagro, Museo Arqueologica, Madrid. **Enthroned goddess:** Koszta Joszef Museum, Szentes, Hungary. *Venus of Lespugue:* Musée des Antequites Nationales, St. Germain-en-Laye, France

P. 26, **Homeric poem:** A. de Vries, *Dictionary of Symbols and Imagery,* New York: American Elsevier Publishing Co., 1974

P. 27, **Spindle whorl drawing:** After J. Deshayes, "Bulletin de Correspondance Hellenique," XCII, 1968. **Drawing of goddess, front and back:** Marija Gimbutas, *The Gods and Goddesses of Old Europe, 7000–3500 B.C.,* Berkeley: University of California Press, 1974 (after figurine, National Museum, Belgrade, Yugoslavia). **Drawing from tomb urn:** Drawn by S. Hogan from Mary Lois Kissel, *Yarn and Cloth Making,* An Economic Study, New York: Macmillan Co., 1918. **Sumerian women making cloth:** Ilse Seibert, *Women in the Ancient Near East,* New York: Abner Schram, 1974 (Damascus Museum)

P. 28, **Exodus excerpt:** Ethyl Lewis, *The Romance of Textiles: The Story of Design in Weaving,* New York: Macmillan Co., 1918. **Cretan procession:** Heraklion Museum, Crete, Greece (photo – André Held, Ecublens, Switzerland)

P. 29, **Navaho legend:** Anthony Berlant and Mary Kahlenberg, *Walk in Beauty,* Boston: New York Graphic Society, 1977. **Navaho weavers:** The Smithsonian Institution, Photo #2434, Bureau of American Ethnology, Washington, D.C. **Egyptian textile workers:** Mary G. Houston, *Ancient Egyptian, Mesopotamian and Persian Costume,* London: Adams & Black, 1972. **Mesopotamian bas relief:** The Louvre, Paris. **Description of textile mill:** Adèle Coulin Weibel, *Two Thousand Years of Textiles,* New York: Pantheon Books, 1952

P. 30, **Homeric quotes:** From Weibel, above. **Detail from Amphora vase:** Courtesy of Museum of Fine Arts, Boston (Henry R. Pierce Fund)

P. 31, **Greek women working:** Metropolitan Museum of Art, New York. **Engraving, Roman women:** Museum Boymans – van Beuningen, Rotterdam

Color plate 1, opposite p. 32, *Dinner Party* **banners:** Designed by Chicago and woven at the San Francisco Tapestry Workshop under the direction of John Pierre Larochette

P. 35, **Carved spirals:** Commissioners of Public Works in Ireland, Dublin

P. 41, **Poetry fragment:** Erich Neumann, *The Great Mother,* New York: Pantheon Books, 1974

P. 42, **Creation myth:** Mircea Eliade, *The Two and the One,* trans. J. M. Cohen, New York: Harper & Row Publishers, 1965

P. 43, **Poetry fragment:** Erich Neumann, *The Great Mother,* New York: Pantheon Books, 1974

P. 45, **Ishtar Gate:** Burkhard Verlang, Ernst Heyer Essen, Haus der Technik, Essen, West Germany

P. 47, **Kali sculpture:** Title, *Goddess Mahathairavi;* Artist, Panjab or Himachal Pradesh, 11th century; Los Angeles County Museum of Art, Pan-Asian Collection

P. 49, **Malayan myth:** Gertrude Whiting, *Old Time Tools and Toys of Needlework,* New York: Dover Publications, 1971. **Cretan Snake Goddess:** Museo Archeologico, Florence

P. 55, **De Pisan quote:** Christine de Pisan, *The City of Women,* trans. Kate Cooper, unpublished, 1979. **Detail, Pergamon Altar:** Staatliche Museen, Berlin (DDR), Antiken-Sammlung. **Dying Amazon:** Archaeological Museum, Piraeus, Greece

P. 58, **Portrait of Queen Hatshepsut:** Courtesy of Museum of Fine Arts, Boston

P. 60, **Fragment of Egyptian fabric:** Cairo Museum, Cairo

P. 63, **Representation of Neith:** Sir Wallis Budge, *The Gods of the Egyptians: Studies in Egyptian Mythology,* Vol. I, New York: Dover Publications, 1904

P. 66, **Antique bridal headdress:** Hebrew Union College Skirball Museum, Los Angeles (photo – Erich Hockley)

P. 67, **Ancient Jewish coin:** From a Dropsie University dissertation; collection of Dropsie University, Philadelphia

P. 69, **Sappho poem:** Mary Barnard, *Sappho: A New Translation,* Berkeley: University of California Press, 1966

P. 70, *Sculpture of Acropolis Maiden:* Acropolis Museum, Athens

P. 75, **Traditional Greek ornamental design:** By permission of Bernard Quaritch, Ltd.

P. 77, **Sculpture of Athena:** Acropolis Museum, Athens. **Drawing of Penelope:** Museo Civica, Cologna Veneta, Italy

P. 80, **Battersea Shield:** Reproduced by permission of the British Library, London. **Celtic Ornamentation:** Norman Ault, *Life in Ancient Britain,* Freeport, New York: Books for Library Press, 1972. **Mirror:** Drawn by S. Hogan from *National Geographic,* May 1977, Vol. 151, No. 5

P. 82, **Sculpture of Boadaceia:** Public square, London (photo – Dr. Susan Rennie)

P. 83, **Fragment of felt hanging:** State Hermitage Museum, Leningrad

P. 84, **Coptic weaving:** Metropolitan Museum of Art, New York (Gift of Helen Miller Gould, 1910)

P. 85, **Coptic tunic:** Metropolitan Museum of Art, New York (gift of George F. Baker, 1890)

P. 92, **Altar frontal and detail:** Helmstedt, Kloster St. Marienberg

P. 93, **Medieval seal:** Staatliche Museen, Berlin (DDR). **Göss chasuble:** Osterreichisches Museum fur Angewandte Kunst, Vienna

P. 94, **Syon cope:** Crown copyright, Victoria and Albert Museum, London

P. 95, **Glove:** Weltliche Treasury, Vienna. **Mitre:** Musée de Cluny, Paris

P. 98, **Detail, Bayeux tapestry:** Musée de la Reine Mathilde, Bayeux, France. **Detail, Giotto painting:** Arena Chapel, Padua, Italy

P. 99, **Tristram hanging:** Kloster Wienhausen. **Sculpture, woman hackling flax:** Chartres Cathedral, France. **Detail, knotted carpet:** Quedlinburg Cathedral Treasury, East Germany

P. 100, **Greek woman:** Adapted from Henry Ling Roth, *Ancient Egyptian and Greek Looms,* Halifax, England: Bankfield Museum, 1951. **Anglo-Saxon women and household work shop:** Thomas Wright, *Womankind in Western Europe from the Earliest Times to the Seventeenth Century,* London: Groombridge & Sons, 1869

P. 101, **High-warp and low-warp looms:** Denis Diderot, *A Diderot Pictorial Encyclopedia of Trades and Industry,* Vol. II, ed. Charles C. Gillespie, New York: Dover Publications, 1959. **Durer engraving, Witch, Goat and Putti:** The British Museum, London

P. 103, **Silk workers, manuscript illuminations, and wool workers:** British Library, London. **Weaving song:** Sibylle Harksen, *Women in the Middle Ages,* New York: Abner Schram, 1975

P. 104, **Manuscript Illumination:** Elise Boulding, *The Underside of History: A View of Women Through Time,* Boulder, Col.: Westview Press, 1976 (redrawn from manuscript, Bibliothèque Nationale, Paris)

P. 106, **Orans figure:** Photo – André Held, Ecublens, Switzerland

P. 107, **Astarte:** The Louvre, Paris

P. 108, **Thecla:** Reproduced by permission of the British Library, London. **Painting of Christ:** Photo – Scala/Editorial Photocolor Archives, New York

P. 112, **Detail of Gundestrop cauldron:** Danish National Museum, Copenhagen

P. 113, **Cross of Muiredach:** Commissioners of Public Works in Ireland, Dublin

P. 118, **Mosaic from Ravenna:** Photo – Scala/Editorial Photocolor Archives, New York

P. 119, **Hagia Sophia:** David Talbot Rice, *Art of the Byzantine Era,* New York: Frederick A. Praeger, 1963

P. 120, **Portrait of Theodora:** Photo – Scala/Editorial Photocolor Archives, New York

P. 125, **Example of opus teutonicum:** Courtesy of The Art Institute, Chicago

P. 128, **Abbess' coins:** Staatliche Museen, Berlin (DDR), Münzkabinett, **Valkyrie excerpt:** Peter Andreas Munch, *Norse Mythology, Legends of Gods and Heroes,* trans. Sigurd B. Hustredt, New York: American Scandinavian Foundation, 1926

P. 131, **Nuns weaving:** Elise Boulding, *The Underside of History: A View of Women Through Time,* Boulder, Col.: Westview Press, 1976 (drawing from Italian manuscript, Biblioteca Ambrosiana, Milan)

P. 134, **Sicilian quilt:** Museo della Casa Fiorentina Antica, Florence

P. 135, **Egyptian vase:** The Louvre, Paris

P. 136, **Mesopotamian cylinder seal:** Roger Cook, *The Tree of Life: Symbol of the Center,* London: Thames and Hudson, 1974. **Jewish menorah:** Alexander Eliot, *Myths,* Berkshire, Eng.: A McGraw-Hill Co-publication, 1976. **Roman tree:** Erich Neumann, *The Great Mother,* Princeton, N.J.: Princeton University Press, 1974 (from an engraved gem, Vatican Library). **Coronation mantle:** Kunsthistorisches Museum, Vienna. **Siberian myth:** Roger Cook, *The Tree of Life, Symbol of the Center,* London: Thames and Hudson, 1974

P. 137, **The Dream of the Virgin:** Pinacoteca Nazionale, Ferrara, Italy

P. 140, **Unicorn tapestry:** Metropolitan Museum of Art, The Cloisters Collection, New York

P. 143, **Medieval refrain:** Sophie Drinker, *Music and Women,* New York: Coward-McCann, 1948

P. 144, **Painting of Mary:** Staatliche Museen, Berlin (DDR)

P. 145, **Chartres cathedral:** Gemäldegalerie, Bildarchive Foto Marburg, Marburg-Lahn, Germany

P. 149, **Example of opus anglicanum:** Kunsthistorisches Museum, Vienna

P. 150, **Illumination and quote by Hildegarde:** Karen Petersen and J. J. Wilson, *Women Artists: Recognition and Reappraisal from the Early Middle Ages to the Twentieth Century,* New York: Harper & Row, 1976

P. 155, **Manuscript illumination:** Bibliothèque Nationale, Paris

P. 156, **Women being hanged:** By permission of the British Library, London

P. 156–57, **Tale of Habitrot:** Katherine M. Briggs, *The Anatomy of Puck,* London: Routledge & Kegan Paul, 1959

P. 157, **Habitrot:** Joseph Jacobs, *More English Fairy Tales,* London: Nutt, 1890 (courtesy of Pantheon Books, division of Random House, New York

P. 159, **Bargello chair:** Museo Nazionale, Florence. **Traditional Bargello pattern:** Sherlee Lantz, *A Pageant of Patterns for Needlepoint Canvas,* New York: Atheneum, 1973

286

P. 161, Bargello wastebasket: Elsa Williams, *Bargello: Florentine Canvas Work*, New York: Litton Educational Publishing, 1967 (reprinted by permission of Van Nostrand-Reinhold Co.)

P. 163, Assisi work: Courtesy of Cooper Hewitt Museum, The Smithsonian Institution's National Museum of Design, New York

P. 165, Italian velvet: Courtesy of The Art Institute of Chicago. **Renaissance painting:** Morrison Collection, Fonthill, So. Ontario, Canada

P. 166, Elizabeth's prayer book: Bodleian Library, Oxford, England

P. 167, Portrait of Elizabeth I: Reproduced by kind permission of the Marquess of Tavistock and the Trustees of the Bedford Estates, England

P. 169, Jacket and detail: Crown copyright, Victoria and Albert Museum, London. **Lady Montagu quote:** Gertrude Whiting, *Old Time Tools and Toys of Needlework*, New York: Dover Publications, 1971

P. 172, *Judith Beheading Holofernes*: Pitti Palace, Florence (photo – Scala/Editorial Photocolor Archives, New York)

P. 174, Bizarre Silk: Metropolitan Museum of Art, New York (Rogers Fund)

P. 176, Drawing of schoolgirls: By permission of the British Library, London

P. 177, Traditional sampler (lettering): Concord Antiquarian Society, Concord, Mass.

P. 178, Traditional stitch patterns: Crown copyright, Victoria and Albert Museum, London

P. 179, Dutch sampler (basket): Philadelphia Museum of Art, Whitman Sampler Collection (given by Pet, Inc.). **Needlework rhyme:** Ethel Stanwood Bolton and Eva Johnston Coe, *American Samplers*, New York: Dover Publications, 1973

P. 184, De Gournay quotation: From "Grief des Dames," by Marie le Jars de Gournay (quoted by Elise Boulding, *The Underside of History*, Boulder, Col.: Westview Press, 1976. **Embroidery of Henry VIII:** Maidstone Museum and Art Gallery, Maidstone, England

P. 185, Morell's embroidery: Swiss National Museum, Zurich. **Pattern book:** Harriet Bridgeman and Elizabeth Drury, ed., *Needlework: An Illustrated History*, New York: Paddington Press, Ltd., 1978

P. 186, Bed hanging: Crown copyright, Victoria and Albert Museum, London. **Julia Calverley's screen:** The National Trust, Wallington, Northumberland, England

P. 187, Engraving: Metropolitan Museum of Art, New York. **Needlework chair:** Yvonne Hackenbroch, *English and Other Needlework, Tapestries and Textiles in the Irwin Untermyer Collection,*

Cambridge, Mass.: Harvard University Press, 1960. **Mary Lamb quote:** Anthea Callen, *Women Artists of the Arts and Crafts Movement: 1870–1914*, New York: Pantheon Books, 1979

P. 188, Peruvian weaving: The Textile Museum, Washington, D.C.

P. 189, Colonial kitchen: Courtesy of the Library of Congress, Washington, D.C. **Berlin work:** Crown copyright, Victoria and Albert Museum, London

P. 190, Sweat shop: Courtesy of the Library of Congress, Washington, D.C. **Black textile workers:** Works Projects Administration, National Archives, Washington, D.C. **Child laborer in mill:** Courtesy of the Library of Congress, Washington, D.C. **Ueghorn poem:** M. B. Schnapper, *American Labor: Pictorial Social History*, Washington, D.C.: Public Affairs Press, 1972

P. 191, Carlyle and Morris quotes: Anthea Callen, *Women Artists of the Arts and Crafts Movement: 1870–1914*, New York: Pantheon Books, 1979. **Women embroidering:** Birmingham School of Art, Birmingham, England (photo – Alan Crawford)

P. 192, Victorian painting, *Family Circle*: Private collection, Copenhagen. **"Reticule" and "Quilted Bed Pocket":** S. F. A. Caulfield and Blanche E. Saward, *Encyclopedia of Victorian Needlework*, Vol. II, New York: Dover Publications, 1972

P. 196, Angelica Kauffmann, *Fame Decorating the Tomb of Shakespeare*: Reproduced from the Collection of Lord Exeter (photo: Courtauld Institute of Art, London). **Traditional mourning picture:** *Mourning Becomes America: Mourning Art in the New Nation*, catalog prepared by Anita Schorsch, Clinton, N.J.: The Main Street Press, 1976

P. 198, Urn: Drawn by S. Hogan from Erich Neumann, *The Great Mother*, Princeton, N.J.: Princeton University Press, 1974. **Egyptian fresco:** Barbara S. Lesko, *The Remarkable Women of Ancient Egypt*, Berkeley: B.C. Scribe Publications, 1978

P. 199, Greek vase painting: By courtesy of the Vatican Museums

P. 204, Beaded dress: Bureau of Indian Affairs, U.S. Department of the Interior, Washington, D.C. **Sioux parfleche painting:** Reproduced by permission of The University Museum, University of Pennsylvania, Philadelphia

P. 205, Quillwork box: The University Museum, University of Pennsylvania, Philadelphia

P. 206, Cradle board: From the collection of the Denver Art Museum

P. 207, Hopi tale: Alice Marriott and Carol Rachlin, *American Indian Mythology*, New York: Thomas Y. Crowell Co., 1934. **Indian song:** *Songs of the Tewa*, trans. Herbert Joseph Spinden, New York: The Brooklyn Museum, 1933

P. 209, Caroline Herschel's drawing: Reproduced from Michael A. Hoskin, *William Herschel and the Construction of the Heavens*, by permission of W. W. Norton & Co. (© 1963 by Oldbourne Book Co., Ltd.)

P. 210, Abigail Pett's crewel work: Crown copyright, Victoria and Albert Museum, London. **Marjorie Biggs' *Peaceable Kingdom*:** Church of Our Savior, San Gabriel, Calif.

P. 211, Drawing of telescope: Photo – Palais de la Decouverte, Paris

P. 212, Stumpwork example: Crown copyright, Victoria and Albert Museum, London

P. 222, Moore quotation: Norman Yetman, *Life Under the "Peculiar Institution": Selections from the Slave Narrative Collection*, New York: Holt, Rinehart & Winston, 1970. **Fon hanging:** John Michael Vlach, *The Afro-American Tradition in Decorative Arts*, Cleveland: The Cleveland Museum of Art, 1978. **Powers' appliqué Bible quilt:** Courtesy of Museum of Fine Arts, Boston (bequest of Maxim Karolik)

P. 223, Pieced quilt: Philadelphia Museum of Art (given by Mrs. Horace Wells Sellers)

P. 224, Women's weave: Collection of Ms. Alexandra C. Cole, Santa Barbara, Calif.

P. 229, Suffrage march: Courtesy of the New Jersey Historical Society, Newark

P. 230, Crazy quilt: The Smithsonian Institution, Washington, D.C.

P. 231, *Quilting Bee*: C. Kurt Dewhurst, Betty MacDowell, and Marsha MacDowell, *Artists in Aprons: Folk Art of American Women*, New York: E. P. Dutton and Museum of American Folk Art, 1979 (Spelce Family Collection). **"The Original Cubist":** New York Sun: Museum of Modern Art, New York

P. 233, Mola: Virginia Bath Churchill, *Embroidery Masterworks*, Chicago: Henry Regnery Co., 1972

P. 237, Dickinson poem: *"I'm Nobody! Who Are You?": Poems of Emily Dickinson for Children*, wings Mills, Md.: Stemmer House Publishers, 1978

P. 239, Lacemakers: Charlotte Kellogg, *Bobbins of Belgium*, New York: Funk & Wagnalls, 1920. **Noblewoman making lace:** The Louvre, Paris. **Wedding veil:** Marian Powys, *Lace and Lace Making*, Boston: Charles T. Branford Co., 1953

P. 240, *Woman's Mission*: The Tate Gallery, London. **Scott poem:** Sir Walter Scott, *Marmion*, 1830. (Quoted by Martha Vicinus, *Suffer and Be Still: Women in the Victorian Age*, Bloomington, Ind.: Indiana University Press, 1973

P. 241, Factory: Culver Pictures. **Hood excerpt:** Thomas Hood, "Song of the Shirt" from Vicinus, above. **Quote from**

millworker: William Cahn, *Pictorial History of American Labor*. **The Seamstress:** Courtauld Institute of Art, University of London

P. 244, Amelia Bloomer: Elizabeth Ewing, *Dress and Undress: A History of Women's Underwear*, New York and London: Drama Book Specialists and B. T. Batsford, 1978. **Photograph of Dame Ethel Smyth:** Barbara Grier and Coletta Reid, ed., *Lesbian Lives: Biographies of Women from "The Ladder,"* Oakland, Calif.: Diana Press, 1976 (used by permission). **Drawing of rib cage:** Adapted from Thomas Hess and E. C. Baker, *Art and Sexual Politics*, New York: Macmillan, 1973. **Sackville-West quotation:** Vita Sackville-West, quoted by Nigel Nicholson, *Portrait of a Marriage*, New York: Atheneum Publishers, 1973

P. 245, Traditional women's pockets: Old Sturbridge Village, Mass.

P. 246, Birth-control advocate: Beryl Suitters, *Be Brave and Be Angry*, London: International Planned Parenthood Federation, 1973

P. 247, Kollwitz' *Tower of Mothers*: Private collection, West Berlin. **Sanger quote:** Margaret Sanger, *The New Motherhood*, London: Jonathan Cape, 1922

P. 252, Romaine Brooks' *L'Amazone*: Musée du Petit Palais, Paris

P. 253, Tiffany bowl: Metropolitan Museum of Art, New York (gift of H. O. Havermeyer, 1896)

P. 258, Nin quotation: Anaïs Nin, *The Diary of Anaïs Nin*, Volume 2 (1934–1939), New York: Harcourt, Brace and World, 1967. **Life drawing class:** Courtesy of Pennsylvania Academy of the Fine Arts, Philadelphia

P. 265, Leonardo da Vinci's *Last Supper*: Santa Maria delle Grazie, Milan. **Bayeux Tapestry detail:** Musée de la Reine Mathilde, Bayeux, France

P. 266, Medieval painting: The Pierpont Morgan Library, New York. **Matisse painting:** Patricia Easterbrook Roberts, *Table Settings, Entertaining and Etiquette*, New York: Viking Press, 1967 (photo – Peter A. Juley & Son)

P. 267, Altar cloth: Collegiate Church, Castell'Arquato, Italy

P. 268, Chalice: Corpus Christi College, Oxford, England. **Paten:** Walmer, Kent, England. **Infant Christ on Paten:** Serbian Monastery of Chilandari, Mont-Athos (photo: Archives Photographiques, Paris). **Traditional luncheon setting:** Courtesy of Valentine Museum, Richmond, Virginia

P. 269, Seder: Mae Shafter Rockland, *The Jewish Party Book*, New York: Schocken Books, 1978 (photo – Bill Aron)

P. 270, Traditional altar: St. Augustine-by-the-Sea, Santa Monica, Calif.

287

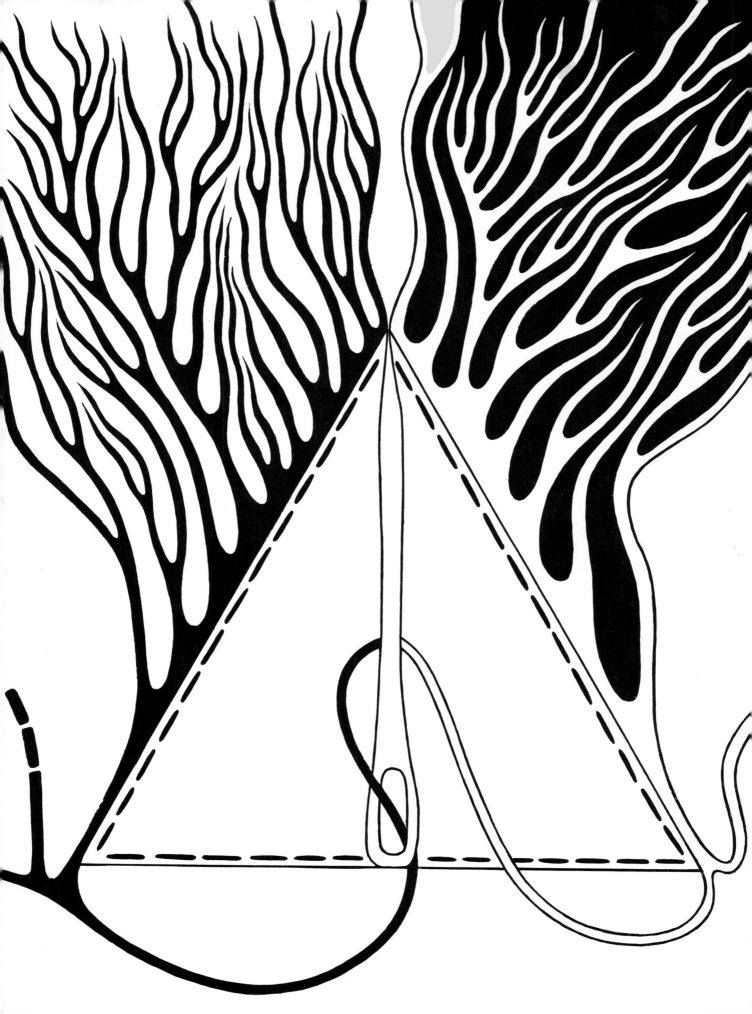